Infectious Diseases in Critical Care Nursing

Prevention and Precautions

Inge Gurevich, RN, MA
Coordinator
Infection Control Department
Winthrop-University Hospital
Mineola, New York

Aspen Series in Critical Care Nursing
Kathleen Dracup, Series Editor

AN ASPEN PUBLICATION ®
Aspen Publishers, Inc.
Rockville, Maryland
1989

Library of Congress Cataloging-in-Publication Data

Gurevich, Inge.
Infectious diseases in critical care nursing:
prevention and precautions/Inge Gurevich.
p.   cm.

"An Aspen Publication."
Includes bibliographical references.
ISBN: 0-8342-0083-X
1. Communicable diseases--Nursing. 2. Nosocomial infections.
3. Intensive care nursing. I. Title.
[DNLM: 1. Communicable Disease Control--nurses' instruction.
2. Communicable Diseases--nursing. 3. Critical Care. WY 153
G979i]
RC112.G87 1989
616'.047--dc20
DNLM/DLC
for Library of Congress   89-17613
CIP

The authors have made every effort to ensure the accuracy of the information herein, particularly with regard to drug selection and dose. However, appropriate information sources should be consulted, especially for new or unfamiliar procedures. It is the responsibility of every practitioner to evaluate the appropriateness of a particular opinion in the context of actual clinical situations and with due consideration to new developments. Authors, editors, and the publisher cannot be held responsible for any typographical or other errors found in this book.

Editorial Services: Jane Coyle Garwood

Library of Congress Catalog Card Number: 89-17453
ISBN: 0-8342-0083-X

Printed in the United States of America

1 2 3 4 5

Table of Contents

Foreword

The medical interventions in the critical care setting are by definition intensive; so too is the risk of exposure to infectious agents. There are few areas in the hospital that have a greater potential for infectious disease transmission than intensive care. Critical care personnel rendering care to their patients expose themselves and their other patients to a variety of contagious, infectious diseases. There is, therefore, a need for a book to educate critical care personnel in controlling the spread of the infections that they deal with every day. This book clearly fills that long-standing need.

Infectious Diseases in Critical Care Nursing contains much useful information on the principles of infection control as they apply to critical care nursing. Particularly important are the sections on specimen collection and the interpretation of results, which are always problematic. The sections on isolation and precautions are perhaps its main strengths. There are also unique sections about the pregnant nurse and the relationship between Infection Control and the critical care nursing staff. While this book is not intended to be a definitive treatise on infection control, it may be used as a quick reference to infection control practices germane to critical care. It is a unique guide for those who daily wage war against a persistent and ubiquitous microbial presence.

Burke A. Cunha, M.D.
Chief, Infectious Disease Division
Winthrop-University Hospital
Mineola, NY

Introduction

Unnecessary exposure to infection is a familiar and potentially serious problem in critical care units and elsewhere in the health care setting. Usually descriptions of infectious diseases are confined to pathophysiology, diagnosis, and treatment of infection. High-risk populations, transmission, protective measures, pre- and postexposure prophylaxis are rarely addressed. These aspects of an infectious disease, however, greatly concern nurses, who are responsible not only for their own protection and that of other health care workers, but also for the safety of patients and visitors. These concerns are addressed in this book. Chapter review questions help readers assess their knowledge of the topics discussed.

Most of the topics were chosen with special emphasis on the needs of critical care nurses. These needs have been evidenced by questions to the author, who is an experienced infection control practitioner in a 530-bed hospital. The approach to each topic is based on the vast knowledge required by nurses if they are to use appropriate precautionary measures without sacrificing good patient care practices. Each chapter contains descriptions of the various pathogens, their sources and modes of transmission, the patient populations most likely to be infected, as well as preexposure and postexposure prophylaxis.

The book is divided into three parts. In the first chapter in Part I actual unnecessary exposures to patients with meningitis, tuberculosis, and disseminated zoster are described. All three infections could have been avoided if they had been recognized sooner by the patients' physicians or if the nurses had been familiar with the factors that predispose patients to these specific infections. Therefore, in Chapter 2 the immune system is described with emphasis on how deficits in the system, especially of the T and B lymphocytes, provide a measure of predictability for certain infections in patients.

Many questions about the collection of culture specimens and how to interpret the results are answered in Chapter 3. Examples are provided to show how laboratory reports can influence patient care practices by differentiating pathogens from ''normal flora.''

In Part II, each chapter deals with a specific transmissible disease such as meningitis, hepatitis, and the acquired immunodeficiency syndrome (AIDS). These infections are encountered again and again in a nurse's career, and the material is presented in the context of the needs of the critical care nurse. The information from Part I is incorporated into each of these chapters so that the connection between who is a high-risk patient and why can be clearly understood. The early warning signs for each infection and diagnosis, transmission, and prevention are discussed. Preexposure and postexposure prophylactic measures and their hazards are also described where applicable.

In Part III, pregnancy and infectious diseases are discussed in relationship to the potentially adverse fetal outcomes of a maternal infection. The issues of transfer to a "safe" area and refusal to care for infectious patients are examined. A discussion of toxoplasmosis and other infections not related to critical care but of importance to pregnant nurses is also included. Chapter 12 is a summation of the epidemiologic aspects of infectious diseases, different approaches to Isolation and Precautions, and how a cooperative collegial relationship between nurses and the infection control practitioner can be of mutual benefit to staff and patients. Some readers may wish to read Chapter 12 before approaching the information on the clinical infections in Part II; for others it will provide a summary of the information previously alluded to in less detail.

Caring for patients with infectious diseases has always been, and will always be, an integral part of professional nursing. Nowhere is the maxim "forewarned is forearmed" more applicable than in the critical care setting. This book can be used as a quick reference or can aid in providing an in-depth understanding of a wide range of important topics related to infectious diseases. It is hoped that it will prove to be a valuable addition to any nurse's library.

Part I

Infectious Diseases: Related Topics

In Chapter 1 three examples are provided of unnecessary exposure to patients with transmissible infections. The role of the functional and dysfunctional immune system in the infectious process is described in Chapter 2. Chapter 3 is a review of the microbiology of infectious diseases, which should help critical care nurses to improve their skills for the collection and interpretation of their patient's culture specimens.

Chapter 1

The Infectious Patient: Reducing the Risk of Transmission

Infectious diseases are frequently the cause of critical illness, as is the case in meningitis. They may develop because of an underlying condition, such as tuberculosis in Hodgkin's disease, or they may have no connection with the patient's admission, as in a patient with diabetic ketoacidosis who is an asymptomatic carrier of the human immunodeficiency virus.

When an infection is overt and part of the working diagnosis, alert and knowledgeable physicians and nurses can readily carry out precautionary measures to protect themselves and others. Unfortunately, however, when infections are covert and unrecognized or misdiagnosed, inadvertent exposure is likely to occur. This is especially true if patients or their physicians are unaware of a chronic or underlying infection or are not aware of the need to inform others. When patients are admitted on an emergency basis, many factors can contribute to the lack of communication to the staff about underlying infectious conditions. Patients who have been hepatitis carriers for years, a condition that is of little concern in everyday life, may not recognize that an infection such as this may pose a real risk to persons who must have contact with their blood and body fluids during their care in the hospital. Other patients may be faced with a serious or even life-threatening situation, such as shortness of breath, a myocardial infarction, or a car accident. They will therefore understandably be more concerned about those situations than their chronic hepatitis or recently diagnosed tuberculosis. And yet others may be unable to communicate altogether, owing to the nature of their present problem. In such cases, personnel, as well as other patients, may be exposed to an infectious condition for some time before it is recognized or before a pertinent history becomes available from the patient or an informed physician, relative, or friend. In some instances, postexposure prophylaxis may be available, but that in itself may present risks.

The three cases presented in this chapter illustrate what nurses must know when caring for critically ill patients if transmission of infection is to be avoided. Nurses must be able to recognize the obvious and not so obvious manifestations of infectious diseases. They must know which type of patient may fit into a particularly high-risk category for harboring or developing a particular infection, and they must be familiar with the mode(s) of transmission of each disease. Only then can they institute the appropriate protective measures for themselves and others.

CASE 1

Mr. P was a 28-year-old man with leukemia whose present hospital admission was for fever and possible pneumonia. On physical examination, the first-year resident noticed that the patient had a facial rash. The distribution and appearance of the rash resembled herpes zoster (shingles). He informed the attending physician and suggested that Contact Isolation be instituted. The patient's physician "did not want to make the patient feel worse than he already felt," refused to approve the precautions, and changed the diagnosis to "pneumonia and facial cellulitis." The patient's arterial blood gas values deteriorated, and he was transferred to the medical intensive care unit during the evening. A pulmonary consultation was obtained, ventilatory assistance was considered, but antibiotic and other therapies improved the patient's respiratory status toward morning. It was 10 AM before a nurse was able to perform the patient's morning care. By that time the patient had a rash not only on the face but also on his neck, chest, and back, and the nurse called the infection control practitioner. The intensive care unit resident and the infection control practitioner agreed with the nurse that the patient had disseminated zoster, and the patient was placed in Strict Isolation.

Disseminated zoster is extremely contagious and is transmitted in the same manner as chickenpox—by air from the respiratory tract as well as by direct contact with the vesicular fluid and with articles contaminated with the virus. At risk are patients and staff who have not had chickenpox and who are thus susceptible. Of special concern are immunosuppressed patients and pregnant women. The infection control practitioner therefore began a search for all those who may have been exposed to this patient in the 20 hours since his admission and to ascertain their susceptibility status (Table 1-1). Anyone who was not immune by history of having had chickenpox or zoster themselves, or by living with siblings or children who had it, would be tested for antibody. Those who were susceptible would not be able to work from day 10 after their exposure to day 21 (during the incubation period). The search for exposed persons covered not only the intensive care unit but also the emergency department, where the patient was briefly seen before transfer to his room, and the unit on which the patient spent the first few hours after his admission. It included the patient who shared his room in that area and that patient's visitors. Mr. P's family were also questioned when they came to visit him.

Table 1-1 Exposures and Economic Analysis of an Instance of Disseminated Zoster Contact

Title	Number of Persons Exposed/Susceptible	Days of Missed Work	Cost to Hospital
House officers	4/1	11	$1,100
Registered nurses	12/2	22	$1,600
Nursing assistant	1/0	0	0
Laboratory technician	1/0	0	0
Maid	1/1	11	$520
Porter	1/0	0	0
Unit secretary	1/0	0	0
Radiology technician	1/1	11	$500
Secondary case (ECG technician)	1/1	10	$550
Pregnant sister	1/1		$350*
Patient's roommate and visitors	3/0		
Infection control time			$200
Antibody titers			$450
Totals	27/7	65	$5,270

*Patient's pregnant sister was given varicella-zoster immune globulin.

It was discovered that the patient's sister, who had brought him to the emergency department, was pregnant and had not had chickenpox. She, therefore, was given varicella-zoster immune globulin at a cost of $350 and would not be able to visit the hospital during her incubation period. Indications for the administration of varicella-zoster immune globulin are described in Chapter 9. The cost of the investigation, the tests, and the furlough time for the susceptible house officer, radiology technician, maid, and two nurses was $5,270, and 20 full hours of infection control time were required. A secondary case occurred 21 days later because a susceptible ECG technician had been in the intensive care unit but not in the patient's room and had not reported her presence in the unit. She was thus not identified as being a possible contact and in turn exposed many others to her chickenpox.

CASE 2

A 24-year-old woman was brought to the emergency department at 3 PM on a Friday afternoon with a temperature of 102.6°F (39.2°C), nausea, vomiting, and confusion. She was 24 weeks pregnant and had recurrent bouts of *Esche-*

richia coli pyelonephritis. The obstetrics resident admitted the patient to the antenatal unit, ordered blood and urine cultures, and started her on therapy with 2 g ampicillin given intravenously every 4 hours. Ten hours later, at 1 AM Saturday, the patient was transferred to the medical intensive care unit because she was not responding to therapy and was becoming increasingly obtunded. A spinal tap showed a white blood cell count of 450 cells/cu mm with 95% polymorphonuclear neutrophils. The glucose value was 80 mg/dL, the protein concentration was 45 mg/dL, and a Gram stain done by the medical resident was negative. Two hours later the patient required ventilatory assistance and was intubated.

The microbiology laboratory opened at 8 AM on Saturday, and because of the serious and life-threatening implications of meningitis, cerebrospinal fluid specimens were always examined, or reexamined, as soon as possible. At 8:30 AM the laboratory technician called the intensive care unit to report gram-negative diplococci on the Gram stain of this patient's cerebrospinal fluid. At that time, penicillin, 4 million units given intravenously every 4 hours, was added to the ampicillin. No one thought of isolating the patient until 10 AM, when one of the intensive care unit nurses finally instituted Respiratory Isolation. At noon, the microbiology technician phoned the on-call infection control practitioner to inform her of the positive results of the Gram stain. This call was standard hospital policy, a safeguard that had been instituted several years earlier when a patient with a diagnosis of meningococcal meningitis was also not promptly isolated and a resident developed meningitis as a consequence.

The infection control practitioner ascertained that the patient had been placed on Respiratory Isolation but that this had not been instituted until 19 hours after the patient's admission. The nursing supervisor was contacted and asked to obtain the names of all those persons who had been in close proximity to the patient and were possibly eligible for postexposure prophylaxis with rifampin.

Since the meningococcus is transmitted directly person to person via air but does not remain suspended in the environment for prolonged periods, only those in very close contact with a patient are considered at risk.[1] Included are those who give mouth-to-mouth resuscitation, perform fundoscopy, or intubate a patient. Other indications, including prolonged proximity during meal sharing, are listed in Table 1-2. Anyone who is not considered eligible for prophylaxis or does not want to take rifampin, which is not an innocuous drug, should be told to watch carefully for early manifestations of meningitis and to then obtain prompt treatment. More information on meningitis is presented in Chapter 11.

The infection control practitioner investigated all contacts, starting with the emergency department where the nurses on the day and evening shifts had been exposed and the two shifts of nurses involved on the antenatal unit and the intensive care unit. The intravenous therapy team and radiology, respiratory therapy, and electrocardiology department staffs were contacted, and those in

Table 1-2 Hospital Personnel Eligible for Prophylaxis after Exposure to MenIngococcal Meningitis

Those involved in:	Mouth-to-mouth resuscitation
	Intubation of patient
	Oral or fundoscopic examination
	Assisting while the patient is vomiting
	Having the patient breath *directly* on a staff member
Dose:	Rifampin, 600 mg orally for 2 days

charge at that time were asked to telephone everyone who had been on duty and possibly in contact with the patient. Altogether, 42 persons were investigated, 22 of whom had some type of contact with the patient (Table 1-3). Three others could not be reached until the following Monday. Seven of the 22 had a close enough contact with the patient to be considered eligible for prophylaxis, and their names were given to the hospital pharmacist so that the necessary antibiotic (rifampin) would be released. At that time it was discovered that the obstetric resident who admitted this patient had already given rifampin prescriptions to 12 staff members, contrary to hospital policy that only infection control or infectious disease fellows could approve this drug for prophylaxis because of previous experiences with overdosing and inappropriate prescription. Several problems surfaced in connection with the erroneously released rifampin on this occasion also. Two nurses, one a pregnant intensive care unit nurse, could not be reached until late Sunday night. At that time the pregnant nurse had already taken three of the four doses of rifampin that had been issued. Rifampin is contraindicated in pregnancy, but no one had asked her if she was pregnant as the infection control practitioner would have done before approving her for prophylaxis. The other nurse worked in the emergency department, but he did not need the rifampin since he had only pushed the patient's stretcher from the emergency department to the antenatal unit. This nurse's contact lenses had to be replaced because rifampin caused a permanent orange discoloration, another warning the infection control practitioner would have issued. No one had thought to include the patient's roommate on the antenatal unit in the prophylaxis group, even though the patients had shared the same room for several hours. The infection control practitioner contacted the roommate's attending physician and recommended that she receive rifampin prophylaxis if there was no clinical contraindication. The roommate's visitors had been in the room only for about 10 minutes, and they were instructed to notify their private medical doctor and then report any manifestations of upper respiratory tract infection or headache and fever to that physician should they occur.

Table 1-3 Listing of Contacts Eligible for Rifampin Prophylaxis and of Those Who Were Given the Drug Unnecessarily

Person Exposed	Type of Exposure	Needed	Rifampin Given (by Obstetrics Resident)	Problem
Emergency Department				
RN, pregnant	Foley catheter insertion	No	(Yes)	Pregnant
RN	Close patient care	Yes	(Yes)	Gastrointestinal
RN	Transport	No	(Yes)	Contact lenses
Unit secretary	Spoke to family	No	(Yes)	Gastrointestinal
ECG technician	In room; test postponed	No	(Yes)	
House officer/Emergency department	Fundoscopy	Yes	Refused	
House officer/Obstetrics	Close examination	Yes	(Yes)	
Patient	In room	Yes	Yes	
Two visitors of roommate	In room only 10 minutes	No	No	
Antenatal Unit				
Two Radiology technicians	X-ray postponed	No	No	
RN (3–11)	Patient care	Yes	(Yes)	
RN (7–11)	Minimal patient care	No	(Yes)	
Aide	Brought in equipment	No	No	
IV Team RN	Restarted intravenous drip	No	No	Refused
Intensive Care Unit				
House officer	Intubated patient	Yes	(Yes)	Gastrointestinal
Respiratory therapist	Adjusted respirator, suctioned patient	No	(Yes)	
RN (11–7)	Patient care	Yes	(Yes)	Gastrointestinal
RN (11–7)	Took blood pressure	No	(Yes)	
RN (7–3)	Assisted primary nurse	No	No	
Attending private physician	Tested reflexes	No	No	

CASE 3

The third case involves a 59-year-old surgeon with gastrointestinal bleeding who was admitted to the medical intensive care unit from the emergency department. He had a massive gastric ulcer, and when his bleeding could not be controlled medically he underwent surgery and was transferred to the surgical intensive care unit. Two days after surgery, the special chemistry laboratory routinely reported two positive hepatitis B test results to the infection control practitioner. One of these results belonged to the surgeon. The positive hepatitis B surface antigen and hepatitis B core antibody indicated that the patient had hepatitis, either in the late acute/early convalescent stage or as a chronic carrier. In either case, he was potentially infectious.

This type of cooperative relationship between the laboratories and the infection control department serves to ensure that when an infectious condition exists an infection control practitioner is made aware of it so that any possible further transmission can be avoided.

As in the meningitis case previously discussed, the infection control practitioner investigated four questions: (1) Was this patient's infectivity known to hospital personnel and had the patient been placed on Blood and Body Fluid Precautions or all the staff alerted? The answer was no. (2) Did any staff member sustain a needlestick while caring for this patient? (3) Did any of the body fluids of the patient contact nonintact skin or the mucous membranes of any staff member? (4) Was there any indication in the patient's medical record that he had hepatitis? If so, why had he not been placed on Blood and Body Fluid Precautions or, in hospitals where this category is not used, why had the staff not been informed of the possible diagnosis?

Although no one had reported a needlestick to the employee health service in connection with this surgeon, on closer questioning the infection control practitioner found that one emergency department nurse had sustained a small puncture wound from a venipuncture needle used on the patient that had been considered too minute to report. When this was discovered, more than 7 days had passed since the injury and it was, therefore, too late to administer hepatitis B immune globulin. However, several other serious exposures that involved bloody gastric irrigating fluid contact with cuts on the hands of personnel were recent enough to warrant the administration of hepatitis B immune globulin. Indications and procedures for immunoglobulin prophylaxis, which would now also involve administration of hepatitis vaccine, are discussed in greater detail in Chapter 5.

It must be remembered that this incident occurred at the very beginning of the acquired immunodeficiency syndrome (AIDS) epidemic; but there are enough persons even now who do not wear gloves when indicated, and some of the exposures would probably occur even now. Altogether, in the 10 days since the surgeon's admission, 95 persons had direct hands-on contact with him, six of whom had serious exposures. In answer to the question of whether the nurses or physicians should have suspected hepatitis, a chart review revealed that on admission, the patient's bilirubin value was 2.2 mg/dL and that 2 days later, the alanine aminotransferase value was 635 units/mL. Both values are abnormal and should have aroused suspicion among the nursing staff. Indeed, 4 days after the surgeon's admission to the medical intensive care unit the internist recorded his suspicion and ordered the hepatitis screening test. The physician did not, however, order Body Fluid Precautions or discuss the elevations or his suspicion with the nurses. Because of the patient's transfer to the operating room and then to the surgical intensive care unit, the note was not read by the nurses in either area. Until the infection control practitioner called the surgical intensive care unit with the positive result, no one was aware of the risk posed by this patient.

PREVENTION OF UNNECESSARY EXPOSURE TO INFECTIONS

Exposures such as those discussed in the previous cases can be prevented. In the first case, the patient's attending physician acted irresponsibly by refusing to permit institution of appropriate isolation and so did the resident. Anyone who does not wish to directly dispute an attending physician's "no isolation" order should at least have informed the patient's nurse and the infection control practitioner of the patient's infectious condition. Unfortunately, the patient's nurses, on all three shifts, also contributed to the problem by not reading the history and physical, which clearly described a "zoster-like rash on the face with vesicles on the chest." The night nurse wrote that the patient had complained of pain in the chest rash area, and so was clearly aware of the rash. The nurse should have known, as should have both physicians, that patients with leukemia are in a high-risk category for disseminated zoster and thus can become extremely infectious. In fact, the Centers for Disease Control guidelines recommend that immunosuppressed patients, even with localized herpes zoster, be placed on Strict Isolation for that very reason.[2]

Most of the exposures to the patient with meningitis could also have been avoided. If the emergency department and intensive care unit personnel had maintained a high index of suspicion regarding meningitis in a patient with fever *and* confusion, this patient would have been placed on Respiratory Isolation precautions on admission to the emergency department. Respiratory Isolation simply requires that the patient be placed in a private room and that masks be worn. Hospital policy was further ignored by the obstetrics resident, by personnel exposed to the patient, and by the pharmacist when rifampin was ordered, dispensed, and taken without approval. The hospital Infection Control Manual provided clear guidelines regarding employee exposure and indications for and release of rifampin for prophylaxis.

Knowledge about high-risk patients for hepatitis carriage would have alerted the intensive care unit staff to look at the third patient's liver enzyme values. He was born in Taiwan, an area with high hepatitis carriage rates, and had also received prior blood transfusions for other episodes of gastric bleeding. However, beyond that if the physicians and nurses had fulfilled their responsibilities, very few, if any, of the personnel who cared for the patient would have been exposed to the risk of acquiring hepatitis. It was the responsibility of the physician who ordered the hepatitis screening test to order Blood and Body Fluid Precautions for the patient or otherwise alert the staff because of the elevated enzyme levels. Picking up an order for a hepatitis screening test in turn should have alerted the patient's nurse to check the laboratory data or inquire about the reason for the test.

If nurses in emergency departments, trauma centers, and critical care units are to protect themselves and others against their patient's transmissible infections, they should keep in mind several important guidelines. They need to

- Know the groups of patients at high risk for specific transmissible infections; including, but not limited to, AIDS, hepatitis, pulmonary tuberculosis, meningitis (meningococcal and *Hemophilus influenzae*), and varicella zoster.
- Become familiar with the covert or subtle manifestations as well as overt signs and symptoms of the common and transmissible infectious diseases.
- Maintain a high index of suspicion. Nurses should read the physicians' notes and laboratory results that can alert them to the presence of infection.
- Know the mode(s) of transmission for the more common and serious infections.
- Treat all blood or body fluids as potentially infectious.
- Follow hospital policies regarding institution of precautions or isolation to prevent such transmission.
- Institute specific precautionary measures on *suspicion*, by themselves, if a physician is not available. By the time an infection is diagnosed, a lot of exposures may already have taken place.
- Inform and consult with the infection control practitioner as soon as possible, especially if inadvertent exposures may have occurred. Sometimes, prophylaxis is limited to a narrow time frame. Exposures such as needlesticks should always be documented, no matter how insignificant or embarrassing they may appear.

In most health care facilities, whoever first becomes aware of a patient's potential infectivity, whether it be a physician or a nurse, is responsible for instituting precautionary measures and informing the infection control practitioner. Usually this poses very few problems. In a worst case situation however, as in the disseminated zoster example, the infection control practitioner *must* be consulted. In most institutions, in an emergency situation when a hazard to other patients and personnel exists, the chairman of the Infection Control Committee and/or a designee (usually the infection control practitioner) has the authority to institute precautionary measures, even against the wishes of a patient's physician. Fortunately, this is rarely necessary if the hazard is explained. The precautionary measures are based on scientific data and on the guidelines issued by the Centers for Disease Control. They are the accepted, nationwide standard of care, and no reasonable physician or nurse should ignore them.

The cases discussed in this chapter are only three examples of exposures that occur in the critical care setting. Most exposures are preventable, and it is hoped that with this warning, more of them will be prevented.

REFERENCES

1. Advisory Committee on Immunization Practices. Meningococcal disease—United States. MMWR 1981;30:113–115.

2. Garner JS, Simmons BP. CDC Guidelines for Isolation Precautions in Hospitals. Infect Control 1983;4:245–325.

CHAPTER REVIEW QUESTIONS

1. Critical care nurses should be alerted to a transmissible infection and/or patients should be placed on the appropriate category of Isolation or Precautions
   a. When a test confirms the infectious diagnosis
   b. On suspicion of having a transmissible infection
   c. As soon as a culture has been taken

2. If a patient is suspected of having a transmissible infection but the physician decides not to place a patient on Isolation or Precautions, what should the nurse do?
   a. Call the infection control practitioner.
   b. Put the patient on Isolation or Precautions anyway.
   c. Follow the physician's order.
   d. a and b

3. A patient with a high temperature and change in mentation should be placed on what type of Isolation until meningococcal or *Hemophilus influenzae* meningitis has been ruled out?
   a. Strict Isolation
   b. Resistant Organism Isolation
   c. Contact Isolation
   d. Respiratory Isolation
   e. Acid-fast bacilli Isolation

4. In-hospital postexposure follow-up for hepatitis B and meningitis is best handled by
   a. Emergency department
   b. Employee health service or infection control practitioner

5. A patient with meningitis should be placed on isolation if the cerebrospinal fluid Gram stain shows
   a. Gram-positive cocci
   b. Gram-positive diplococci
   c. Gram-negative diplococci
   d. All of the above

Answers are provided in Appendix B.

Chapter 2

The Immune System and Its Relationship to Infection

It is difficult to imagine that one could read, or write, a chapter about any infectious disease without referring to the immune system. It would be almost impossible to understand or to predict which transmissible infection a patient may harbor or develop if one is not familiar with the functions and malfunctions of the immune system.

Critical illness itself is immunosuppressive to some extent. If nurses are to develop a high index of suspicion of a patient's potential for being infectious, knowledge of deficit-related infections is imperative. Armed with such knowledge, nurses will know what types of infections to anticipate and what to look for, so that they can protect themselves and others in a timely fashion.

Understanding the immune system also helps to interpret diagnostic tests. For example, is a patient infectious if there is a positive hepatitis B core antibody but a negative hepatitis B surface antigen and surface antibody? Why does a diagnosis of cytomegalovirus infection often depend on titers from paired specimens? Can a patient with a nonreactive (negative) purified protein derivative (PPD) skin test have active tuberculosis? And, is a nurse who has never had chickenpox immune or susceptible to chickenpox if a blood test shows a low titer? The answers to these questions are found in this chapter.

COMPONENTS OF THE IMMUNE SYSTEM

It is not entirely correct to look on the immune system as a single entity. There are several systems or parts. The phagocytic inflammatory response is one, the humoral and complement system is another, and the cell-mediated immune system is a third. Each part specializes in a variety of functions. Each plays an important role in preventing or fighting certain infections. But one without the others is severely limited in its efficacy against serious infections, and without the checks and balances they apply to each other's functions the individual response could destroy not only the invading pathogens but the body itself. Thus, in the true sense of the word, the whole internal human immune system is greater than the sum of its individual parts.

The Phagocytic System

The body's first and most familiar defense against an invasive organism are the phagocytic white blood cells, which consist of granulocytes, including eosinophils and basophils, and the primary defenders, the polymorphonuclear neutrophils.[1]

Polymorphonuclear neutrophils originate in the bone marrow at a rate of 10^{11} cells a day and comprise about 50% of while blood cells in the peripheral circulation. A large reservoir of mature cells also remains in the bone marrow for rapid release if needed (Table 2-1).

The normal peripheral neutrophil count in adults varies from 5,000 to 10,000 cells/cu mm, but moderate increases from 15,000 to 25,000 cells/cu mm or more can occur as a result of myocardial infarction or other tissue injury, during labor, with exercise, or during the digestive process and is not considered significant or diagnostic of infection. In newborns, the normal range is between 9,000 and 30,000 cells/cu mm.[2] In the presence of foreign antigens such as bacteria and fungi, or even with other foreign substances such as splinters, chemotactic factors released at the injured site attract neutrophils to the area, where they begin the process of phagocytosis of the foreign substance. This process involves attachment to the organism and is enhanced by opsonins produced by the complement system. Opsonization makes the microorganism more attractive or "tasty" for phagocytosis. After attachment and engulfment, the organism is killed and digested by a variety of processes within the neutrophil.

There is a group of pathogens however that are not destroyed by phagocytosis within the neutrophilic cells. These organisms not only can survive but also can multiply within these white blood cells, and they are therefore called intracellular pathogens. The mechanism of their destruction is discussed later. If necessary, additional neutrophils are released into the bloodstream from the reserves in the bone marrow, resulting in large increases of white blood cells in the circulation, which is known as leukocytosis. The increased blood flow at the site of injury, and the arrival of large numbers of white blood cells in the area, produces the erythema, induration, and purulence that is part of this nonspecific defense mechanism. Pus is a mixture of dead tissue, bacteria, and white blood cells. Should the infection persist, the store of neutrophils will become depleted and the bone marrow will increase its production of new cells. The stages of neutrophil maturation are shown in Figure 2-1 from left to right. The cell begins as a myeloblast and progresses through the other five phases until the mature

Table 2-1 The Differential Granulocyte Count in Infectious Processes

Cell Types	Cells/cu mm	% of Total	Functions and Response
Leukocytes	Adult: 5,000–10,000 Newborn: 9,000–30,000	100	
Polymorphonuclear neutrophils	2,500–6,000	40–60	Early nonspecific response: phagocytosis; increased in inflammatory or infectious conditions; decreased in certain viral infections
Immature neutrophils (stabs, bands)	0–600	0–6	Increased in bacterial and early viral infections; if above 6% = shift to the left
Eosinophils	50–300	1–3	Elevated in allergy and skin and parasitic infections
Basophils	0–100	0–1	Not involved in phagocytosis

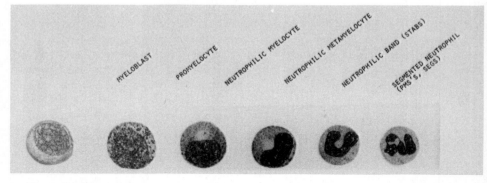

Figure 2-1 Maturation process of polymorphonuclear neutrophils. *Source:* Reprinted from *The Competent Immune System* (p. 152) by I Gurevich with permission of Nursing Clinics of North America.

segmented neutrophil emerges. If the need for leukocytes outstrips the normal maturation time, immature white cells will be released into the circulation in the form of "bands" or "stabs."

When the number of immature cells in the serum exceeds the norm of 0 to 600 cells (or 0–6% of the circulating polymorphonuclear neutrophils) the differential is said to show a shift to the left. Typically, this shift occurs in bacterial infections, while in viral diseases, after an early leukocytosis, the differential shows an increase in lymphocytes (lymphocytosis). A mature neutrophil is able to inactivate 20 bacteria or more, but the immature forms are less efficient. Without the backup of the other parts of the immune system, the infecting organisms could soon overwhelm this first line of defense.

Neutrophil Deficiencies: Causes and Related Factors

A phagocytic response in a healthy, well-nourished person is usually able to contain a localized bacterial infection and to destroy the organisms involved. Deficits may be inherited or acquired and due to a decrease in the absolute number of neutrophils or to qualitative defects that are difficult to assess from the routine white blood cell counts and the differential. They include chemotactic defects and migratory difficulties and can occur in diabetes, rheumatoid arthritis, and Chédiak-Higashi syndrome and from medications such as corticosteroids. The inability to phagocytose or kill organisms may be due to malnutrition in some patients and to the immunosuppressive effect of uremia, cirrhosis, and other disease states.

Patients at high risk for developing leukopenia are those on chemotherapy for tumors or other malignancies and transplant patients.[3] Infections related to neutropenia are usually of bacterial origin, and some are listed in Table 2-2. These

Table 2-2 Granulocyte Deficits and Related Infections

Deficit	Frequent Causes and Diseases	Infection	Pathogen
Leukopenia	Malnutrition Uremia	Pneumonia	*Streptococcus pneumoniae*
	Diabetes mellitus Leukemia Chemotherapy Immunosuppressants Irradiation	Skin and soft tissue Sepsis Perirectal abscesses	Gram-negative organisms*† Staphylococci*†
	Idiosyncratic, drug-related, bone marrow depression	Pharyngitis Esophagitis	*Pseudomonas* species*‡ *Serratia* species*‡ *Klebsiella* species*‡ *Acinetobacter* species*‡
Chemotaxis and other qualitative deficits	Age (related to poor perfusion) Corticosteroids Immunosuppressants		

*Patient's own normal flora
†Hands of personnel
‡"Water bugs" via hands of personnel or equipment

may originate from the patient's own "normal" flora or from sources within the critical care area such as the hands of health care workers and the equipment used in the care of patients. Common pathogens are the gram-negative "water bugs" from respiratory therapy and other water reservoirs. Such infections are of little danger to healthy nurses with intact skin and mucous membranes, but they can be deadly for the patients themselves. Nursing measures to prevent patients from developing nosocomial infections have been well described elsewhere.[4-8]

Since critical illness by itself, and the aging process, is a potent stressor of all systems, including the hematopoietic system, most patients in intensive care units are already in a somewhat "compromised" state. Infections that develop in these patients are rarely contained by phagocytosis alone, and the other arms of the immune system will be required to assist in the process.

The Lymphocyte-Mediated Immune Systems

Lymphocytes originate in the bone marrow from a common progenitor—the stem cell. Thereafter they go through a variety of growth stages until they are differentiated into T and B lymphocytes, as shown in Figure 2-2. T cells complete their maturation process in the thymus; B cells mature in lymphoid tissue and bone marrow.

The T lymphocytes are responsible for cell-mediated immunity, and most live for many years. There is replacement of T cells as they die, but their numbers and functions decline somewhat with age.[9] T cells differentiate "self" from "nonself" and are responsible for "nonself" graft rejection and delayed hypersensitivity, immunologic surveillance for tumor cells, and graft-versus-host rejection. Their diminished numbers and efficacy in the aged may account for the increase in malignancies in that population. Their activities in regard to infection will be described in greater detail later in this chapter.

B cells are mediators of humoral immunity. They are shortlived and replaced about every 16 days. B cells also distinguish "self" from "nonself." When they are not able to make that differentiation they produce the destructive manifestations of autoimmune diseases. B cells are found mostly in blood, whereas T cells reside mainly in lymphoid tissue. The infection-related activities of the B lymphocytes are discussed in detail in the section on humoral immunity.

Both T- and B-cell deficits can be due to inheritance or acquired by disease or therapy directed against the disease. Anything that decreases bone marrow function can decrease the number or efficacy of these two arms of immunity.

Cell-Mediated Immunity

It is difficult to decide which system should be described first because both are equally important. With the appearance of the acquired immunodeficiency

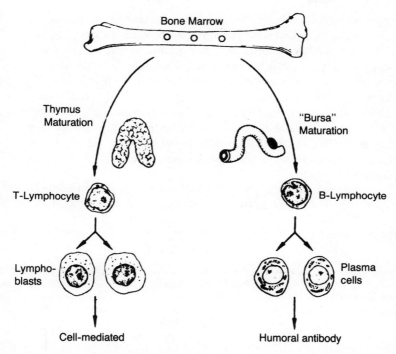

Figure 2-2 T and B lymphocyte differentiation and maturation. *Source:* Reprinted from *The Competent Internal Immune System* (p 156) by I Gurevich with permission of Nursing Clinics of North America, © 1985.

syndrome (AIDS), the T cell has become a familiar topic, and it is therefore helpful to begin with the system it mediates: cell-mediated immunity.[10] Cell-mediated immunity takes many hours to several days to fully evolve because it is a stepwise process. T lymphocytes comprise about 80% of circulating lymphocytes. The remainder reside in lymphoid tissue (the lymph glands) and the spleen. There are several types of T cells: those that mediate delayed hypersensitivity; cytotoxic T cells that kill other cells, especially tumor cells or cells infected by viruses; and those that regulate the immune response.

The sequence of events that follows invasion of tissue cells by a virus or other pathogen begins with cellular secretion of interferons, which quickly attempt to destroy the virus. At the same time, neutrophils and mononuclear macrophages begin the phagocytic processes that also attempt to destroy the invading organism. During this digestive attempt, viral antigen is processed by the macrophages in such a way that it is recognized as ''foreign'' by the T cells circulating in the blood. When T cells meet up with the particular antigen for which they have been programmed since birth, they recognize the antigen and become sensitized to it and are now activated to multiply and produce memory-retaining cells. They also produce lymphokines and interleukins, which, in turn, trigger B-cell responses and multiplication. At the same time, cytotoxic T cells attack the virus-infected cells of the body and they are assisted by the helper T cells. The helper T cells provide added stimuli to B cells to begin antibody production.

Without a regulatory mechanism to halt the immune response, the immune system would go on and possibly destroy its host. It is the function of the suppressor T cells to turn off the production of cytotoxic cells and to signal the B cells to stop production of antibody, so as to prevent overkill or autoimmune processes of destruction.

The interactions between T and B lymphocytes and macrophages are shown in Figure 2-3. The whole cycle takes several days, and some of the clinical

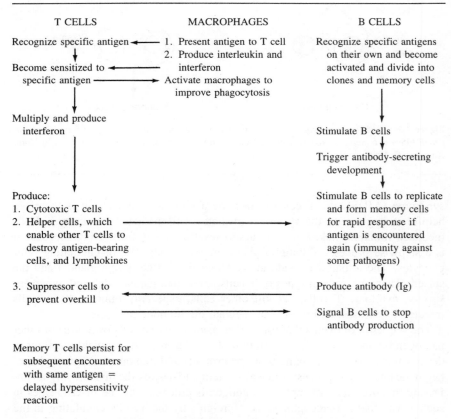

Figure 2-3 Actions and interactions of macrophages with T and B lymphocytes.

manifestations that accompany many viral infections are due to the circulating substances produced by the T and B cells.

Delayed Hypersensitivity and the Memory Cell. Although nurses may not be familiar with the name or meaning of delayed hypersensitivity, they are very familiar with one of its manifestations, the positive (or reactive) purified protein derivative (PPD) tuberculin (Mantoux) test. This localized dermal reaction occurs when an antigen is injected intradermally into a person previously sensitized to that antigen by vaccination, exposure, infection, or disease. The reaction is mediated by the "memory" of previously sensitized T cells.

The antigen recalls that memory and activates a response within 48 days that sends T cells, B cells, and macrophages to the site of the injection to destroy what the immune system imagines to be a new infection with an old and previously seen organism. The result is a measurable area of induration. If the person has never been infected with *Mycobacterium tuberculosis* there will be no induration because there are no memory cells to trigger the delayed hypersensitivity or memory response. It takes 2 to 8 weeks to develop memory cells, so persons may have a negative or nonreactive PPD test if the PPD is placed before the memory cells are produced. A negative response may also result if a patient is on corticosteroid therapy or if the cell-mediated immune system is not functioning adequately. Such may be the case if a patient is suffering a concomitant viral infection, especially measles or influenza, at the time the PPD was placed, or it may occur in conditions that destroy cell-mediated immunity, such as AIDS. In order to differentiate a true-negative from a false-response reaction, other skin tests are placed simultaneously to the PPD. Since most adults have had mumps and all have *Candida* as normal flora, these two antigens are frequently chosen. If all tests are negative, the patient is anergic: his or her cell-mediated immune system is not able to recall its memory. If one of the panel tests is positive but the PPD test remains negative, the PPD test may be truly negative.

As mentioned earlier in this chapter, cell-mediated immunity also diminishes with age. As a result, the reaction to a PPD test may wane. Retesting an older person 2 weeks after a first PPD test may "boost" the memory of the aging memory T cell and produce a reactive test if the patient's T cells had a previous encounter with tuberculosis. The PPD itself does not sensitize the patient's cell-mediated immune system in these cases. If the patient is truly negative, the boosting effect will not occur because there will be no "memory" or delayed hypersensitivity to reactivate.

Cell-Mediated Immune System Deficiencies. The T-cell-dependent immune system can have deficits in the quality of its T cells as well as in the number of cells in the system. The effect on the host is the same, namely, a predisposition to infection with intracellular organisms and an increase in certain malignancies.

As previously mentioned, some viruses, fungi, and bacteria are able to survive within phagocytic neutrophils and macrophages, and even multiply within them, and are thus called intracellular pathogens. Many of these pathogens are responsible for the incurable infections that afflict AIDS patients, but they are also responsible for infections in other patients with cell-mediated immune system deficits. Among the bacteria, *M. tuberculosis, M. avium-intracellulare,* and *Salmonella* species are the most frequent pathogens. All of the herpesviruses are intracellular organisms, and so are *Pneumocystis carinii* and *Toxoplasma gondii. Cryptococcus neoformans* and *Candida* species are the most frequently seen fungal infections. A more complete list is provided in Table 2-3. Although deficiencies can be of genetic origin, the discussion here is centered on acquired deficits.

There are two causes of quantitative T-lymphocyte abnormalities: overproduction, caused by lymphoproliferative diseases, and a decrease in numbers. Lymphopenia can be caused by destruction of mature lymphocytes, as is the case in AIDS when the virus destroys the T cells. It can also occur in depression or destruction of the bone marrow, which then prevents reproduction of new cells. Pharmacologic agents, radiation therapy, and malignancy are the major causes (Table 2-4).

There are many factors that can impair the quality of lymphocyte response and action. Vaccines and viral infections, especially cytomegalovirus and the childhood exanthems, are high on any list. Malignancies, such as Hodgkin's disease, decrease not only the number of cells but adversely affect many of their actions and interactions with the humoral immune system. Lymphomas have been found to be the cause and the effect of lymphocyte deficits. Corticosteroids

Table 2-3 Examples of Intracellular Pathogens

Bacteria	Viruses
Mycobacterium tuberculosis	Cytomegalovirus
M. avium-intracellulare	Herpes simplex
Salmonella species	Varicella zoster
Nocardia species	Epstein-Barr virus
Listeria monocytogenes	

Fungi	Protozoa
Candida species	Pneumocystis carinii
Aspergillus species	Toxoplasma gondii
Cryptococcus neoformans	Strongyloides
Coccidioides	Cryptosporidium
Histoplasma capsulatum	

Table 2-4 Causes of Cell-Mediated Immune System Deficits and the Resultant Problems or Infections

Disease or Cause of Decreased Cell-Mediated Immunity	Problem/Infection
Old age	Increase in malignancies Waning of delayed hypersensitivity Increase in reactivation of tuberculosis, zoster, *Listeria monocytogenes*
Splenic defect (sickle cell disease, Hodgkin's disease, splenectomy)	Tuberculosis Disseminated zoster Other intracellular pathogens Encapsulated bacteria (*Streptococcus pneumoniae, Hemophilus influenzae*)
Radiation and chemotherapy	Infections with intracellular pathogens Anergy
Acute and chronic leukemia	Infections with *Pneumocystis*, varicella-zoster, and gram-negative and gram-positive bacteria
Immunosuppressive drugs and corticosteroids for organ transplants	Early: encapsulated organisms Late: Intracellular pathogens, especially cytomegalovirus Anergy

AIDS	All intracellular organisms, especially
	  Candida
	  Mycobacterium
	  Pneumocystis
	  Cryptococcus
	  Cryptosporidium
	  Toxoplasma
	  Cytomegalovirus
	  Salmonella
	Malignancies
	  Kaposi's sarcoma
	  Lymphomas
	  Carcinomas
	Anergy

depress the cytotoxic activity, and inhibition of lymphokine production is among their other effects on T cells. Cyclosporins and other agents administered to prevent allograft rejection also prevent T-cell responses to other foreign agents. It is important to remember that cell-mediated immune functions will also be impaired if humoral immunity and the complement systems are compromised.

Regardless of the cause of immunosuppression, patients with T-cell deficits are at high risk of developing infections that may contribute not only to their own morbidity and mortality but may also be transmissible. These infections include tuberculosis, disseminated zoster, herpesvirus infection, salmonellosis, and cytomegalovirus infection. Nurses should be alert to the early signs of these diseases, as discussed in the appropriate chapters, in order to protect themselves and others.

Humoral Immunity

Humoral, or antibody-dependent, immunity is mediated by the B lymphocytes. While cell-mediated immunity is mostly directed against viruses and other intracellular organisms, the antibody system is directed mainly against bacteria. There is, of course, the ability to destroy viruses and bacteria within both systems, and, as mentioned previously, there is considerable interdependence between these two arms of the immune system (see Figure 2-3).

As with the T cell, there are several ways in which the B cell protects the body. It may promote opsonization, which makes any organism more attractive and more accessible to the phagocytes of the other immune system. It may stimulate the complement system, which induces lysis of the pathogen, or it may produce antibody to neutralize the invaders and thus destroy their ability to infect other cells. It is antibody production that will be described in detail here for three reasons: (1) antibody production is the main function of the B cell; (2) it is also the basis for understanding a nurse's and a patient's measurable immunity to certain transmissible infections, which, in turn, will influence protective measures; and (3) antibody measurements (titers) are used in the diagnosis of certain infectious diseases, and correct interpretation of results is important.

Immunoglobulins. B cells produce five classes of immunoglobulins (antibodies). Their functions are listed in Table 2-5. Only IgM and IgG are discussed here.

Each B cell is programmed genetically to recognize only one antigen. When this antigen, for example, the hepatitis A virus, comes in contact with the B cell that carries the hepatitis A virus recognition factor or immunoglobulin, they bind together much as a key fits into a lock. Other antigens, labeled B and C in Figure 2-4, cannot achieve this "fit" because the B cell shown in the figure is not programmed to recognize or bind them. This binding sensitizes the B cell and triggers the immune response, which ultimately results in production of hepatitis

Table 2-5 Human Immunoglobulins with Some of Their Functions

IgM
- Is the first to respond to primary infections
- Is not transplacentally transferred
- Activates complement and lysis of organisms
- Neutralizes some viruses

IgG
- Responds slowly to a first infection but very rapidly to subsequent encounters with same organisms
- Is transferred transplacentally to the fetus
- Stimulates production of opsonins
- Neutralizes viruses
- Is the major component of commercial globulins (i.e., immune serum globulin, hepatitis B immune globulin)

IgA
- Is the major component of mucosal secretions (tears, saliva, bronchial and intestinal secretions)
- Inhibits bacterial adherence to mucosal surfaces (deficits predispose to infections in the listed areas)

IgE
- Mediates allergic reactions (immediate hypersensitivity vs. T-cell delayed hypersensitivity)

IgD
- Functions not established

A virus specific antibody. Other B cells will be programmed for *Hemophilus influenzae* recognition, others for staphylococci, and so on. It is possible that a B cell may never meet up with the specific antigen for which it is programmed, and unless immunity is provided by the cell-mediated immune system, as may happen with tuberculosis, the person remains susceptible to that infection. For example, someone who has never been exposed to tetanus will have no antibody to that organism because the B cell programmed to produce tetanus antibody has not been sensitized to it. If it is deemed desirable to protect a person against a potential infection, a vaccine can be given if one is available. Vaccines may consist of the antigen or organism itself in its original, attenuated, or killed form (e.g., measles, rubella) or just part of the antigen (e.g., the hepatitis B vaccine). These antigens, in whatever form, will be bound by their particular B cells, and the resultant antibody will produce protection or immunity against subsequent infection with that organism. Unfortunately, lasting immunity to all organisms is not achievable, although subsequent infections are usually milder.

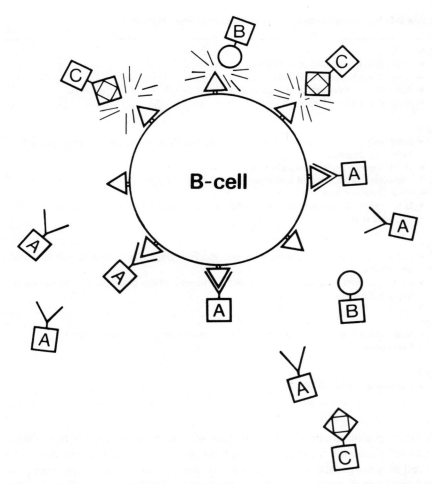

Figure 2-4 Antigen "A" binding to B cell with antibody "A" receptor site shaped to provide an appropriate "fit." This B cell does not have receptors for B and C antigens. *Source:* Reprinted from *The Competent Internal Immune System* (p 157) by I Gurevich with permission of Nursing Clinics of North America, © 1985.

Immunoglobulins and Diagnosis. There are many ways of diagnosing an infection. The most accurate method is culture of the organism; another method is serologic detection of antigens and antibodies. Some organisms are difficult or slow to grow on culture, or good specimens are difficult to obtain. *Legionella* species are a good example of these limitations. Viruses must be grown in tissue cultures. Not all hospitals have virology laboratories, and the process of diagnosis is time consuming, costly, and in some instances, as in the identification of the human immunodeficiency virus, dangerous. In those instances, a variety of antibody tests and counts (titers) are used, but antigen determinations are becoming more efficient and their use will soon become more extensive.

Antibody titers also help determine the susceptible or immune status of patients and nurses and must be understood. The first antibody of the humoral response is IgM. It takes up to 10 days to produce measurable titers, and because IgM titers rise rapidly and decline rapidly they must be measured during the acute phase or they may be missed. If the same pathogen is encountered again at a later time, there will be no significant and sometimes no measurable IgM titer. Because cytomegalovirus is of some concern to pregnant women, which of course includes nurses and physicians, this is used as an example along with hepatitis A virus. During a first infection, cytomegalovirus-specific IgM and hepatitis A virus–specific IgM will become measurable within about 10 days after exposure and their presence denotes an acute, first-time infection. Cytomegalovirus or hepatitis A virus IgG titers become detectable later in the acute phase because they increase at a slower rate than IgM. It is IgG that carries the memory of previous exposures, and in most immunocompetent hosts it persists throughout life. Subsequent exposure to cytomegalovirus or hepatitis A virus will jog the memory of the previously sensitized B cell, and specific IgG titers will be produced very rapidly and in large amounts.

In the case of hepatitis A and many other infections, the presence of specific IgG titers denotes past infection of an indeterminate time. It indicates recovery and immunity to future infections with that organism. This immunity occurs because on subsequent exposure the slow B-cell sensitization process does not need to be repeated and the rapid IgG response is able to neutralize the organisms very quickly and before they are able to cause a new infection or disease.

Practical application of this principle is the testing of nurses for titers to rubella, measles, chickenpox, and hepatitis B. If they do not have titers to these four organisms, they are susceptible and may acquire (or transmit) these infections from or to their patients. In most states, nurses may not work in a hospital if they are susceptible to rubella because of the teratogenic effect of infection in the first trimester. It is advisable for susceptible nurses to receive available vaccinations for measles and hepatitis B.

Unfortunately, the presence of antibody is not protective against reinfection with some organisms. Such is the case for some bacterial infections (e.g., staphylococcal and pseudomonal infections and gonorrhea). It is also true for infections with some viruses, such as cytomegalovirus and herpes simplex types 1 and 2. It is true, however, that a subsequent infection with the same virus will be less severe than the first and also somewhat less likely to cause congenital infections.[11] Antibody is also not protective against reactivation of latent or dormant infection with these viruses, as well as the Epstein-Barr and varicella-zoster viruses. In the case of the varicella-zoster virus, chickenpox is the first manifestation of infection with the virus. Zoster, or shingles, in its localized or disseminated form is the reactivated form of varicella.

How does one know whether an infection with these viruses is a primary infection or due to reinfection or reactivation? Here, virus serology or antibody titers can be of great help. Several methods are available, and the criteria for their interpretation must be provided by the laboratory.

In the case of cytomegalovirus or herpes simplex virus, IgM will usually indicate a recent primary infection. The finding of IgG, however, only shows that a previous infection had occurred. It cannot denote the presence of reinfection or reactivation. If one remembers that IgG titers will increase with a second infection or reactivation, it becomes obvious that a second IgG titer taken 3 to 5 weeks after the first acute titer will be elevated if the present manifestations are due to the suspected organism. These are called paired titers, and they must be processed by the same laboratory at the same time to achieve interpretable results. A fourfold or greater rise in titer from the acute phase specimen to the second specimen can be diagnostic.[12] Similar measurements can be used for suspected infections with *Legionella* species and other organisms that are often difficult to grow on culture, but most of these are not transmissible to others and are not described here.

In many instances the presence of IgG antibody means that the infection has resolved and the pathogen is destroyed. The presence of hepatitis B surface antibody is such an example, as are others already described. However, the presence of antibody in some infectious diseases not only does not prevent reinfection or reactivation but also may not prevent others from acquiring the infection. During periods of reactivation of herpes simplex virus, cytomegalovirus, and zoster virus, persons are shedding the virus and can transmit the disease to others. Even asymptomatic shedding of some organisms may occur in the presence of antibody. Examples of shedding that pertain to critical care nurses and their patients are nasal staphylococcal or streptococcal carriage by nurses that cause infections in infants or adults; asymptomatic carriage of the meningococcus or *Hemophilus influenzae*; inapparent but prolonged shedding of cytomegalovirus by patients or nurses; chronic hepatitis B carriage or disease in the presence of IgM antibody to the hepatitis B core antigen; and carriage of human immunodeficiency virus in antibody-positive persons with or without the clinical features of AIDS. Patients are at high risk for such carriage and shedding, and protective measures are described in the chapters that deal with specific infections.

Humoral Immunity in the Neonate. Unlike IgM, IgG is transported across the placenta from mother to fetus. Because the neonate's immature immune system is not able to manufacture its own IgG, maternal antibody protects the infant against infections only the mother herself had, and even this protection wanes with time. By 3 to 6 months, maternal antibody has almost disappeared and the infant has begun to produce its own IgG (Figure 2-5).[13]

All neonatal intensive care nurses know that neonates are at particularly high risk for bacterial infections. The reason becomes obvious when one remembers that the humoral system is most effective against extracellular bacteria, and this system is least developed at birth. The immaturity of the system and the fact that infants, unlike adults, have not been exposed to bacteria during normal gestation, makes them very susceptible to bacterial and some viral infections after birth. In the immediate neonatal period, *Escherichia coli* and group B streptococci pose the greatest risk because these bacteria can be acquired during passage through the birth canal. In the immediate postnatal period, special concerns arise from other bacteria, such as *Staphylococcus aureus*.

Infants have also not been exposed to the meningococcus and to *Hemophilus influenzae* and have not, therefore, developed antibody to these pathogens after

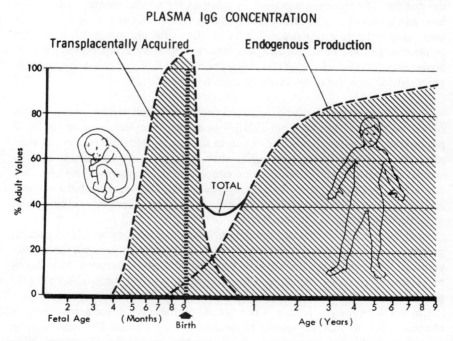

Figure 2-5 Plasma IgG concentrations at different ages. *Source:* Reprinted with permission from *Pediatric Clinics of North America* (1977;24:288), Copyright © 1977, WB Saunders Company.

maternal antibody protection has waned. This places them at extra high risk for these two infections. A further example of how long it takes for humoral immunity to mature completely is its unresponsiveness to certain vaccinations. That is why the first *Hemophilus influenzae* vaccine that became available could not be administered before a child was 24 months of age because it could not elicit an effective antibody response in the immature system. Recently, a *Hemophilus influenzae* vaccine that is effective at 18 months has been developed and will provide earlier protection from this virulent pathogen.[14]

Adults are at a much lesser risk of *Hemophilus influenzae* infections because they have been exposed to the organism from early childhood and are able to mount an adequate immune response before the infection can affect their nervous system and cause meningitis. Antibody thus produced can protect them throughout life.

A final example of the protective value of antibody is the passive immunity transmitted by administration of certain antibodies after an exposure. Hepatitis B immune globulin, zoster immune globulin, and other antibodies confer temporary protection, but they have half-lives of between 14 and 28 days only. Even if they do not totally prevent acquisition of the infection, they will ameliorate the disease. The incubation periods of diseases for which passive antibody has been administered may be prolonged. Hepatitis B could occur as long as 8 months later, and varicella could occur 4 days or more after the usual 10- to 21-day incubation period. Thus, patients and nurses who were given protective antibodies may become infectious after longer periods of time and should be carefully observed for manifestations of the disease involved.

Humoral Immunodeficiency. A natural decline in B-cell performance probably occurs with increasing age, but to a lesser degree than that ascribed to T-cell performance and stimulation. Response to foreign antigens diminishes, as does secretion of antibody. Because aging often decreases tissue perfusion and increases neuropathy, infections become established more easily and are often not noticed or treated as promptly. Together with the suppression of the internal immune systems, these factors are responsible for the increased morbidity and mortality from infection in the elderly.

At the other end of the age spectrum, congenital deficits such as agammaglobulinemia do not permit prolonged survival of such children, who soon succumb to fatal infections. In between these age extremes, humoral deficits can be caused by diseases or pharmacologic agents that affect the lymphocyte progenitor cells and that would, at the same time, decrease T-cell efficiency.

Chronic lymphocytic leukemia is a lymphoproliferative disease that produces abnormal B cells that are unable to produce memory cells. They can also be immunologically defective and produce only low levels of antibody, resulting in infections due to *Streptococcus pneumoniae, Neisseria meningitidis,* and localized pyogenic infections. Of these, only meningococcal infections pose a risk to critical care nurses.

Throughout this chapter the importance of the immune system in relationship to its interaction with the whole has been stressed. An excellent example of the interdependence of the cell-mediated and antibody-mediated systems is provided in AIDS patients. Although the human immunodeficiency virus destroys mostly T cells, in the presence of hypergammaglobulinemia patients with AIDS are unable to combat their old infections and do not produce effective antibody levels against new infections. The reasons for this are not quite clear but must be sought in the inability of the T cells to successfully trigger B-cell production of antibody.

CONCLUSIONS

When the immune systems of critically ill patients have been compromised, either congenitally or by diseases or therapeutic regimens, the body loses its ability to resist infection. Some of these infections are transmissible to those who take care of the patient. It is, therefore, important to be able to predict with some certainty which type of infection a patient might be harboring or developing. Early awareness can result in prompt institution of protective measures as soon as suspicion of an infection is entertained.

One aspect of infection prevention has not been discussed in this chapter. It is an omission not easily sustained by one who is charged to protect patients as well as personnel from infection, but it is hoped that critical care nurses are already aware of, and that they already follow, policies and procedures designed to prevent nosocomial infections in patients. Even without emphasis on patient protection, the material presented in this chapter should heighten their awareness of the fragility of the immune system in their critically ill patients and reinforce their aseptic patient care techniques.

REFERENCES

1. Densen P, Mandell GL. Granulocytic phagocytes. In Mandell GL, Douglas RG, Bennett JE (eds). Principles and Practice of Infectious Diseases, 2nd ed. New York: John Wiley & Sons, 1985.

2. Newland JR. Leukocytosis: Gauging its significance and tracing the cause. Consultant 1984;May:221–237.

3. Reheis CE. Neutropenia: Causes, complications, treatment and resulting nursing care. Nurs Clin North Am 1985;20:219–225.

4. Tafuro P, Gurevich I (eds). Infections in the compromised host. Nurs Clin North Am 1985;20:143–260.

5. Centers for Disease Control. Guideline for prevention of catheter-associated urinary tract infections. Am J Infect Control 1983;11:28–33.

6. Centers for Disease Control. Guideline for prevention of surgical wound infections. Am J Infect Control 1983;11:183–193.

7. Centers for Disease Control. Guideline for prevention of nosocomial pneumonia. Am J Infect Control 1983;11:230–239.

8. Centers for Disease Control. Guideline for prevention of intravascular infections. Am J Infect Control 1983;11:183–193.

9. Wechsle ME: The senescence of the immune system. Hosp Pract 1981;16:53–64.

10. McLeod R, Wing EJ, Remington JS. Lymphocytes and macrophages in cell-mediated immunity. In Mandell GL, Douglas RG, Bennett JE (eds). Principles and Practice of Infectious Diseases, 2nd ed. New York: John Wiley & Sons, 1985.

11. Pass RF, Stagno S, Divorsky ME, et al. Excretion of cytomegalovirus in mothers: Observations after delivery of congenitally infected and normal infants. J Infect Dis 1982;146:1–6.

12. Menegus M, Douglas RG. Viruses, rickettsiae, chlamydiae and mycoplasmas. In Mandell GL, Douglas RG, Bennett JE (eds). Principles and Practice of Infectious Diseases, 2nd ed. New York: John Wiley & Sons, 1985.

13. Miller ME, Stiehm ER. Immunology and resistance to infection. In Remington JS, Klein JO (eds). Infectious Diseases in the Fetus and Newborn, 2nd ed. Philadelphia: W.B. Saunders, 1983.

14. Immunization Advisory Committee. Update—Prevention of Haemophilus influenzae type b disease. MMWR 1988;37(2):13–16.

CHAPTER REVIEW QUESTIONS

1. An elevated white blood cell count (>10,000 cells/cu mm) is usually a sign of viral infection.
   a. True
   b. False

2. Cell-mediated immunity is regulated by
   a. T lymphocytes
   b. B lymphocytes
   c. Chemotaxis
   d. The complement system

3. In order to destroy intracellular pathogens, macrophages must have assistance from
   a. B lymphocytes
   b. T lymphocytes

4. Antibodies are not protective against reinfection with which virus?
   a. Varicella-zoster
   b. Hepatitis A
   c. Measles
   d. Herpes simplex

5. A patient is said to be anergic when the immune system does not "remember" a previously encountered infection. Anergy is due to a deficit in
   a. Polymorphonuclear neutrophils
   b. Macrophages
   c. T lymphocytes
   d. B lymphocytes

Answers are provided in Appendix B.

Chapter 3

Collection of Culture Specimens and Interpretation of Results

Patients in intensive care units undergo a great many tests. When a patient has a serious infection the identification of the pathogen and the antibiotic to which it is sensitive is a matter of great urgency. More than any other test results, culture results can truly become a matter of life and death. Because they can so profoundly affect the medical and nursing care of the patient, and because culture results can only be as good as the specimens submitted, the emphasis in this chapter is on what might be called "bedside microbiology."

Infections and pathogens most commonly encountered in the critically ill patient are discussed along with what constitutes an appropriate specimen, the correct methods for collection, transport, and storage of specimens; the interpretation of the culture reports; and the implications some results may have on the nursing care of the patient.

Cultures are usually ordered by a physician, but in critical care units nurses can often initiate the taking of a culture.

INDICATIONS FOR TAKING A CULTURE

Infectious conditions can often be diagnosed at the bedside before any tests or cultures are taken simply by the clinical presentation of the patient. Two examples are an infected wound and a case of meningitis. However, sometimes just establishing that an infection is present is not enough. There are many organisms that can cause meningitis, and, of course, the physician must treat the cause of the infection to effect a cure. To do that correctly there must be an antibiotic sensitivity report, which, in turn, can only be provided if a culture has produced a pathogen that can be tested against groups of antibiotics. Sometimes, an antibiotic agent can be chosen simply by examination of a smear or stain of the specimen if it contains the pathogen.

In a patient with clinical meningitis, antibiotic therapy must be started within 30 minutes if bacterial infection is suspected. It should not take much more time than that to obtain a cerebrospinal fluid sample and perform a Gram stain. If the Gram stain shows gram-positive cocci in pairs, *Streptococcus pneumoniae* is the likely organism and penicillin would be the antibiotic of choice. If there are small, pleomorphic gram-negative rods, *Hemophilus influenzae* is the most likely organism and ampicillin and chloramphenicol will be administered in most cases. In 24 hours when an organism has been grown on culture and 24 hours after that when the sensitivity results are available, the chloramphenicol may be discontinued if the *Hemophilus influenzae* is sensitive to the ampicillin or vice versa. Sensitivity studies are always required because pathogens can become resistant to almost any antibiotic. The main reason for taking a culture is to determine *specific* antimicrobial therapy. If treatment does not depend on the culture result, as might be the case if removal of a suture might simply release a collection of pus from a wound that will then just require some irrigation, is a culture still needed? Often, a culture is not necessary. However, pathogen identification occasionally may be indicated for reasons other than for therapy (Table 3-1).

For example, a number of infants in an intensive care nursery may have pustules. It is important to know if the pathogen is the same in all cases; if this is so, one can determine the possible source and take corrective action. Or, there may be a sudden increase in bacteremias in patients in an intensive care unit due to *Pseudomonas cepacia*, an organism that is found only sporadically under normal circumstances. The origin of this organism may be a contaminated antiseptic solution. Without knowing the pathogen, a source cannot be found.

In a teaching hospital, pathogen identification is an educational tool. For example, it can help residents differentiate between organisms most likely to cause nosocomial pneumonia in patients on ventilatory assistance and those that cause pneumonia in patients admitted to the hospital from the community. The organisms involved are usually quite different.

Table 3-1 Indications for Taking a Culture

Selection of an effective antibiotic

Establishment of a differential diagnosis and adjustment of medical and nursing care

Identification of a pathogen for purpose of

- Teaching physicians and patients
- Tracing contacts
- Tracing an epidemic and establishing a source
- Determining the need for isolation (rarely needed, mostly for meningitis and tuberculosis)

Occasionally, a culture result can also assist in the decision to institute or discontinue isolation. A patient on respiratory isolation precautions for meningitis whose Gram stain shows gram-positive cocci does not require isolation, but if the Gram stain demonstrates certain gram-negative organisms (*Neisseria meningitidis* or *Hemophilus influenzae*), isolation must be continued.

In the interest of cost containment and effective use of already-stressed laboratories and nursing personnel, it is important to know when not to take a culture because it would be of questionable or no value. A nurse may be curious to know what organisms are causing a decubitus infection, but if the treatment is going to be wound irrigation with normal saline or an iodophor antiseptic solution and the application of a triple antibiotic ointment, regardless of what organisms may be found, a culture is not indicated. A culture report is also not necessary to determine if a patient requires Secretion-Drainage Precautions or Contact Isolation; the amount or type of drainage determines the category.[1]

The cost of performing a culture and sensitivity in materials and personnel time is about $65 in the New York City area. In a study my colleagues and I did in 1986, 53% of cultures instituted by physicians and 94.5% of those instituted by nurses did not result in any change in therapy or there was no evidence in the progress record that the results had been reviewed and considered in the treatment. In other words, the patient's treatment was not affected by one third or more of the cultures.[2]

INFORMATION REQUIRED BY THE LABORATORY

Before a culture specimen is sent for bacteriologic evaluation, certain information needs to be provided, and it is usually the patient's nurse who fills out the voucher or requisition.

1. *Is the patient on antibiotics, and what type?* Ideally, a culture specimen should be obtained before antibiotics are administered, since the growth pattern, morphology of the colonies, and spread of growth of a pathogen can be greatly affected by antibiotics. The information, therefore, reassures the technician that the unusual form is not due to a strange organism. Special growth media may also be necessary. In a more clinical application, the laboratory technician will alert the physician if the sensitivity test reveals that the pathogen is resistant to the antimicrobial agent being administered. If the infection is responding to the antibiotic, a change may not be necessary, but often the information is very important.
2. *What type of organism is suspected?* This information can greatly speed up the identification of a pathogen if special media or different incubating temperatures are required. For example, special media are necessary to

successfully grow *Legionella* species from a patient with pneumonia and *Campylobacter* species require both special media and a higher temperature for incubation. The information can also alert laboratory personnel to handle certain specimens with greater care, as with some of the mycoses, which can pose a real hazard in the laboratory, as can *Salmonella typhi, Brucella, Francisella tularensis*, and others.

3. *The underlying disease of the patient.* In the case of an animal bite, for instance, *Pasteurella multocida* is a common pathogen. Special media are needed to grow the organism, and a culture report will be available 24 hours earlier if time is not lost subculturing the organism. In a sputum specimen the absence of white blood cells on Gram stain would normally prevent processing of the specimen because it would be regarded as saliva not sputum. If, however, the laboratory is informed that the patient is leukopenic, the absence of white blood cells would be expected and the specimen would be processed, preventing delay of appropriate therapy.

4. *The time of collection.* Fastidious or fragile organisms may die, or slowly growing pathogens may be overgrown by those with more rapid growth. Therefore, specimens collected from all patients, but especially from those who are critically ill due to an infectious process, should be transported to the laboratory without delay. Blood and cerebrospinal fluid should never be refrigerated, whereas urine should be so stored if it cannot be processed within 30 minutes.

5. *Proper labeling.* If a patient is on Precautions or Isolation, the specimen should have a label affixed to inform those who will handle it in transit or for processing. Although all specimens should be handled with great care in the laboratory, technicians are occasionally careless and a special reminder is helpful.

COMPARATIVE VALUES OF BODY SITES FOR PATHOGEN RECOVERY

External surfaces of the body and the gastrointestinal tract (mouth to rectum) are highly colonized with each person's "normal flora." These commensal organisms are useful to the body in a variety of ways, but they can also become "opportunistic" pathogens when an opportunity presents. When a specimen for a culture is taken from one of these highly colonized sites, it is difficult to interpret which organisms represent the normal flora and which have become the etiologic agent for the infection. Wound and skin cultures and eye, stool, and vaginal cultures all fall into this category. Cultures from these sites are, therefore, difficult to interpret, must be very carefully obtained, and may not really be needed unless specific antimicrobial therapy is to be directed at the pathogen.

Slightly more helpful are cultures of urine and sputum. The area where the infection occurs (the bladder or kidney and the lung) is usually free of organisms. Without an invasive maneuver to obtain such specimens, they have to pass through passageways that contain many colonizing organisms and will, therefore, also be difficult to interpret.

The most useful and probably the most easily interpretable results are obtained from body sites that are normally organism free or sterile. If care is taken to avoid contamination of these specimens, any organism found on culture is a presumed pathogen. This information is summarized in Table 3-2.

BLOOD CULTURES

The blood is probably the most frequent site cultured in febrile and critically ill patients. This is not surprising, because a patient with a positive blood culture is by definition critically ill. Depending on the site of origin of the pathogen, bacteremia can be very responsive to antimicrobial therapy because the antibiotic comes in direct contact with the pathogen in the blood, if it does not have to penetrate into other tissues such as the lungs, abscesses, or meninges. Even though the pathogens are within the bloodstream, they are there intermittently and not usually in high numbers. Their identification is, therefore, volume dependent.[3] It takes 30 mL or three blood cultures of 10 mL each to obtain the pathogen in 99% of cases. A blood culture should, therefore, consist of 8 to 10 mL sent to the laboratory either in a sterile vacutainer or subdivided into two bottles containing media for aerobic and anaerobic processing.[4,5] The top of the vacutainers or bottles should be disinfected with alcohol or povidone-iodine prior to inoculation with the blood. If the commercial media in use requires a greater or lesser volume of blood, the laboratory should so inform the staff.

Table 3-2 Specimens: Their Value in Relationship to the Normal Microbial Load of the Site

Normally Sterile	Sterile Site → Colonized Passageway	Highly Colonized Areas
Blood	Lung → oropharynx (sputum)	Skin
Cerebrospinal fluid	Kidney and bladder → urethra (urine)	Mucous membranes
Pleural cavity		Oropharynx
Peritoneal cavity		Small and large intestine
Synovial fluid		Eye surfaces and ear
		Urethral meatus
		Vagina

The three blood cultures rule has another advantage. It helps to differentiate a contaminant from a potential pathogen. If one specimen contains *Staphylococcus epidermidis* or any other organism that is commonly present on the skin and can thus be a contaminant and the two other cultures show no growth, there is a greater likelihood that the single culture really does represent a contaminated specimen. If, however, two show the organism and only one does not, it is much more likely to be the pathogen. (In very young children and infants, 5 mL is usually adequate, and it is most often inoculated directly into the bottle containing the aerobic culture medium). At least two of the three cultures should be obtained from different sites, about 15 minutes apart. The ideal timing for a blood culture is just *before* an anticipated fever spike, but this is rarely possible. If all three cultures are negative, the patient remains febrile, and no diagnosis has been made, then repeat cultures after 24 hours may be necessary. This is especially true if the patient has already received antimicrobial therapy.

It is extremely important to use strict aseptic technique to obtain all cultures, but especially those from normally sterile areas. A contaminated specimen representing a false-positive result may lead to therapy for the wrong pathogen. It would be tragic for a patient to suffer a reaction to an antibiotic that is not needed or not appropriate, and it can be equally risky to have to delay appropriate therapy while awaiting the result of a repeat culture. Intensive care nurses often draw blood cultures, and the following technique should be followed:

1. Wash hands.
2. Put on clean gloves for protection. Sterile gloves are not necessary.
3. Prepare the site with tincture of iodine, alcohol, povidone-iodine, or chlorhexidine. Povidone-iodine may be preferable because it is nonstaining, has prolonged antibacterial action (as long as the brown color persists), and does not evaporate as quickly as alcohol. Start at the intended venipuncture site and work in ever-enlarging concentric circles for 30 seconds. Let the antiseptic dry.
4. After obtaining the specimen, if a syringe and needle was used, change to a new sterile needle and disinfect the container prior to gently injecting the blood. Label each specimen according to the order in which it was obtained and initial it. Do not refrigerate blood specimens.

Taking blood cultures from intravascular lines such as triple-lumen catheters is not recommended except in patients in whom no other site is accessible.[6] In such cases, at least 5 mL of fluid must be withdrawn via the disinfected port and then discarded before the blood is withdrawn with a new syringe for culture.

If an intravascular line is suspected of being the source of the patient's fever, the old line should be removed and, if necessary, a new line should be inserted at a different site. If a new access site cannot be found, cultures should be drawn *simultaneously* from the catheter and a peripheral venipuncture site. If there is a quantitative difference of bacterial growth between the sites (i.e., the catheter specimen yields the greater number of organisms), then the line is most likely the source of the infection and there is little choice but to remove it. In order to obtain such quantitative comparisons, the microbiology laboratory must be consulted since a special procedure is required.

If an intravenous catheter is removed because it is believed to be the focus of infection, the laboratory may be requested to perform a semiquantitative culture of the catheter tip.[7] Before placing the aseptically obtained tip in broth and incubating it, the laboratory technician will roll the tip on an agar plate. If more than 15 colony-forming units are identified, or if there is confluent growth where the catheter was rolled, the catheter was most likely the source of the infection.

It is important to remember in blood as in most other cultures that infections are usually caused by a single pathogen. Polymicrobial growth mostly represents contamination of the specimen, and a repeat culture may be required. Repeat cultures delay therapy, waste time and money, and represent poor utilization of laboratory sources. Obtaining a good specimen is an important responsibility of the critical care nurse. It is also important to remember that any and all organisms can become opportunistic pathogens and that none, including *Staphylococcus epidermidis*, can always be dismissed as contaminants. This is especially true in patients with indwelling lines or foreign bodies such as vascular grafts or prostheses. Careful site preparation to prevent contamination of specimens is more important than ever in these patients. Bacterial, fungal, and most viral pathogens in a patient's blood pose little risk to nurses. The two exceptions are the hepatitis B virus and the human immunodeficiency virus. While accidental needlesticks or cuts with instruments used on patients should always be avoided, patients with positive bacterial or fungal blood cultures do not require handling in any special way, except those with meningococcemia.

CEREBROSPINAL FLUID CULTURES

Lumbar punctures are always performed by a physician, and nurses have very little to do with the collection of the specimen. Nurses may be asked to transport the specimens to the laboratory and must remember that these samples should never be refrigerated.

It takes at least 24 hours for organisms to grow, and identification of a specific infective agent may take even longer in some instances. Obviously, when a patient's diagnosis is a possible meningitis, therapy with an appropriate antibiotic must be started as soon as possible. Therefore, the Gram stain is a very vital aid to a rapid presumptive diagnosis and treatment and is usually done as soon as the specimen reaches the laboratory. A negative Gram stain does not rule out bacterial meningitis, while a positve Gram stain is diagnostic.

Of greater concern regarding nursing care is the patient with meningitis due to *Hemophilus influenzae* and *Neisseria meningitidis*, because both are transmissible to other patients and staff. If bacterial meningitis is suspected, the patient should be on Respiratory Isolation unless the Gram stain can rule out these organisms. *Hemophilus influenzae* on Gram stain is a small, pleomorphic gram-negative rod, while the meningococcus is seen as gram-negative diplococci. If the patient has been on antibiotics or if the preliminary Gram stain is done or interpreted by someone other than an experienced microbiology technician, the findings of any organism should be suspect until a culture can be read. It is truly better to be safe than sorry in these cases.

SPUTUM SPECIMENS

As any experienced infection control practitioner can attest, there are far too many sputum cultures being sent to the laboratory. Many of them are sent by critical care nurses without a physician's prior order. Sputum cultures are extremely difficult to interpret, and testing should be reserved for patients with pneumonia or other signs of lower respiratory tract infections, not simply because a patient on ventilatory assistance has copious amounts of what is often described as foul-smelling or purulent sputum. The primary intent of any culture should be the treatment of an infection through the selection of a specific antibiotic agent to which the pathogen is sensitive.

Unless the patient is intubated, a deep cough is required to produce a good specimen. Early morning specimens are the most desirable, and the patient should be supervised during specimen collection if at all possible. Sputum specimens are usually Gram stained to differentiate true sputum from saliva. If there are more than 10 epithelial cells and fewer than 25 leukocytes, then the specimen most likely is saliva. Sputum cannot be labeled as purulent by visual means alone: white blood cells are needed since they represent true pus, and a good number are needed to show that there is indeed an inflammatory response to a lower respiratory tract infection. It is very important to let laboratory personnel know if a patient is leukopenic, because in the absence of circulating peripheral leukocytes the body may not be able to mount an inflammatory response to a respiratory tract infection and there may be very few, if any, white blood cells in a real sputum specimen under these circumstances. The sputum may, therefore, be labeled erroneously as saliva.

The oropharynx is highly colonized with normal flora (Table 3-3).

During sleep, even in a normal and healthy person, some organisms may be aspirated, and if conditions are right or a large enough number are aspirated,

Table 3-3 Commonly Identified Normal Flora of the Mouth and Oropharynx

Gram-Positive Organisms	Gram-Negative Organisms
Coagulase-negative staphylococci, including *Staphylococcus epidermidis* *Staphylococcus aureus* *Streptococcus pneumoniae* (pneumococcus) β-Hemolytic streptococci, not group A Diphtheroids	*Bacteroides* species *Hemophilus* species *Neisseria* species, including *N. catarrhalis* and *N. meningitidis*

they may produce a pneumonitis. This is frequently how pneumococcal and *Hemophilus influenzae* pneumonia originates. In hospitalized patients, the normal gram-positive organisms are replaced with additional gram-negative rods. It occurs especially rapidly in the critically ill patient and in those who are intubated. Any of these organisms can then become "opportunistic pathogens" and become the etiologic agent in nosocomial pneumonia.

Since expectorated sputum must pass through the highly colonized oropharynx and mouth, it is often difficult to tell which are colonizing organisms and which are pathogens. For example, a sputum culture report from a patient with pneumonia acquired in the community may read as follows:

Moderate normal flora, moderate *Streptococcus pneumoniae*

In this case, it is fairly easy to decide that the pneumococcus is the etiologic agent. But, how would one interpret this report from a patient who had a respiratory arrest 10 days ago, has been on ventilatory assistance ever since, and is now febrile?

Moderate normal flora, moderate *Pseudomonas*, abundant enterococcus, few *Acinetobacter* species, moderate *Staphylococcus aureus*, few yeast

Here the Gram stain may be of some help if it shows that one or other of the organisms is predominant, because on culture the more aggressive bacteria might just grow faster than a less aggressive type. The Gram stain for the above culture read:

Moderate WBCs; few epithelial cells; few gram-positive cocci in clusters, pairs, and chains; moderate gram-negative rods; few to moderate yeast

This Gram stain seems to show that there is some inflammatory response (the abundant leukocytes), that the abundant enterococcus and streptococci (gram-positive cocci) were not present on the Gram stain, that there were moderate gram-negative rods (*Pseudomonas* or *Acinetobacter*), that there was no predominant organism on either the culture or Gram stain, and that there was much mixed flora. Here, clinical collaboration with the culture results is helpful, and we know that a patient in whom *Staphylococcus aureus* or *Pseudomonas* is the cause of a nosocomial pneumonia is septic and may develop some cavitary disease. This patient had only a low-grade fever, and the chest roentgenogram did not show an infiltrate, consolidation, or cavitation. Therefore, this polymicrobial mix was probably representative of colonization of this patient's respiratory passages, rather than demonstrating any one organism as the cause of nosocomial pneumonia at this time. Microbial predominance in a sputum specimen is also influenced by any antibiotics being administered to the patient, because the drug may inhibit some organisms and let others proliferate.

Unless obtained by transtracheal aspiration, which bypasses the colonized upper passages, sputum cultures are very difficult to interpret and the clinical presentation and radiologic findings must always be taken into consideration. And, without evidence of pneumonia, expectorated sputum specimens are of no, or at best questionable, value and should be avoided.

Patients with pneumonia do not require isolation, with a few exceptions. However, respiratory secretions that harbor colonizers that may become potential pathogens for other patients should be handled with gloves, and hands should be washed between caring for each patient to prevent spread of hospital organisms, especially those that may be resistant to antibiotics. The exceptional pneumonias requiring respiratory isolation are those due to the meningococcus, the tubercle bacillus, *Staphylococcus aureus*, and group A streptococci and in infants and children, *Hemophilus influenzae* pneumonia. Respiratory isolation precautions should be maintained for between 24 and 48 hours after the institution of effective therapy in infection with *Mycobacterium tuberculosis*.[1] Effective therapy means that the patient is being given an antibiotic to which the pathogen is sensitive *and* that the patient is showing clinical improvement in response to this therapy. All cases of nosocomial pneumonia and all patients on respiratory and other isolation should be reported to the hospital's infection control practitioner.

Sputum collection and interpretation for acid-fast organisms is discussed in detail in Chapter 7.

URINE CULTURES

As in sputum specimens, the area in which the urine originates is usually free of bacteria, but in a voided specimen and, to some extent, in a specimen from an indwelling urinary catheter, the passageway has its resident or normal flora. As in many other types of specimens, far too many urine samples are routinely sent for culture. In the study performed at my institution only 54% (68 to 125) of urine cultures were subsequently read, discussed in the progress notes, or shown to influence the treatment of the patient.[2] Although medical texts still advise the use of urine cultures prior to instituting therapy,[8] this pertains more to community-acquired urinary tract infections, not to patients without specific indications such as dysuria or flank or costovertebral angle pain. Of course, dysuria cannot be established in patients with indwelling urinary catheters, and so any fever seems to elicit a urine culture. The maxim holds that in the patient with suspected nosocomial urinary tract infection in the intensive care unit, cultures should be obtained *if* specific antimicrobial therapy is intended to be based on the culture report. Exceptions are as follows:

1. If the patient is febrile and has had urinary tract manipulation within the previous 2 days
2. If the patient is symptomatic (pain in the flank, costovertebral tenderness, or dysuria)
3. If the patient is immunosuppressed
4. If an obstruction is present
5. If the blood culture reveals an organism considered to be a urinary tract pathogen
6. If there is pyuria or hematuria on urinalysis
7. If no other site for the infection can be found

One must remember that this pertains only to patients in intensive care settings with suspected nosocomial urinary tract infections.[9]

Collection of the Specimen

Few patients in intensive care units escape insertion of a catheter, and collection of a specimen via catheter is simple. It must be done in an aseptic manner from the sample port. The port should be well disinfected with alcohol or povidone-iodine and 5 mL of urine withdrawn with a sterile syringe. The urine should be sent to the laboratory within 20 to 30 minutes or refrigerated. It can remain in the syringe for a short period. If the syringe has been labeled with the patient's name, it can be used to transport the specimen to the laboratory. A culture specimen should *never* be taken from the collection bag or urine meter. A concomitant urinalysis can be helpful in the interpretation of culture results and is explained later in the chapter. More volume of urine will, however, be necessary for urinalysis. A clean catch or midstream specimen is very difficult to obtain from a patient in bed. If this kind of specimen is required, the nurse should assist the female patient and instruct the male patient to cleanse the urethral meatus and adjacent areas with soap and water, rinse off the soap, and "catch" the urine in a sterile container after first having voided a few milliliters into a bedpan or urinal. The first voiding in the morning will probably contain most organisms and should be used when possible. Otherwise, an interval of about 2 hours should lapse to allow reaccumulation of organisms in the bladder.

Interpretation of Results and Patient Care Implications

Interpretation depends somewhat on the following (Table 3-4):

- The clinical picture
- Corroborative cultures (blood showing the same organisms as urine—urosepsis)
- Simultaneous microscopic examination or urinalysis. Ten or more white blood cells and the presence of bacteria can corroborate the presence of inflammation, which, in turn, can be ascribed to infection.
- The method of collection of the specimen
- The number of colony-forming units

Suprapubic catheterization is usually performed only on the newborn. It is the most accurate method to obtain a specimen that is the least likely to become contaminated. Any organisms on such a culture can be interpreted as a pathogen.

Table 3-4 Interpretation of Urine Cultures

Colony-Forming Units	Voided Specimens	Catheter Specimens
<1,000	Normal flora, not significant	Not significant, unless specimen is obtained by suprapubic catheter
10^4 (10,000)	Probably colonization/ contamination	Significant only if patient is symptomatic (see text) and urinalysis has >10 white blood cells
>10^5 (100,000)	Significant bacteriuria	Possible urinary tract infection Clinical correlation needed (see text) Urinalysis helpful

Multiple Species} More than three different species implies contamination or overgrowth

Midstream and voided urines have to pass through the urethra, the distal third of which is highly colonized with skin, genital, and, in the female, intestinal flora (Table 3-5). Therefore, 10^4 colony-forming units are considered normal unless the female patient has severe dysuria and 10^5 colony-forming units or more are usually considered significant if a single pathogen is encountered. Polymicrobial growth, meaning three or more species, is usually not processed for identification and sensitivity testing, since this represents contamination or overgrowth in most cases. In a catheterized specimen, 10^5 colony-forming units is considered significant.

The common urinary pathogens originate in the distal urethra, the female perineum, the vagina, and the intestine. They are normal flora for those areas, but when they enter the bladder they may turn into opportunistic pathogens. In catheterizd patients they may migrate into the bladder along the mucous sheath that envelops the catheter. It is possible to inoculate the bladder with a large number of organisms from the urine collection bag if urine from the bag or even the tubing is allowed to flow back into the bladder. Therefore, uninterrupted downhill flow of the urine at all times is absolutely necessary. In addition, organisms may have been transmitted via the hands of intensive care unit personnel who handle the catheter and from irrigating solutions and other water reservoirs.

In general, avoidance of indwelling catheters is the best method of preventing nosocomial urinary tract infections, but in a critically ill patient this is not always possible. Therefore, critical care nurses can employ other good patient care

---

Table 3-5 Commonly Implicated Organisms in Urinary Tract Infection and Colonization, According to Their Most Likely Origin

Urethra (Vagina Only)	*Intestinal*	*Hands of Personnel and Intensive Care Unit Environment (Water Reservoirs)*
Coagulase-negative staphylococci	Enterococci	*Pseudomonas* species
Diphtheroids	*Escherichia coli*	*Serratia marcescens*
(*Lactobacillus* species)	*Klebsiella* species	*Acinetobacter* species
Streptococci	*Proteus* species	*Staphylococcus aureus*
(*Candida* species)	*Candida*	All those in the other two columns
(*Gardnerella* vaginalis)	Coagulase-negative staphylococci	
	Diphtheroids	
	Streptococci	

practices to help the prevention of nosocomial urinary tract infections by hydrating the patient as much as the clinical condition allows and maintaining an acid urine (cranberry juice is still the suggested method). Individual urine measuring devices should be used for each patient, and they should be rinsed and dried between use to prevent multiplication of "water bugs" such as *Pseudomonas* species, *Acinetobacter* species, and *Serratia* species. Handwashing before and after handling of indwelling catheters and urine collection bags remains basic to good patient care.

WOUND, SKIN, AND SOFT TISSUE CULTURES

The normal inhabitants of the skin are the staphylococci, several *Corynebacterium* species, aerobic and anaerobic streptococci, and *Candida* species. In addition, gram-negative organisms are transiently present from the intestinal tract and, in hospitalized patients, from the hands of personnel. It is, therefore, not surprising that it is extremely difficult to obtain a specimen from superficial wounds, decubiti, ulcers, and so on that contain only a single organism, which is the presumed pathogen. Instead, many organisms will be recovered and any one of these could be a pathogen. In general, cultures of the skin or superficial wounds should therefore be avoided.[10] If a culture must be taken, and if polymicrobial growth is to be avoided, it is important to first remove the old drainage with sterile 4 × 4-inch gauze pads and nonbacteriostatic sterile water or saline and then to express or swab any new drainage for the culture specimen. If a large area is involved, as in a decubitus, it is better to run the swab around the inner (advancing) edge of the infected site. The swab should be placed in a transport medium immediately to prevent drying and death of the organism during transport and storage. It is also important to remember that a culture should be sent ony if individual antimicrobial therapy is to be prescribed and an outbreak situation is suspected, in which case the infection control practitioner should be informed.

Safe Transport of Specimens

The safety of those who transport specimens to and within laboratories must be kept in mind. Specimen containers must be tightly closed and leakproof or must be placed into a second container or bag. The outside of the container should be free of blood or body fluids. If necessary if can be wiped clean with alcohol or other disinfectant and/or double bagged. Within the laboratory all specimens should be processed as if they were infectious, and a caution sticker or label for any specific category of isolation or precautions is usually not required. However, hospital policies pertaining to any such requirement should be followed.

Interpretation of Results and Patient Care Implications

Superficial wounds, stasis ulcers, and decubiti are often irrigated with standard solutions of saline or hydrogen peroxide, followed by application of antiseptic or triple-antibiotic ointments, regardless of the culture results. Cultures are, therefore, not required for the treatment of those cases. Culture orders should not be sought out of curiosity or routinely and should be questioned for intent if they have been written. It is not possible to identify the etiologic agent of an infection in the presence of polymicrobial growth. In the example given in question 2 at the end of the chapter, any of the organisms could be an opportunistic pathogen or simply represent overgrowth of normally present flora. The swab was obviously used without first removing the organisms that were colonizing the surface. In a deep-seated infection, such as an abscess where colonization is uncommon, an aspirated specimen of pus should be obtained after the entry site is cleansed; the air is then expressed from the syringe, and the syringe is labeled and taken to the laboratory at once. Or the specimen can be transferred into an oxygen-reduced vial or other special anaerobic container to determine the presence of anaerobes, which may not survive to grow on culture. In these specimens, polymicrobial growth (two or three organisms) is not unusual. Abscesses are usually caused by intestinal bacteria, which consist of both aerobes and anaerobes. They exist synergistically in abscesses: the aerobes reduce the oxygen content of the area, which furthers the growth of the anaerobes.

Nurses and physicians sometimes erroneously believe that a culture result can help in deciding what, if any, category of precaution or isolation is required. Since all skin, intestinal, or environmental organisms can cause infections of wounds, skin, or soft tissue, and since all can be transmitted by hands of personnel and by contaminated instruments or equipment, the category of precautions depends on two criteria: (1) the amount of drainage and (2) whether the infected area is covered and the pus contained. For major infections in which there is a moderate or large amount of drainage, and/or drainage is not covered by a dressing or not contained by a dressing, Contact Isolation (or Wound and Skin Precautions) are indicated. In the absence of dressings or containment, a private room is necessary, even for minor infections. For wounds with scant or little drainage, Secretion Precautions suffice.[1] The policies of each institution should be followed, and the infection control practitioner notified. If critical care nurses understand the need for the private room for uncovered wounds or skin infections such as shingles on the face (the reason being that these are more easily dissem-inated into the environment), the choice of category becomes obvious.

STOOL CULTURES

Patients who are admitted with gastrointestinal infections alone rarely require placement in intensive care units. However, if they are admitted to the unit, stool cultures will be necessary to identify an etiologic agent if the patient is ill enough to require antibiotic treatment for the infection. Fresh stool samples should be sent to the laboratory as soon as the patient is admitted. The stool sample should be examined for fecal leukocytes and bacterial pathogens. The absence of white blood cells or bacterial pathogens does not rule out an infectious etiology for the diarrhea. If organisms other than *Salmonella, Shigella*, or *Cam-pylobacter* are suspected, the laboratory should be informed, as is also the case for *Giardia* species and other ova and parasites. Ova and parasites are rarely found in stool samples in the United States and should be sought only if a patient has traveled to endemic areas or has features that are suggestive of such an infection. More than one specimen may be required, but rarely more than three.

Clostridium difficile is normally the cause of antibiotic-associated diarrheal disease. It should be suspected in patients whose diarrhea develops 3 days or more after their admission, especially if they have been on antibiotic therapy or chemotherapy or have been taking other agents that affect the balance of normal bowel flora. *Clostridium difficile* antitoxin tests or complement fixation can be requested from the laboratory, but stool cultures for this organism are not done.

Enteric pathogens, other than those already mentioned, are *Cryptosporidium* and *Isospora belli*. Both are being noted more frequently because they tend to infect patients with the acquired immunodeficiency syndrome. In patients on antibiotics, there may be no normal enteric flora or there may be predominance of *Pseudomonas* species or some other bacterium that is resistant to the antibiotic being administered. This overgrowth, other than *Clostridium difficile* in adults and possibly *Escherichia coli* in neonates, is usually not the cause of the diarrhea. It is possible that both the *Clostridium difficile* toxin and antigen tests may be negative, even in the presence of antibiotic-associated diarrhea or pseudomem-branous colitis. Regardless of the culture or test results, unless the diarrhea can be ascribed to a noninfectious etiology by the physician, patients with diarrhea should be kept on Enteric Precautions until the diarrhea resolves. It is important to remember that ulcerative colitis and other chronic conditions can be exacer-bated by intestinal infections, and these patients should not be exempt from Enteric Precautions. The infection control practitioners should be notified of patients with diarrhea, since some gastrointestinal infections are reportable to the local health department.

YEAST OR *CANDIDA* REPORTS

One other point of discussion is important. In critically ill patients, especially those on antimicrobial therapy, *Candida* or other yeast species may occasionally be found on cultures. This is not unusual since the antibiotic will suppress normal bacterial flora and permit growth of these organisms, which are also present in small numbers in a variety of body sites. It is difficult with a single culture to differentiate fungal infection or invasive disease from colonization. Invasive candidiasis is a very serious infection, and diagnosis usually requires repeatedly positive cultures from more than one site or from the blood. Candidemia does occur in patients on parenteral nutrition and strict asepsis is mandatory for these patients. Patients with fungal sepsis do not require precautions or isolation because it is the susceptibility of the individual host that causes the infection to develop, not any external transmission.

In the intensive care unit, the collection of a clinically relevant specimen for culture and sensitivity testing is usually the responsibility of the patient's nurse. A culture result is only as good as the specimen on which it is based, so obtaining and transporting these specimens is a serious responsibility. Because appropriate antibiotic regimens can be lifesaving, nurses must be knowledgeable about the timing and correct methods of specimen collection. Since the patient's nurse is also very often the first to see the culture result and may have to act on it, nurses must also be able to interpret culture reports and institute appropriate patient care practices indicated by these results. Speedy action on the nurse's part can improve the patient's chances of survival and prevent exposure of others to certain transmissible pathogens.

REFERENCES

1. Garner JS, Simmons BP. CDC guidelines for isolation precautions in hospitals. Infect Control 1984;4(S):245–349.

2. Cunha BA, Gurevich I, Tafuro P. Cost effective utilization of microbiology data. Hosp Physician 1986;22:19–24.

3. Washington JA. Blood cultures: Principles and techniques. Mayo Clin Proc 1974;50:91–98.

4. Ilstrup DM, Washington JA. The importance of volume of blood cultured in the detection of bacteremia and fungemia. Diagn Microbiol Infect Dis 1983;1:107–110.

5. Weinstein MP, Reller LB, Murphy JR, Lichtenstein KA. The clinical significance of positive blood cultures. Rev Infect Dis 1983;5:35–53.

6. Tafuro P, Colburn D, Gurevich I, et al. Comparison of blood cultures obtained simultaneously by venipuncture and from vascular lines. J Hosp Infect 1986;7:283–288.

7. Maki DG, Weiss CE, Sarafin HW. A semiquantitative culture method for identifying intravenous catheter-related infection. N Engl J Med 1977;296:1305–1309.

8. Sobel JD, Kaye D. Urinary tract infections. In Mandell GL, Douglas RG, Bennett JE (eds). Principles and Practices of Infectious Diseases, 2nd ed. New York: John Wiley & Sons, 1985.

9. Stamm WE. When should we use urine cultures? Infect Control 1986;7:431–433.

10. Bartels JH, Weinstein MP. Appropriate use of the microbiology laboratory in the diagnosis of infectious diseases. Infect Control 1987;15:187–195.

CHAPTER REVIEW QUESTIONS

1. The most important reason for taking a culture is to
   a. Determine whether a patient requires isolation
   b. Establish appropriate antibiotic therapy
   c. Identify the pathogen

2. The following culture report from a decubitus ulcer is posted on a patient's chart.

   Abundant *Proteus morganii*, few *Serratia marcescens*, moderate *Staphylococcus aureus*, moderate *Staphylococcus epidermidis*, few *Streptococcus viridens*, moderate *E. coli*, abundant *Enterococcus*.

   Which is the pathogen causing the patient's infection?
   a. Abundant *Enterococcus*
   b. Moderate *Staphylococcus aureus*
   c. Moderate *E. coli*
   d. Cannot tell from this report

3. Based on the above culture report, the patient should be placed on
   a. Wound and Skin Precautions
   b. Contact Isolation
   c. Drainage Secretions Precautions
   d. Cannot tell from the culture report alone.

4. When a sputum specimen is not processed by the microbiology laboratory the reason may be because
   a. The sputum specimen was not refrigerated
   b. No pathogens were seen on Gram stain
   c. The patient is leukopenic and the laboratory was not informed
   d. There were too many white blood cells seen on the Gram stain

5. In adults, no fewer than three blood cultures should be ordered because
   a. Isolation of an organism is often volume dependent
   b. Three cultures can help differentiate a contaminant from a pathogen in some instances
   c. a and b

Answers are provided in Appendix B.

Transmissible Infections: Protecting the Nurse and Others

Each chapter in Part II deals with an important and transmissible infectious disease. Chapters are organized so that the range of clinical manifestations for each pathogen is described along with its relationship to the immune system of susceptible, high-risk populations.

A unique aspect in these chapters is the emphasis on maintaining a high index of suspicion based on early recognition of these infectious diseases. Only by prompt and early institution of precautionary or isolation measures can their transmission be prevented. For those nurses who suffer an inadvertent exposure, applicable postexposure prophylaxis with its potential benefits and hazards is also included.

Chapter 4

The Acquired
Immunodeficiency
Syndrome

At the present time, compared with most other epidemics, the one caused by the human immunodeficiency virus (HIV) is numerically insignificant if no less tragic in human terms. In the Middle Ages, the Black Death killed one third of the population in Europe within 4 years. Malaria causes 200 million cases every year, and millions of these patients die. The great influenza epidemic of 1918 killed more than 20 million persons all over the world in a few months.[1] AIDS has killed only about 60,000 persons of a total of 95,000 reported cases in the 9 years since it was identified.[2] And yet, more than any of its predecessors, the AIDS virus has changed the life-styles of millions of Americans and the patient care practices of nurses and physicians. Some of these changing practices are the result of sound scientific knowledge, but others are based on unrealistic fears and propagated myths. AIDS is not caused by an airborne virus like tuberculosis or meningitis, yet some nurses will not even enter the room of a patient who is merely being tested for antibody to HIV without wearing a mask, gown, and gloves. And although HIV is not nearly as infectious as hepatitis B virus, some physicians will wear gloves while taking a history and performing a physical on an HIV-negative drug abuser. However, they will draw blood without using gloves from a 68-year-old Chinese woman with primary liver cancer who is most likely a chronic carrier of hepatitis B virus. This type of behavior can be explained in part by the almost certainly fatal outcome of infection with HIV and the fear it therefore produces. A poll of medical students revealed another reason for wearing inappropriately excessive protective apparel, namely, the negative attitude of the students toward the life-style and behaviors of the majority of those infected with HIV.[3]

What is known and not known about HIV and how this knowledge affects nurses and other health care providers are reviewed in this chapter. Although the emphasis is on issues related to the workplace, some other aspects are also included with the hope that nurses who are considered experts in their communities can influence the attitudes and behavior of patients, their families and friends, and others where necessary.

TERMINOLOGY

Medical terms are not always used correctly and can be confusing. Therefore some definitions are in order. A person can be infected with HIV without being aware of it and without symptoms. He or she is then an asymptomatic carrier. Serum antibody will be present in that case but may not necessarily be detectable by presently available tests. The same is true for the hepatitis B virus. Once infected, the person is infectious. Some infected persons may remain asymptomatic for many years. They may at any time develop a limited set of signs and symptoms such as lymphadenopathy and fatigue, which has been called the AIDS-related complex (ARC) and is often called "pre AIDS." It is not until certain opportunistic infections, central nervous system manifestations, or cancers develop in addition to the lymphadenopathy that a person is said to have AIDS. Thus, AIDS implies clinical disease but is often used somewhat loosely to describe HIV carriers without disease.

THE IMMUNODEFICIENCY VIRUSES

The immunodeficiency viruses are retroviruses. Retroviruses are well-known pathogens among animals, with the feline leukemia virus being a familiar example. In 1981, the first human retrovirus was discovered and named human T-cell lymphotropic virus III (HTLV-III).[4] Others followed, among them HTLV-II and HTLV-IV (Table 4-1). HTLV-III was renamed the human immunodeficiency virus 1 (HIV-1), often also called the AIDS virus. In 1988, when HIV-2 was implicated as the serologic agent of the first American AIDS case not due to HIV-1, concerns resurfaced that we really do not know enough about the AIDS viruses to say for sure how to prevent work-related transmission. These fears are unjustified and can be allayed by the facts and by historical perspective. There are many other examples of how the transmission of unidentified viruses and bacteria can be determined and preventive measures tailored to that knowledge. The spread of legionnaires' disease was established as airborne on epidemiologic data alone long before the first and subsequent *Legionella* organisms (there are now more than 20 species) were identified. New ones are still being discovered and named. Similarly, the three non-A, non-B hepatitis viruses have still not been identified but, as with HIV, it is known how they are spread. It is expected that more non-A, non-B hepatitis viruses and more human immu-

Table 4-1 Comparison of the Human Immunodeficiency Retroviruses

Virus	Clinical Diseases
HTLV-I	Micosis fungoides
	Bone lesions
	Lymphoma
	Acute T-cell leukemia (Southern Japan)
	5% immunosuppressive candidiasis, pneumocystis
HTLV-II	Hairy cell (B-cell) leukemia
	8% immunosuppressive
	No neurologic disease
HTLV-III = HIV-1	Lymphoma
	Kaposi's sarcoma
	Adenocarcinoma of colon
	Neurologic disease (similar to visna in sheep)
	95% immunosuppression
	Opportunistic infections (AIDS)
HTLV-IV = HIV-2	Very similar to HIV-1

nodeficiency viruses will be identified as testing mechanisms become more refined and sensitive.

One of the several remaining mysteries about the HIV is its exact origin, although Africa is the most likely place. A related question is how the virus was introduced into the United States. Theories abound, and these riddles may never be solved.

MECHANISMS OF IMMUNODEFICIENCY IN AIDS

One of many issues being studied and debated is how the virus induces such devastating immunosuppression. Originally it was believed that there were preceding or co-infections with other viruses such as cytomegalovirus or hepatitis B virus and that the HIV was then able to attack an already stressed immune system. At one time the blame was placed on abuse of amyl nitrate, a drug commonly used in the homosexual community.

Shortly thereafter, it was recognized that HIV-1 had an affinity for the CD4 antigen, a protein on T lymphocytes and certain other cells, and that its destruction of the helper T cell caused the profound cellular immune deficiency (see Chapter 2). Nurses are familiar with the fact that lymphopenia is severe in AIDS, and there is an inverse helper-to-suppressor ratio. Since the helper T cell aids in the destruction of invading pathogens and circulating cancer cells, patients with reduced numbers of helper T cells eventually succumb to infections produced by intracellular pathogens and to various forms of malignancy. Patients are also anergic, having lost their cellular memory and ability to mount a delayed hypersensitivity reaction.[5] What happens to the presumably noninfected B cells? Why do they not produce antibody and destroy those viruses that have evaded the cell-mediated immune system? The reasons are not totally clear, but there are several theories. Partly it may be that the virus undergoes "antigenic drift," changing its genetic structure sufficiently to make the neutralizing effect of antibodies produced by the B lymphocytes ineffective. It is this capability that makes vaccine development difficult. Such mutations occur in the flu virus and in the visna virus (a slow virus that infects sheep). Among other factors is the important role played by the T cell in eliciting an adequate humoral immune system response. When T cells are infected and depleted, B cells do not receive the stimulus for appropriate antibody production, and although there is general hyperglobulinemia, the antibody is not effective and is not directed against newly encountered infections.[6]

Related to the incompetence of the B lymphocytes is the issue of a vaccine. If the virus is able to achieve antigenic drift, will a single vaccine ever be effective?

And this in turn raises another question. Should asymptomatic HIV carriers and AIDS patients be vaccinated with live or attenuated virus vaccines? If the immune system cannot contain invading pathogens, how will it handle vaccine-introduced viruses? Even if this type of vaccine does not itself cause the very infection it is intended to prevent, is the risk worth the chance that the humoral system will fail to produce effective new antibody without the usual assistance of the T cell? Recommendations for vaccination of children and adults with live or attenuated vaccines are constantly being revised, and any information given here will not necessarily remain accurate in years to come. In March 1988, recommendations by the Centers for Disease Control were that measles, mumps, and rubella vaccines are indicated for previously unvaccinated and susceptible children, adolescents, and young adults, even those with symptomatic HIV infection.[7] It is hoped that these infections can indeed be prevented because they can be deadly when they occur in HIV-infected persons.

CLINICAL MANIFESTATIONS

The purpose of describing clinical manifestations of the other infectious diseases in this book is to provide nurses with the knowledge needed to recognize the early and sometimes subtle signs of transmissible infections. Once the signs and symptoms are recognized, precautionary measures can be instituted until the suspicions are confirmed or dispelled. With AIDS, this is hardly necessary for several reasons. If, as recommended, universal precautions are observed for all patients, it matters little whether a patient's AIDS is recognized or not—at least as far as the further protection of personnel is concerned. In addition, when a physician suspects AIDS, he or she usually communicates these suspicions to other health care workers, because everyone recognizes the need to take precautions.

A brief summary of the major manifestations of AIDS is included here, but the disease is much more complex than can can be described in this chapter.

The Primary Infection

Acute infection with HIV-1 and probably HIV-2 produces a mononucleosis-type syndrome of varying severity after an incubation period of 2 to 8 weeks. Symptoms may range from almost unnoticeable fatigue to meningoencephalitis (Table 4-2).[8] Seroconversion from negative to HIV antibody positive follows exposure and infection by 6 to 12 weeks.[9]

Table 4-2 Frequent Manifestations of Acute HIV Infection and AIDS

HIV Infection	*AIDS*
Early manifestations (%) (at seroconversion)	Generalized and persistent lymphadenopathy
Fever (76.9)	Fever and night sweats
Lethargy and malaise (66.7)	Fatigue
Anorexia (66.7)	Central nervous system involvement
Sore throat (56.4)	Opportunistic infections
Photophobia (56.4)	Lymphoid interstitial pneumonia (children)
Myalgia (56.4)	Failure to thrive (children)
Headache (48.7)	Organomegaly (liver and spleen)
Arthralgia (48.7)	Malignancies
	Primary lymphoma (brain) (children)
Later manifestations	Other lymphomas
Weight loss (46.2)	Kaposi's sarcoma
Swollen glands (43.5)	Other cancers
Retro-orbital pain (38.5)	
Diarrhea (38)	
Dehydration and nausea (38.8)	
Maculopapular rash	
Meningoencephalitis	
Peripheral neuropathy	

Source: Archives of Internal Medicine (1988;48:945–949), Copyright © 1988, American Medical Association.

Patients may recover completely and remain asymptomatic for varying lengths of time, for 10 to 15 years in some cases. They are, however, infectious.

The Syndrome and Related Opportunistic Infections

Eventually, most of those persons infected will develop any one or a combination of symptoms, usually starting with generalized lymphadenopathy, fatigue, anorexia, and weight loss. The lymphadenopathy will persist, and the weight loss (called slim disease in Africa) must be unintentional, be independent of caloric intake, and be greater than 10% of body weight. Central nervous system dysfunction may precede or follow opportunistic infections and may be due to the virus itself or to other central nervous system infections. *Toxoplasma gondii*, cytomegalovirus, and *Cryptococcus neoformans* are probably the most common infectious causes, but any organism can be involved, especially those that are "intracellular" pathogens. Neoplasms of the central nervous system are also common. Nearly 40% of patients develop neurologic complication during their illness, and at least 10% manifest neurologic symptoms before the diagnosis of AIDS is made.[10]

Pneumonia due to *Pneumocystis carinii*, cytomegalovirus, or *Mycobacterium tuberculosis* is frequently present, as is chronic intractable diarrhea. Oral thrush or invasive esophageal candidiasis afflicts almost all AIDS patients, and other common infections and the necessary precautionary measures are listed in Table 4-3.[10]

Malignancies in AIDS

Kaposi's sarcoma was the first cancer to be associated with AIDS. But there are others, which is not surprising. As described in Chapter 2, T lymphocytes are responsible for immunologic surveillance, which differentiates self from nonself and thus identifies tumor cells as nonself. As the T-cell population declines naturally with age and in deficiencies of cell-mediated immunity, older and immunodeficient populations tend to have a higher prevalence of malignancies. AIDS patients fall into the latter category and are, therefore, at risk for several types of cancer. In addition, there is ever-growing evidence that viruses in general, and retroviruses in particular, are the etiologic agents of many cancers in animals and humans. Feline leukemia is a well-known retrovirus that causes malignancy in cats. In humans, T-cell leukemia viruses (HTLV-I and HTLV-II) are the etiologic agents of lymphomas and leukemia (see Table 4-1).[4] HIV-1 causes not only Kaposi's sarcoma and lymphoma but also adenocarcinoma of the colon.

Table 4-3 Common Infections in AIDS Patients and Precautionary Measures to Prevent Their Spread

Organism	Site(s) of Infection	Precautions in Addition to Universal Precautions
Bacteria		
Mycobacterium avium-intracellulare (MAI)	Lungs and disseminated	None
Mycobacterium tuberculosis (MTB)	Lungs and glandular	Respiratory Isolation or Acid Fast Isolation (pulmonary tuberculosis)
Salmonella species	Gastrointestinal and disseminated	Enteric Precautions
Fungi		
Candida albicans	Oral, esophageal, disseminated	None
Cryptococcus neoformans	Central nervous system, disseminated	None
Protozoa		
Cryptosporidium	Gastrointestinal tract	Enteric Precautions
Toxoplasma gondii	Central nervous system, disseminated	None
Pneumocystis carinii	Lungs	None
Viruses		
Cytomegalovirus	Retina, lung, disseminated	Handwashing
Herpes simplex	Mucocutaneous, disseminated	Contact Isolation (disseminated), Drainage Secretion Precautions (local)
Herpes zoster	Skin (local), disseminated	Strict Isolation (immunosuppressed patient likely to disseminate)

Source: Author

MODES OF TRANSMISSION

Infectivity of Body Fluids

In order to understand why only some body fluids are considered infectious and why some exposures result in infection while others do not, the needs of pathogens in general and those of HIV in particular must be understood. The virus was first isolated from T lymphocytes and other cells that expressed the T4 protein. It has now also been found in macrophages and B lymphocytes, in endothelial cells, as well as in glial cells of the brain. It is believed, but not proved that HIV not established within a cell, so called cell-free virus, is usually not infectious. The theory is that cell-free virus when found in body fluids is present only in small concentrations or titers and that these small numbers are usually not infectious. This theory is borne out by studies that have isolated HIV in low quantities from plasma, serum, saliva, tears, and urine, but experiments and epidemiologic studies have not found any cases that can be ascribed to contact with only these fluids. The only exception of cell-free but infectious fluid is cerebrospinal fluid, which contains virus at high titers.[11] Virus-infected cells are present in blood and semen, and these are two well-known routes of transmission. Virus-infected cells are also present in organs and body tissues, vaginal secretions, and probably amniotic fluid.

Prerequisites to HIV Infection

The success of HIV in establishing an infection depends on certain criteria. The first is the size of the viral inoculum (the number of viruses that enter the host). There are parallels to this requirement in other infections. For example, the hepatitis B virus can establish an infection with a miniscule inoculum, and in order for typhoid fever to develop only 10^1 (100) *Salmonella typhi* are required. In contrast, *Salmonella* enteritis requires a much larger inoculum of 10^7 to 10^9 organisms.

The second requirement is the length of exposure or its frequency needed to establish an infection. A single brief exposure to virus on a mucous membrane is unlikely to cause infection, but frequent exposure to infectious semen, which is sticky and persists in its mucosal contact, is much more likely to result in infection. The same is true of a patient whose intravenous fluid is contaminated by a nurse's hands with only a few *Staphylococcus epidermidis* organisms. The bactericidal action of the blood can usually clear those few organisms. But what if the fibrin sheath that adheres to a triple-lumen catheter becomes colonized with *S. epidermidis*? Over time, more and more staphylococci will be shed into the bloodstream from this nidus until the frequent exposure to increasing numbers of organisms establishes a staphylococcal bacteremia.

Lastly, there must be T cells or other cells with appropriate binding sites at the portal of entry to which the virus can adhere or attach itself. This is also true of most other pathogens.

Transmission

Modes of HIV transmission were established on epidemiologic grounds long before the virus was identified as the etiologic agent of AIDS. Suspected modes that were confirmed at a later time were those related to transfusion of blood and clotting factors and to intrauterine or perinatal infection. This was not surprising because transmission closely resembled that of hepatitis B virus and the delay in establishing the transfusion and perinatal routes was due to the long incubation period for the appearance of AIDS at a time when antibody tests were not available.

No additional modes of transmission have been established. If anything, many theoretically possible modes of spread have been ruled out, the main ones being casual contact with infected persons and transmission by mosquitoes.

Early in the epidemic, and using hepatitis B virus as the model, all body fluids were considered to be potentially infectious. Epidemiologic studies and the research cited earlier have resulted in removal of some body fluids from the list (Table 4-4).[11,12]

Mechanisms of pathogen transmission in general are described in detail in Chapter 12. Therefore, details about transmission in this chapter will be confined to HIV.

Only direct airborne transmission of HIV occurs. Unlike tuberculosis, chickenpox, variola, and some other infections, HIV cannot remain airborne for distances beyond about 3 feet, and it does not travel on air currents from room to room. It can theoretically be transmitted by sputum and saliva if they contain visible blood during intubation and suctioning or in other situations where the distance is very close,[10,12] although there are no documented cases. Therefore, doors of AIDS patients' rooms need not be kept closed and patients can walk in halls.

Certain direct contacts with infectious body fluids can be a very efficient mode of HIV transmission (see Table 4-4). Especially risky is contact with blood, semen, or vaginal secretions. The risk is less with other fluids that are noninfectious unless they are visibly bloody. Vertical transmission in utero or perinatally is another very efficient mode for HIV transmission.

Although sexual transmission is not a hazard in intensive care units, it deserves detailed discussion because it illustrates one of the concepts discussed in Chapter

Table 4-4 Body Fluids Designated as Infectious and Noninfectious for the Human Immunodeficiency Virus

Infectious	Noninfectious (Unless Visibly Bloody)
Blood* and blood products*	Saliva
Semen*	Sputum
Vaginal secretions*	Nasal secretions
Any body fluid containing visible blood	Vomitus
Fluids	Urine
Peritoneal	Feces
Amniotic	
Pericardial	
Synovial	
Cerebrospinal fluid	
Pleural	
Human breast milk? (for infants only)	
Any tissue or organ	

*Body fluids considered as infectious by the Occupational Safety and Health Administration

Source: Reprinted from Morbidity and Mortality Weekly Report (1988;37:377–387), 1988, US Centers for Disease Control.

12, that concerning portals of entry. Pathogens require a portal of entry in order to cause infection. In fact, skin is a very effective barrier against penetration by most pathogens. Mucous membranes are more easily damaged and breached, and sexual transmission of HIV is a good example of this.

Although female-to-male transmission can occur, it is less frequent than male-to-male or male-to-female transmission. The reason becomes clear when one considers that the receptive mucosa of the vagina or rectum offers a large area for absorption compared with that of the skin of the penis.[13] In addition, intact (penile) skin is a protective barrier against most organisms, whereas mucosal areas are more delicate and absorbent. In sexually active persons, such as prostitutes or those practicing frequent anal intercourse, the mucosa is more likely to be inflamed, fissured, or otherwise damaged. If there is preexisting dermal or mucosal inflammation, especially from other sexually transmitted diseases, ready access for the HIV is available to T cells and others present during an inflammatory response to infection.[14]

Reports abound about single exposures to body fluids of HIV-infected persons that have not resulted in transmission. Nonsexual examples of transmission are provided in the section concerned with the risk of HIV transmission to health care workers.

The virus is also effectively transmitted in utero and perinatally.[15] Thus, some children are born with the infection and others develop it after birth. Breast milk is known to contain the virus, and nursing infants ingesting a large quantity of contaminated breast milk may acquire the infection. Health care workers are not considered at risk from handling breast milk if they wear gloves.

Indirect transmission via shared needles in abusers of intravenous drugs is very efficient because the criteria of a large inoculum and frequent exposure via a breached defense mechanism (the skin) are met. Much less efficient is transmission to health care workers by accidental needlestick, because the inoculum of virus is much smaller and one hopes there is only a single such exposure. Theoretically, contaminated patient care equipment or instruments could also result in indirect transmission, but no such occurrences have been documented.

Food has been ruled out as a vehicle of transmission and so have insects. Most effective in destroying the mosquito myth is the evidence from Africa. In the areas affected, the death rate is very high in the newborn to 5-year-old age group (maternally acquired infection) and in those from 15 to 45 years old (sexually acquired infection). It is very low between 6 and 14 years of age and in those over 45 years of age. It is highly unlikely that mosquitoes would selectively bite only those populations who are in the two high mortality age groups and would not bite those between 5 and 14 years or over 45 years. Another study in Belle Glade, Florida, also disproved the contention that insects were the vectors of transmission in that outbreak.[16]

HIGH-RISK POPULATIONS

Risk is closely tied to the modes of transmission. Percentages in various risk categories published in 1984 have changed very little over time. The changes that have taken place are not due to miscalculations of the original rates of risk but to the drastic change in life-styles of the male homosexual community. Their risk factor has decreased somewhat, and a greater percentage of risk has now been assigned to abusers of intravenous drugs. Hemophiliacs and blood transfusion recipients are still counted among high-risk groups, but that risk has also decreased since testing of donated blood was instituted. Unfortunately, tests are not always reliable and the risk can therefore not be completely eliminated. Haitians are no longer designated as a separate group but fit into the other categories according to the mode of acquisition for each person. The difference has been absorbed by heterosexuals and infants at risk.

Of greatest interest to nurses is the 4.5% category listed as "other." This category includes persons who cannot be placed in a known risk group and includes health care workers exposed in the workplace. The percentage has remained stable. After 8 years of caring for thousands of HIV-positive patients, the percentage of this "other" category would have increased if health care workers were at increased risk from patient exposures.

RISK TO HEALTH CARE WORKERS

Intensive studies of the risk to health care workers have been conducted. Many nurses and physicians have preconceived ideas about the patients they consider to be at high risk. Sometimes the preconceived risk is realistic, owing to the admitted life-style of the patient involved. At other times the judgment is based on appearances (e.g., men wearing an earring or long hair or male or female patients with tattoos). In general, nurses are less likely to be concerned about patients who seem conservative, middle-aged, married, and with children. Both beliefs have proved incorrect and are risky. The blood and body fluids of *all* patients must be considered potentially infectious and handled accordingly, regardless of appearances.

HIV ACQUISITION IN CRITICAL CARE

The risk of acquiring HIV from health care–related activities is far less than 1%.[17] In contrast, the risk of hepatitis B virus acquisition after a needlestick from a seropositive patient is 25% to 30%.[18] An interesting confirmatory case occurred during bronchoscopy when one of the assistants sustained a needlestick from a patient with AIDS and hepatitis B. After 15 months, no HIV conversion had occurred but the bronchoscopist developed hepatitis B.[19]

By June 1987, 883 health care workers with serious exposures to blood or body fluids of AIDS patients had been reported to the Centers for Disease Control and have been followed by this organization to assess the rate of HIV acquisition from such exposures. Of those followed, 708 (80%) sustained needlesticks and 175 (20%) had mucosal or open wound exposure. The National Institutes of Health have followed 453 exposures due to needlesticks and mucous membrane exposures. A study at the University of California followed 129 health care workers with similar exposures. Of all these, only one worker seroconverted.[20-22] In addition, 8 other health care providers who denied other risk factors and who reported needlesticks or exposure to blood and body fluids of AIDS patients have seroconverted. Two of these did not use any protective measures during prolonged care of AIDS patients.[23] Three further seroconversions were subsequently reported by the Centers for Disease Control.[24] These deserve a detailed description because they illustrate some of the important principles of HIV transmission.

One emergency department nurse applied prolonged pressure to an arterial site. She did not wear gloves and had blood on her chapped hands for 20 minutes before washing it off. The other two conversions occurred in laboratory accidents. Two laboratory phlebotomists were spattered with HIV-positive blood on the face and in the mouth. One worker had facial acne. She seroconverted; the other did not. In the third accident, the hands and forearms of a laboratory technician were covered with blood from an HIV-positive patient's specimen. The technician had dermatitis on one ear and may have touched it with the bloodstained hand. This worker subsequently seroconverted while a co-worker exposed during the same accident remained seronegative.

These last three cases confirm the statement in this and other chapters that intact skin is an excellent barrier against most infections, including HIV. Damaged skin is a serious risk factor and in order to deny the virus access to cellular binding sites should never be exposed to blood and body fluids of any patient.[25] Altogether, in the United States, 12 health care workers without other obvious risks, some of whom were seronegative at the time of their exposure, have seroconverted by the beginning of 1989, for a risk of less than 1%. To further illustrate the relatively low risk of seroconversion from exposure of intact skin, 1,231 dentists and dental hygienists were enrolled in a survey to determine the prevalence of HIV antibody in this relatively high-exposure population. Only one dentist was seropositive. He was not aware of having treated any seropositive patients but admitted that he rarely, if ever, wore gloves when providing dental care.[26] Most of the others interviewed in this survey also did not wear gloves.

There is great concern among critical care personnel about the potential of HIV transmission from the sputum and saliva of patients. Even before the removal of these body fluids from the Universal Precautions list, there was substantial evidence of their noninfectivity. Extensive studies of family members of AIDS patients showed no seroconversions among nonsexual family contacts. These contacts included children, siblings, and parents of hemophiliacs and other AIDS patients.[27-30] Obviously, if saliva were a risk factor, family members would be at high risk because eating utensils, towels, and other articles are often shared in families and young children are involved with much hand to mouth contact. A cashier who was bitten by an HIV-positive customer whom she was assisting during a seizure has also remained seronegative and so have two persons who provided emergency mouth-to-mouth resuscitation to an AIDS patient.[31,32] This is not meant to imply, however, that mouth-to-mouth resuscitation of an infected person is ever advisable.

PREVENTIVE MEASURES

By this time, all nurses, physicians, and other health care workers should be familiar with and conscientiously observing Universal Precautions, as mandated by the Occupational Safety and Health Administration.[33] These laws are based on the Centers for Disease Control guidelines that have evolved over a period of years. In 1983, the Centers for Disease Control suggested that Blood and Body Fluid Precautions be observed for patients known or suspected of having an infection due to bloodborne pathogens, which included the hepatitis B virus and HIV.[34]

When it became evident that a social and medical history could not reliably identify all patients infected with bloodborne pathogens, the Centers for Disease Control began to develop a series of guidelines called universal precautions. This series was assembled into a single document in 1987 and has been further updated in 1988. The 1987 document and the 1988 update are reproduced in their entirety in Appendix A of this book. They are informative and should be read by everyone.[12,23] The Occupational Safety and Health Administration laws are based on the 1987 document. Both are guided by the knowledge that body fluids from all patients can be potentially infectious, regardless of the patient's diagnosis or test results, and that HIV, the hepatitis B virus, and other bloodborne pathogens must enter the body percutaneously (including via damaged skin) or permucosally and may also be transmitted via the placenta or perinatally.

Universal Precautions

Only those aspects of the guidelines that pertain specifically to intensive care personnel are reproduced here. However, some items that elicit many questions and concerns for intensive care unit staff, or problems for infection control practitioners, are discussed in some detail.

The first statement of importance concerns the routine use of "appropriate barrier precautions to prevent skin and mucous membrane exposure when contact with blood or other body fluids of any patient is anticipated." Since that blanket statement was made in 1987, the update of 1988 has provided a listing of those body fluids that are not considered infectious and to which Universal Precautions do not apply (see Table 4-4).

"Gloves should be worn for touching blood and body fluids, mucous membranes, or non-intact skin of all patients, for handling items or surfaces soiled with blood or body fluids, and for performing venipuncture and other vascular access procedures." According to the Centers for Disease Control and contrary to rumors, latex or vinyl gloves offer equal protection.

Gloves should be changed after contact with each patient. Personnel should *not* wear gloves outside a patient's room, unless they are putting them on specifically to dispose of or clean contaminated articles. Gloves should not be washed and reused because they often have minute holes and when washed a "wicking" effect may draw fluid from the outside to the inside surface of the glove.

"Hands should be washed immediately after gloves are removed." This is very important because gloves have imperfections that may allow the virus to pass through. ''Health care workers who have exudative lesions or weeping dermatitis should refrain from all direct patient care and from handling patient care equipment until the condition resolves.'' This is for the protection of the worker *and* the patient. Two more measures are also highly recommended: (1) any cut or damaged skin area should be covered at all times with an impervious dressing that is frequently changed; and (2) no one should touch his or her mouth, nose, or eyes in the workplace with unwashed hands.

Other barriers consist of masks or protective eyewear, which ''should be worn for procedures that commonly result in the generation of droplets, splashing of blood or other body fluids, or the generation of bone chips.'' Masks, gloves, and eye protectors should be kept on crashcarts and at other strategic locations. In addition, ''gowns or aprons made of materials that provide an effective barrier should be worn during invasive procedures that are likely to result in the splashing of blood or other body fluids.'' Bathing patients, getting them out of bed, or taking blood pressures is not included in that list of procedures. ''Needles should not be recapped, purposely bent or broken by hand, removed from disposable syringes, or otherwise manipulated by hand. After they are used, disposable syringes and needles, scalpel blades, and other sharp items should be placed in puncture-resistant containers for disposal . . . located as close as practical to the use area.'' Intravenous piggy-back needles should be handled with great care, and no needles may ever be discarded in waste containers or left among soiled linen.

Universal Precautions further require that ''hands and other skin surfaces should be washed immediately and thoroughly if contaminated with blood or other body fluids.'' If skin of hands or other body surfaces is not intact or mucous membrane splashes occur, the procedures listed under postexposure follow-up should be observed.

Blood spills should be cleaned up promptly. Any detergent and water or disinfectants are suitable. The cloths and gloves used are considered highly contaminated. After the area is cleaned, an Environmental Protection Agency hospital-approved disinfectant may be applied. The least expensive and probably most easily available and effective of these is sodium hypochlorite (household bleach 5.25%) in a 1:10 solution. Sodium hypochlorite is inactivated by the protein in blood and must be applied to a cleaned area for effective decontamination and left to dry. The same is advisable for other disinfectants. Other disinfectants that have also been found effective are listed in Table 4-5.[35]

Pregnant Personnel

Questions often arise about pregnant physicians and nurses. The Centers for Disease Control states the following:

Table 4-5 Disinfectants Active Against HIV

Agents	Recommended Concentration
Sodium hypochlorite	0.5%
Sodium hydroxide	30 mM
Glutaraldehyde	1%
Hydrogen peroxide	1%
Ethyl alcohol	50%
Isopropyl alcohol	50%
Lysol	1%
Chlorhexidine gluconate/ethanol mix	4/25%
Quaternary ammonium chloride	1%
Nonoxynol-9 (spermicidal)	1–5%

Source: Infection Control (1983;4:258–325), Copyright © 1983, Charles B Slack Inc.

Pregnant health care workers are not known to be at greater risk of contracting HIV infection than health care workers who are not pregnant; however, if a health care worker develops HIV infection during pregnancy, the infant is at risk of infection resulting from perinatal transmission. Because of this risk, pregnant health care workers should be especially familiar with and strictly adhere to precautions to minimize the risk of HIV transmission.

Refusal to provide care for AIDS patients has been addressed by the American Medical Association and American Nurses Association and is summarized in an article by Fowler.[36] Refusal of individual employees to care for AIDS victims because of concern about being infected is best addressed by the personnel department of each institution. According to at least one opinion, such refusal is a breach of the employment contract.[37] Moreover, exempting pregnant physicians and nurses from caring for AIDS patients is tantamount to implying that the precautionary protocols are not protective,[38] and thus it would be unfair to expect nonpregnant personnel to care for these patients as well.

Other AIDS-Related Infections

In addition, patients with AIDS may suffer from a variety of other infections. If these infections are transmissible, such as pulmonary tuberculosis or diarrhea, the appropriate categories of precautions or isolation approved for other hospital patients should be observed.

POSTEXPOSURE PROTOCOL

The Centers for Disease Control have put forth the following suggestions (see Appendix A for complete text):

If an accidental needlestick injury occurs, or there is significant contact of a patient's blood with mucous membranes or nonintact skin surfaces, the health care worker should wash the affected area thoroughly.

The exposure should then be reported to the employee health service or infection control practitioner.

If the source (patient) does not have a previous diagnosis of AIDS or a positive HIV antibody test, a clinical and social assessment of the patient's risk factors for AIDS should be undertaken. In the presence of any such factor, the patient should be told of the health care workers' exposure and an informed consent should be obtained for taking an HIV antibody test. The patient and the health care worker should be counseled regarding the implications of positive or negative results.[9]

Whether or not the test is obtained from the patient, the health care worker should consider obtaining a test himself or herself.[39] In order to ensure complete confidentiality of test results, it might be preferable for physicians and nurses to be tested at an off-site test center rather than at their own institution. If the initial test is negative, the health care worker should be followed for a "flulike" illness for 2 weeks to 2 months. This has been the usual time for HIV infection to develop after a known exposure. Repeat HIV tests at 1, 3, and 6 months are recommended.[23,40]

The usual protocol for possible concomitant hepatitis B exposure should also be observed. As previously discussed, the risk of work-related HIV conversion has been less than 1% in contrast to hepatitis B conversion, which is considerably higher, between 20% and 30%.[17]

One note of warning: serum immunoglobulins (γ-globulin, hepatitis B immune globulin, and others) may contain HIV antibody along with other antibodies.[41] They do *not*, however, contain live viruses of any kind. Therefore, anyone who has received immunoprophylaxis should be aware that they may test positive for HIV antibody. Such passively administered antibody has a half-life of about 28 days. It usually disappears within 3 to 6 months. However, a positive HIV antibody result would naturally be of great concern to anyone, and this potential source should be brought to the attention of immunoglobulin recipients.

ROUTINE TESTING FOR HIV ANTIBODY

One of the questions often asked of infection control practitioners is why all hospitalized patients cannot be routinely tested to determine their HIV antibody status. Any knowledgeable infection control practitioner will, in turn, ask such a questioner what he or she would do differently in the care of a patient who had tested positively. Thoughtful physicians and nurses often will then realize that the precautionary measures they use should not be affected in any way; others will still reply that they would just "be more careful." This is a dangerous attitude because it is well known that test results have a high false-negative rate and at present there is a 2- to 3-week delay in availability of test results. The false sense of security a negative test result may impart may prevent personnel from taking appropriate and consistent precautions.

The cost–benefit ratio of indiscriminately testing the 35 to 40 million patients who are admitted annually to hospitals in the United States is also extremely questionable.[42] Few, if any, type of tests these days costs less than $10. Even at $5 a test, the $185 million expended would not buy greater safety for physicians or nurses. All the health care workers with documented needlesticks or exposures to blood and body fluids who were followed by the Centers for Disease Control, the National Institutes of Health, or at the University of California, knew that their patients had AIDS or were HIV antibody positive. If this prior knowledge of risk did not prevent these accidents, why would test results on all patients make a difference? Furthermore, the cost of unnecessarily mandated tests will be borne directly or indirectly by everyone through increased insurance rates and hospital charges.[43] And what should be done with the test results? To whom should they be revealed? Certainly physicians and nurses providing direct care for the patient need to know, not necessarily to institute appropriate precautions, which should be universal, but to institute effective therapeutic regimens and patient counseling. However, experience has demonstrated that in a hospital it is difficult to confine such information to those who need to know.

There is increasing evidence that HIV antibody conversion may not occur for up to 36 months after infection, at least in homosexual men. Therefore, many infectious patients may have a false negative test result; a negative antibody test does not definitively rule out infectivity.[44]

CONFIDENTIALITY AND THE RIGHT TO KNOW

Theoretically, the diagnosis of any patient's condition is confidential. In general, however, this information is widely available and patients often discuss their diagnoses with roommates and visitors and even with the maid or x-ray technician. Usually this lack of confidentiality has little impact on their future lives. Quite the contrary is true for breaches of confidentiality in regard to a positive HIV antibody test or a diagnosis of AIDS.[45] Disclosure can have catastrophic implications. Infected children are excluded from schools, families become divided, and friends are lost. Loss of jobs and insurance benefits can be devastating, not only to the patient but also to society. If large numbers of otherwise healthy persons were to lose employment and insurance because of a positive HIV antibody test, can society afford to support them for the next 5 to

15 years until they develop the debilitating features of AIDS and die? Surely it would be preferable for these persons to remain productive taxpayers until they can no longer support themselves.

Many states are arriving at the same conclusions and are enacting statutes that prohibit disclosure of test results without the patient's permission.[46,47] Physicians are authorized in some states to inform the person's sexual partners and those who have shared intravenous needles with him or her that they may have been exposed to HIV. They may usually do so without disclosing who the contact was. This is also the procedure used for other sexually transmitted diseases.

Physicians and nurses should be supportive of such requirements, and 5.8% of adults reported to the Centers for Disease Control as having AIDS are health care workers.[22] Although less than 1% of these acquired the virus in the workplace, if their names became known they, too, might be excluded from employment and insurance. They would probably be shunned by friends and co-workers, even though they pose no risk to those with whom they work or have only casual contact. This very fear has kept many nurses and physicians from reporting work-related HIV exposures and accidents, which in turn decreases their chances of receiving adequate compensation if such an unfortunate exposure were to result in HIV infection. Contrary to some assertions, confidentiality need not conflict with the rights of others. These others should follow safe work procedures in the hospital and safe sexual practices in their private lives.

Patients in high-risk groups should be encouraged to be tested on a voluntary basis. Then, if discrimination against HIV-infected persons is reduced or eliminated, more patients will follow the counseling they should all receive: that they should abstain from transmitting the virus to others either sexually or through shared intravenous use of needles and that they should inform their dentists, physicians, nurses, and other health care workers of their seropositivity or infectious status.

CONCLUSIONS

The AIDS epidemic is not going to go away. The high mortality rate and the stigma attached to infected persons have changed the life-styles of large segments of the American population. It has also changed patient care practices in hospitals.

The AIDS virus can be transmitted in the workplace. Accidental needlesticks and spattering of blood with certain potentially infectious body fluids onto non-intact skin or mucous membranes must be avoided. Although the risk of acquisition of the virus is low, it must be recognized and reduced to its absolute minimum. By conscientiously and unfailingly adhering to the precautionary measures proposed by the Centers for Disease Control, mandated by the Occupational Safety and Health Administration, and outlined in this chapter, critical care nurses can continue to provide the high quality of care they usually render to all their patients, without endangering their own health.

REFERENCES

1. Thomas E. Plagues, man and history. Newsweek 1988; May 9:65–66.

2. Centers for Disease Control. Quarterly report to the Domestic Policy Council on the prevalence and rate of spread of HIV and AIDS in the United States. MMWR 1988;37:223–226.

3. Kelly JA, St. Lawrence J, Smith S. Medical students' attitudes towards AIDS. J Med Educ 1987;62:549–556.

4. Gallo R. The virus-cancer story. Hosp Pract 1983;18:79–89.

5. Buckley RH. Immunodeficiency diseases. JAMA 1987;258:2841–2850.

6. Laurence J. The immune system in AIDS. Sci Am 1985;253:84–93.

7. Centers for Disease Control. Revised measles/mumps/rubella immunization recommendations for persons infected with HIV. MMWR 1988;37:181–183.

8. Tindell B, Barker S, Donovan B, et al. Characterization of the acute illness associated with human immunodeficiency infection. Arch Intern Med 1988;48:945–949.

9. Centers for Disease Control. Public Health Service guidelines for counseling and antibody testing to prevent HIV infection and AIDS. MMWR 1987;36:509–514.

10. Lawrence J. Bacterial infection in AIDS. Infect Med 1987;4:299–304.

11. Levy JA. The transmission of AIDS: The case of the infected cell. JAMA 1988;259:3037–3038.

12. Centers for Disease Control. Update. Unusual precautions for prevention of transmission of hepatitis B virus and other bloodborne pathogens in health-care settings. MMWR 1988;37:377–387.

13. Winkelstein W, Lyman DM, Padian N, et al. Sexual practices and risk of infection by the human immunodeficiency virus. The San Francisco men's health study. JAMA 1987;257:325–330.

14. Quinn TC, Mann JM, Curran JW, et al. AIDS in Africa: An epidemiologic paradigm. Science 1986;955–963.

15. Rubinstein A, Bernstein L. The epidemiology of pediatric acquired immunodeficiency syndrome. Clin Immunol Immunopathol 1986;40:115–121.

16. Castro NG, Lieb S, Jaffe HW, et al. Transmission of HIV in Belle Glade, Florida: Lessons for other communities in the United States. Science 1988;239:193–197.

17. Friedland GH, Klein RS. Transmission of the human immunodeficiency virus. N Engl J Med 1987;317:1125.

18. Valenti WM. From ritual to reason and back again: OSHA and the evaluation of Infection Control. Infect Control Hosp Epidemiol 1988;9:289–299.

19. Gerberding JL. Transmission of hepatitis B without transmission of AIDS by accidental needle stick. N Engl J Med 1985;312:5.

20. Henderson DK, Saah AJ, Zak BJ, et al. Risk of nosocomial infections with human lymphotropic virus type III lymphadenopathy-associated virus in a large cohort of intensely exposed health-care workers. Ann Intern Med 1986;104:644–647.

21. Gerberding JL, Bryant-LeBlanc CE, Nelson K, et al. Risk of transmitting the human immune deficiency virus, cytomegalovirus, and hepatitis B virus to health-care workers exposed to patient with AIDS and AIDS-related conditions. J Infect Dis 1987;156:1–8.

22. McCray E. The cooperative needlestick surveillance group. Occupational risk of the acquired immune deficiency syndrome among health-care workers. N Engl J Med 1986;314:1127–1132.

23. Centers for Disease Control. Recommendations for prevention of HIV transmission in health-care settings. MMWR 1987;36(3S):3S–18S.

24. Centers for Disease Control. Update: Human immunodeficiency virus infections in health-care workers exposed to blood of infected patients. MMWR 1987;36:285–288.

25. Fuchs D, Hansen A, Reibnegger G, et al. HIV seroconversion in health-care workers. JAMA 1987;258:2525–2526.

26. Kline RS, Phelan J, Friedlander GH, et al. Low occupational risk for HIV infection for dental professionals. In: Abstracts from the 3rd International Conference on AIDS, Washington, DC, 1985.

27. Martin K, Katz BT, Miller G. AIDS and antibodies to HIV in children and their families. J Infect Dis 1987;155:54–58.

28. Biberfeld G, Bottiger B, Berntorp E, et al. Transmission of HIV infection to heterosexual partners but not to household contacts of hemophiliacs. Scand J Infect Dis 1986;18:497–500.

29. Friedland GH, Saltzman BR, Rogers MF, et al. Lack of HTLV III/LAV infections to household contacts of patients with AIDS or AIDS-related complex with oral candidiasis. N Engl J Med 1986;314:344–349.

30. Fischl MA, Dickinson CM, Scott GB, et al. Evaluation of heterosexual partners, children, and household contacts of adults with AIDS. JAMA 1987;257:640–644.

31. Drummond JA. Seronegative 18 months after being bitten by a patient with AIDS. JAMA 1986;256:2342–2343.

32. Saviteer SH, White CG, Cohen MS. HTLV III exposure during cardiopulmonary resuscitation. N Engl J Med 1985;313:1605.

33. Enforcement procedures for occupational exposure to hepatitis B virus, human immunodeficiency virus, and other bloodborne infectious agents. CPL 2-2-44, U.S. Department of Labor, OSHA, Washington, DC.

34. Garner JS, Simmons BP. Guidelines for isolation precautions in hospital. Infect Control 1983;4:258–325.

35. Martin LS. Disinfection and inactivation of the human T-lymphotropic virus type III/LAV. J Infect Dis 1985;152:400–403.

36. Fowler MDM. Acquired immunodeficiency syndrome and refusal to provide care. Heart Lung 1988;17:213–215.

37. Dubois IA, Lozano M. AIDS and the neonatal ICU. Neonatal Network 1986; December:39–41.

38. Regan W. Legally speaking: Refusing to treat AIDS victims. RN 1983;46:22–24.

39. Kuhlis TL, Cherry JD. The management of health-care workers' accidental parenteral exposures to biological specimens of HIV seropositive individuals. Infect Control 1987;8:211–223.

40. Brennan TA. The acquired immunodeficiency syndrome (AIDS) as an occupational disease. Ann Intern Med 1987;107:581–583.

41. Gockle DJ, Rasta K, Pollack W, Schwartzer T. HTLV-III antibody in commercial immunoglobulin. Lancet 1986;1:37–38.

42. Barry J, Cleary P, Fineberg H. Screening for HIV infection: Risks benefits and the burden of proof. Law Med Health Care 1987;14:259–267.

43. Cleary PD, Barry MJ, Mayer KH, et al. Compulsory premarital screening for the human immunodeficiency virus. JAMA 1987;258:1757–1761.

44. Imagawa DT, Lee MH, Wolinsky SM, et al. Human immunodeficiency virus Type I infection in homosexual men who remain seronegative for prolonged periods. N Engl J Med 1989;320:1458–1462.

45. Gostin L, Curran WJ. AIDS screening, confidentiality, and the duty to warn. Am J Public Health 1987;77:361–365.

46. Lewis HE. Acquired immunodeficiency syndrome—State legislative activity. JAMA 1987;253:2410–2414.

47. Dickens BM. Legal limits of AIDS confidentiality. JAMA 1988;259:3449–3451.

CHAPTER REVIEW QUESTIONS

1. The risk of HIV infection due to an accidental needlestick is
   a. Less than 1%
   b. Between 1% and 5%
   c. About 10%
   d. Unknown

2. Latex and vinyl gloves
   a. Are equally protective
   b. May be washed for reuse
   c. a and b

3. A blood spill in the intensive care unit should be handled as follows (using any hospital-approved disinfectant or 1:10 solution of sodium hypochlorite).
   a. Clean the spill up with the disinfectant.
   b. Clean the spill up, then spread disinfectant over the area and let air dry.
   c. Flood the spill with disinfectant, let stand 5 minutes, then wipe dry.

4. The Centers for Disease Control considers the following body fluids as infectious for HIV.
   a. Synovial, cerebrospinal fluid, pleural, peritoneal, amniotic
   b. Urine, saliva, sputum, tears
   c. Blood, semen, vaginal secretions
   d. a and c
   e. All of above

5. When caring for a patient with AIDS, gloves should be worn for
   a. Bathing the patient and making the beds
   b. Feeding the patient
   c. Emptying the Foley catheter bag
   d. None of the above
   e. All of the above

6. In Belle Glade, Florida, the only identified risk factor for the high rate of HIV infection was the presence of large numbers of mosquitoes in 1982.
   a. True
   b. False

7. Infants or young children have become infected with HIV
   a. By sharing dishes and towels and toothbrushes in the family
   b. By close contact with an infected family member other than their mother
   c. Before or during birth from an infected mother
   d. All of the above

8. Testing all intensive care unit patients for HIV antibodies would provide greater protection for nurses and physicians in those units.
   a. True
   b. False

Answers are provided in Appendix B.

Chapter 5

Hepatitis B and Delta Hepatitis

Viral hepatitis can have a significant impact on a person's health, and in the United States it ranks third in prevalence among communicable diseases that are reportable. The causative agents are the hepatitis A, B, delta, and non-A, non-B viruses (Table 5-1).These viruses are hepatotropic, which means that they demonstrate a distinct preference for the liver. They invade and replicate in liver cells, but integrated hepatitis B viral DNA has been demonstrated in pancreatic, renal, and skin cells and in semen. The significance of these findings, however, is not clear, whereas the role of hepatitis B virus in the liver has been well established.[1]

The hepatitis viruses, like other viruses, cannot reproduce by themselves as bacteria and fungi do. They require living tissue cells for this process. After penetrating a hepatocyte, the hepatitis viruses induce the host cell to synthesize viral particles, which in turn are released to infect other liver cells. Hepatitis viruses, unlike some other viruses, do not generally destroy their host cells in the process of replication but may injure some of them. These changes cause inflammatory reactions by the immune system. As the virus tries to destroy the virus-infected hepatocytes, liver function can become compromised and the clinical entity of hepatitis is manifested.

There is significant variability in the severity of disease, the clinical manifestations, the length of incubation, and the types of complications and the sequelae among the hepatitis viruses. Hepatitis B and the delta virus will be described in this chapter; hepatitis A and hepatitis non-A, non-B are described in Chapter 6. Although hepatitis A is not a common problem in critical care it does cause viral hepatitis and needs to be differentiated from hepatitis B.

HEPATITIS B

HEPADNA Viruses

The human hepatitis B virus is one of a group of hepatotropic DNA (HEPADNA) viruses. This HEPADNA group includes three other viruses that

Table 5-1 The Hepatitis Viruses—Three Different Groups

Enteroviruses

Hepatitis A

HEPADNA Viruses

Human Hepatitis B virus
Animal Hepatitis B virus
Delta Hepatitis

Non-A, Non-B Viruses
Enteric Virus NANB
Other NANB

cause hepatitis in woodchucks, ground squirrels, and ducks. These viruses are species specific, however, and only the hepatitis B virus infects humans. They are grouped together because of certain similarities in replication, pathogenesis, and sequelae. All are DNA viruses, but unlike other such viruses their replicating mechanisms resemble those of the retroviruses, of which the human immunodeficiency virus is presently the most familiar. The HEPADNA viruses also share the ability to cause silent infections, to persist within the host cells in an asymptomatic carrier state, and to cause persistent or progressive disease. There is some evidence that the human and the woodchuck hepatitis viruses may be responsible for development of hepatocellular carcinoma.[2]

Clinical Manifestations

When hepatitis B virus enters the body it penetrates the host's liver cells and begins the process of replication by inducing the cells to synthesize new viral particles. These, in turn, are released and go on to infect other liver cells. The clinical signs and symptoms known as hepatitis are caused by the vigorous response of the body's competent immune system in an attempt to destroy the liver cells that harbor the virus. Some manifestations, such as the prodromal serum sickness–like syndrome, are caused by the formation and deposition of antibody–antigen complexes. In the absence of such an immune response, the virus may persist and the patient may become a carrier.

After a long incubating period of 6 weeks to 6 months, one of three typical clinical patterns may develop. Over 50% of infections are inapparent. They go unnoticed or cause only minor symptoms of fatigue. In anicteric hepatitis, onset of more noticeable manifestations is gradual. Ninety percent of patients are fatigued and complain of malaise and anorexia. Eighty percent will have nausea, which may lead to some weight loss. Patients may describe a feeling of abdominal fullness, discomfort, or pain. There may be hepatomegaly and occasionally splenomegaly. Fever may be present, with a temperature usually below 102°F (38.9°C). The third type of pattern includes development of jaundice. Scleral icterus, dark urine, and clay-colored stools precede frank jaundice by about 5 days in patients who develop this type of hepatitis. There may be involvement of other organ systems, as demonstrated by

- Flulike symptoms
- Gastritis or gastrointestinal bleeding
- Depression, peripheral neuropathy
- Glomerulonephritis
- Rashes
- Disturbances of glucose metabolism
- An immune complex–mediated, serum sickness–like syndrome and polyarteritis

These manifestations often occur prodromally and they usually improve or disappear with the onset of jaundice.[3] A very small number of patients develop fulminant hepatitis and die, but most, 80% to 85% of patients, recover completely.

Diagnosis

Nonspecific Tests

In the early stages of hepatitis, as in most viral infections, there may be neutropenia and lymphopenia, which may later develop into lymphocytosis. The presence of 2% to 20% atypical lymphocytes is not uncommon. Prothrombin times may be prolonged, depending on the extent of hepatocellular damage. Levels of liver enzymes, the aminotransferases, will be elevated. Familiarity with the different enzymes is important in order to distinguish between cellular injury of various types and between the possible causes of jaundice. The differential diagnosis includes viral hepatitis, alcoholic cirrhosis, and obstructive conditions of the gallbladder and its ducts. Only viral origin indicates potential infectivity of the patient.

The aspartate aminotransferase (AST) (or serum glutamic oxaloacetic transaminase [SGOT]) level becomes elevated when there is extensive cellular damage of any kind. Critical care nurses are familiar with such elevations in patients with myocardial infarctions. The greater the insult, the higher the AST value will be. This is also true after bone fractures or other cellular trauma. Alanine aminotransferase (ALT) (or serum glutamic pyruvic transaminase [SGPT]), however, is more specific for liver damage because this enzyme is released only from injured hepatocytes. Therefore, in acute viral hepatitis, ALT will have significantly higher elevations, up to 50 times of the normal values, than AST. This is also true in chronic disease, although elevations will often be less dramatic. In most acute cases, the ALT level will become elevated late in the incubation period and drop off gradually during the late acute stage. Bilirubin elevations can be seen in any type of liver involvement. When the value rises above 2.5 mg/dL the patient may show clinical icterus. In alcoholic liver disease, the AST value will be higher than the ALT value and the liver will be enlarged in 92% of patients.

The alkaline phosphatase value is useful in differentiating the jaundice of viral hepatitis from that caused by obstructive cholestasis, cholelithiasis, or cancer of the pancreas or gallbladder. In obstructive jaundice the alkaline phosphatase value will be elevated to a greater extent (up to a greater than 10 times normal) than the ALT value. The ALT level will usually be normal or minimally elevated, up to about three times of its normal value.

An example of how an unnecessary exposure to a patient with hepatitis B could have been avoided if the patient's nurses had been aware of the significance of their patient's aminotransferase elevation is given when high-risk patient groups are discussed later in this chapter.

Although past history, exposure, type of onset of disease, clinical manifestations, and nonspecific laboratory tests can all provide a presumptive diagnosis of viral hepatitis, a definitive diagnosis can only be made by virus-specific serologic tests, including radioimmunoassay, enzyme-linked immunoabsorbent assay (ELISA), immune adherence, and others.

Serodiagnosis

The serodiagnostic markers are related to the structure of the virus shown in Figure 5-1. The virus is a double-shelled DNA virion, which has also been called the Dane particle. One of the structural components of the outer surface or shell is the hepatitis B surface antigen (HBsAg). This is a protein produced in great amounts in more than 75% of infected patients. It represents presence of virus in the liver cells and thus makes the patient infectious. The surface antigen can be isolated from serum and is used to identify certain stages of infection. Depending on the presence or absence of other markers, it can denote acute infection, asymptomatic carriage, or chronic persistent and progressive disease. The nonacute sequelae will be discussed in more detail later. The HBsAg value will fall below detectable levels in the normal progression of the disease by the 8th to the 12th week.

The inner core of the virus contains two proteins identified as hepatitis B core antigen (HBcAg) and hepatitis B e antigen (HBeAg). HBcAg is the first to be produced after a new infection, but it remains in the liver cell and is not detectable

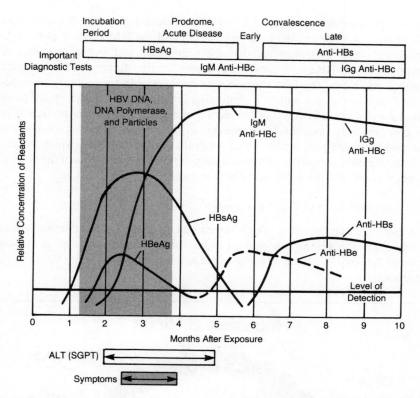

Figure 5-1 Diagrammatic presentation of the structure of the hepatitis B virus and its markers. *Source:* Reprinted with permission of Abbott Laboratories, North Chicago, Illinois.

in serum. Therefore, it does not help in the diagnosis of hepatitis B. HBeAg is a product of degradation of the core and a good indicator of infectivity.[4,5] Its role in chronic hepatitis and maternal-child transmission is discussed later in the chapter.

Other core components are the viral DNA and DNA polymerase, which is the enzyme whose presence represents an ongoing process of viral replication. Both of these components would be better indicators of a patient's infectious status, but the tests are usually too complex to be performed routinely in most laboratories.

As discussed in Chapter 2, the humoral immune system, mediated by the B lymphocytes, normally produces antibodies or immunoglobulins when a foreign antigen is encountered. Indeed, in immunocompetent patients, this response is also triggered in hepatitis B. When a newly infected liver cell begins to synthesize the first protein of the hepatitis B virus (the core antigen), the B-cell system will produce antibody to the core protein—first of the IgM class, then the IgG anti-HBc. These antibodies are detectable in serum and aid in diagnosis of hepatitis B. Anti-HBc IgG remains detectable for life. In persistent or chronic ongoing infections, the IgM fraction may be detectable for prolonged periods of time and indicates a patient's continuing infectivity. Similarly, synthesis of HBeAg will eventually result in production of anti-HBe. The e antibody, unlike the core antibody, eventually disappears. In the normal course of events, the last antibody to be produced at about 3 months will be anti-HBs, which usually indicates resolution of the infection and immunity.[5] The correlation of the clinical manifestations and serologic markers is shown in Figure 5-2.

Serologic Markers and Clinical Staging[6]

A patient's hepatitis B serology screen can have six different combinations (Table 5-2). The results can be used to interpret or determine at what clinical stage of disease the patient is being tested and whether he or she is likely to be infectious.

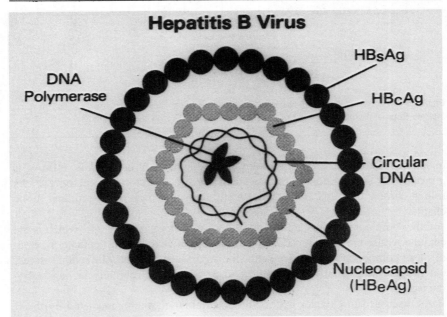

Figure 5-2 Serologic evaluation of hepatitis B. *Source:* Reprinted with permission. Hollinger FB, Serologic Evaluation of Viral Hepatitis. *Hospital Practice*, 22(2):106, 1988, Illustration by Mr. Albert Miller.

Table 5-2 Antigen–Antibody Combinations as Aids to Diagnosis and Establishment of Infectivity in Hepatitis B

Serologic Marker in Order of Appearance			Stage of Clinical Disease	Is Patient Infectious
HBsAg	Anti-HBc	Anti-HBs		
+	−	−	Early acute infection Asymptomatic carriage Chronic persistent or progressive hepatitis	Yes
+	+	−	Late acute infection Asymptomatic carriage Chronic persistent or progressive hepatitis	Yes
−	IgM +	−	Window period (early convalescent stage) Asymptomatic carriage Chronic persistent or progressive hepatitis	Yes
−	IgM − IgG +	−	Convalescence Asymptomatic carriage Chronic persistent or progressive disease	No No ?
−	+	+	Recover, immunity	No
−	−	+	Vaccine response Patient may have received hepatitis B immune globulin within past 6 months; patient may not be immune, depending on antibody titer	No
+	+	+	Asymptomatic carriage Chronic hepatitis with an immune-deficient response Possible reinfection with a different antigenic strain of hepatitis B virus Patient may have been given hepatitis B immune globulin for an exposure but subsequently developed hepatitis	Yes

1. The patient is positive for HBsAg only. This can represent (a) the late incubation period or early acute stage; (b) the asymptomatic carrier state, or (c) chronic hepatitis of the persistent or active-progressive kind. The patient should be considered infectious.
2. HBsAg and anti-HBc are positive. The patient may be in the late acute or early convalescent phase; this finding may represent asymptomatic carriage or chronic persistent or progressive hepatitis. The patient should be considered infectious.
3. Anti-HBc alone is positive. This may represent the window phase in the normal progression of hepatitis B, when the HBsAg has disappeared but the anti-HBs has not yet become detectable. It is a common finding in early convalescence. The antibody to the HBcAg may be of the IgM or IgG class depending on the time at which the test is done. The patient may be an asymptomatic carrier or have asymptomatic persistent or progressive hepatitis:
   a. In the presence of IgM anti-HBc the patient is considered infectious due to ongoing viral infection.
   b. In the absence of IgM anti-HBc, IgG will be present and the patient is not considered infectious. However, blood for donation will not be accepted.
   A fourth possible, but rare, explanation would be that the patient may have received an anti-HBc positive blood transfusion. If the unit of blood did not contain the virus, the passive antibody will be cleared from the patient's blood in about 2 months. Retesting a patient who is only positive for anti-HBc and is not known to be a chronic carrier in about 3 months will help with staging of the patient's clinical status.
4. Both anti-HBc and anti-HBs are positive. This represents recovery and immunity. The patient is not considered to be infectious.
5. Only anti-HBs is present. This is an unusual finding. It probably does not represent a past hepatitis B infection because such an infection would have produced core antibody, which usually persists for life. Therefore this finding suggests a response to the hepatitis B vaccine (the vaccine contains HBsAg and therefore the only immune response is production of anti-HBs) or the patient may have received a prophylactic dose of hepatitis B immune globulin (HBIG). In both instances the patient is not infectious. The surface antibody titers in vaccine response may decline to unprotective levels and after HBIG administration will disappear entirely in 2 to 3 months.
6. All three markers (HBsAg, anti-HBc, and anti-HBs) are positive. Concurrent antigen and antibody markers are being reported with increasing frequency. The most likely explanation is the patient is suffering ongoing acute or chronic hepatitis to which the immune system is producing some antibody but in amounts insufficient to eliminate the virus.[7] Or there is

the possibility of reinfection with a different antigenic subtype. However, since there is known cross-immunogenicity for all subtypes, this explanation has not been substantiated. It is not known whether patients who are positive for all three markers are infectious.[8] It would be safer to consider the patient infectious and not to accept blood for donation from patients who are HBsAg positive.

DELTA HEPATITIS

Any discussion of hepatitis B, its outcomes, transmission, high-risk groups of patients, and prophylaxis, requires an understanding of the role of the delta agent, because this virus can be intimately involved in all these aspects of hepatitis B.[9]

The highly pathogenic delta virus was identified in 1976. In contrast to the hepatitis B virus, it is cytopathic and highly destructive for the liver cells. The delta virus, however, is an incomplete or defective RNA virus that is totally dependent on the hepatitis B virus for its replication and effect. This means that the delta virus cannot cause hepatitis in the absence of established hepatitis B.

Clinical Delta Hepatitis

There are two types of delta infection. Both are clinically indistinguishable from other types of hepatitis. One occurs simultaneously with hepatitis B infection. In this type of acute co-infection, there will be two aminotransferase elevations about 6 weeks apart. The first peak signals the release of circulating delta antigen (delta-Ag) and the cytopathic effect of this virus on the liver cells. The second peak coincides with the appearance of anti-HBc and anti-delta IgM. This type of co-infection usually resolves uneventfully and anti-delta IgM and IgG disappear very quickly, although occasionally the IgG will persist for 1 to 2 years. It is not clear whether there is a higher incidence of fulminant hepatitis with delta co-infection, but in some studies the presence of delta virus markers is found with increasing frequency in fulminant cases.[10]

The second type of delta hepatitis occurs as a result of superinfection in a patient who has preexisting hepatitis B. The patient may be an unknown, asymptomatic carrier or someone with chronic hepatitis B. A new delta virus infection mimics hepatitis B and is indistinguishable on clinical grounds. It can be differentiated from acute hepatitis B because acute anti-HBc (IgM) is absent and anti-delta IgM or IgG may be detectable.

In patients with chronic hepatitis B, a superinfection with delta virus is more likely to be severe or fulminant or lead to progression of damage in an already compromised liver.[11]

OUTCOMES AND SEQUELAE

The complexity of hepatitis B is further enhanced by the range of different outcomes (Table 5-3). In most cases it is a self-limiting disease and 85% of infected adults recover completely within 2 to 3 months. A small percentage (about 1%) of patients suffer massive hepatic necrosis with progressive liver failure. Encephalopathy, decrease in liver size, and death are part of this fulminant picture. Comparatively benign sequelae may consist of a clinically insignificant but persistent hyperbilirubinemia, while others include asymptomatic (chronic) carriage and chronic persistent hepatitis. The more serious sequelae are chronic active hepatitis, cirrhosis, and hepatoma.

It is this potential for sequelae that produces such concern about the acquisition of hepatitis B virus by nurses and other personnel in the critical care setting.

The Asymptomatic (Chronic) Carrier State

The majority of asymptomatic carriers are healthy and unaware of the fact they were ever infected with the hepatitis B virus. Most cases are detected accidentally. These carriers are, however, considered to be infectious. The frequency of this state is greatly influenced by the age at which a person is initially infected and somewhat less by the state of his or her immune system. Eighty to 90% of neonates, especially males, who are infected perinatally will develop asymptomatic or chronic persistent hepatitis.[12] Presumably the reason for this

---

Table 5-3 Possible Outcomes of Hepatitis B Infection in the United States

1. Self-limiting disease (80%–85%)
   Uneventful recovery
   Cholestatic persistence
   Prolonged hepatitis
   Post-hepatitis bilirubinemia

2. Fulminant hepatitis—death (0.5% to 1%)

3. Chronic conditions (15%)
   Asymptomatic carriage
   ↓
   Hepatoma—death
   Chronic persistent hepatitis
   Chronic active (or progressive) hepatitis
   ↓
   Cirrhosis
   ↓
   Death

carriage is the inability of the neonate's immature immune system to recognize the hepatitis B virus as nonself and therefore it will fail to develop an immune response to destroy the virus. This inability to develop an inadequate immune response is also to blame for other chronic carrier states, which in adults is 5% to 8%.[12]

Worldwide, the pool of chronic hepatitis B virus carriers is about 200 million persons, or 5% of the world's population, with the greatest numbers in the underdeveloped nations. It is in those neonatally infected persons that primary liver cancer or hepatoma is most likely to develop. These healthy persons do not have evidence of ongoing viral replication but may have an integrated form of hepatitis B virus DNA within their liver cells. In time, it is this integrated form that may undergo malignant transformation. The relative risk of developing hepatocellular carcinoma in a neonatally infected Asian carrier is 217 to 1.[13] This is an extremely high risk. In comparison, the risk of developing lung cancer for a smoker in the United States is "only" 10 to 1. The importance of these data to health care personnel will be more evident during discussion of high-risk patient populations.

Chronic Persistent and Chronic Progressive Hepatitis

Hepatitis is diagnosed as being chronic when HBsAg persists for 6 months or more, accompanied by persistent, but usually low, elevations of serum amino-transferases. Early in the chronic phase, HBeAg is also present in a large number of patients, although it may eventually be replaced by anti-HBe. Diagnosis of chronic progressive, also called chronic active hepatitis, requires persistence of HBsAg and evidence of lobular injury, which usually requires a liver biopsy. Chronicity develops and persists due to the continued presence of hepatitis B virus coexisting with an inadequate immunologic response in the host. Patients with chronic hepatitis B who develop delta virus superinfection are likely to develop more severe or progressive chronic disease because of the significant cytopathic effects of the delta virus on an already chronically affected liver.[9]

Acute exacerbation of hepatitis in a chronically infected person is more likely to occur in HBeAg patients than in those with anti-HBe (91% and 63.5%, respectively), but the clinical and pathologic features are similar.[14] Exacerbation can also be due to a new infection with non-A, non-B hepatitis viruses or delta hepatitis virus. Regardless of acuity or pathogenesis, these patients are considered potentially infectious.

HIGH-RISK POPULATIONS

Up to 1.5% of patients admitted to hospitals are carriers of HBsAg. Of these, 80% to 90% will go unrecognized because they are admitted for reasons unrelated to hepatitis and may not be known as carriers. They pose a serious threat to health care workers unless a high index of suspicion is maintained and precautionary measures faithfully observed.

Case History

The 60-year-old mother of an internist on staff at a large university-affiliated hospital was admitted to the coronary care unit to rule out a myocardial infarction. The patient's history contained the information that the patient had liver cancer, diagnosed 3 weeks prior to admission. Two days after admission, the patient had a cardiac arrest and during resuscitation efforts a nurse stuck herself with a needle used on the patient. Because the patient's liver enzyme values were elevated, a routine hepatitis screening test was ordered on the patient and the incident was reported to the employee health service and infection control practitioner. When the infection control practitioner reviewed the patient's chart and read the history of liver cancer, she checked the patient's birthplace and noted that the patient was born in Taiwan. A telephone call to the patient's physician confirmed the suspicion that she was a HBsAg carrier. When asked why the patient had not been placed on Blood and Body Fluid Precautions (this incident preceded the institution of Universal Precautions by 5 years), the reply was that the patient was "probably not infectious." The patient's son, the internist, was also questioned and his reply was that the patient's physician was in charge of his mother's care! Those who had participated in the patient's care and resuscitation were individually questioned by the infection control practitioner regarding exposure to the patient's blood. One house officer had to be called at another hospital where he had just transferred for his fellowship in pulmonary medicine. This physician reported having eczematous eruptions on his hand and did indeed get the patient's blood on his hands when he was obtaining arterial blood gas samples during the cardiac arrest. Thinking it unimportant, he had not reported this exposure. When, as expected, the patient's HBsAg was reported as positive, the nurse who had stuck herself was susceptible and received prophylaxis with hepatitis B immune globulin and the first dose of vaccine. The resident/fellow was also informed of the patient's positive antigen report and advised to apply for prophylaxis if he was also susceptible. The infection control practitioner further discovered that the patient had undergone the diagnostic liver biopsy at this hospital 3 weeks ago, and follow-up questioning of those who had performed the biopsy and cared for the patient revealed another exposure that could have been avoided had the patient been on Blood and Body Fluid Precautions. Such precautions would have required the wearing of gloves for certain patient contacts. It was now, however, too late to provide postexposure prophylaxis for that person, who was given a list of possible signs and symptoms of hepatitis infection and instructed to report these to the infection control practitioner should they occur within the 6-week to 6-month incubation period. It was also suggested that he report for liver enzyme tests during that period.

This type of unnecessary exposure could have been avoided if the nurses had been aware of the patient's high risk for hepatitis B virus carriage by virtue of her birthplace and her diagnosis of primary liver cancer. Although it was the responsibility of the two physicians to inform the nurses of the patient's potential infectivity, nurses cannot rely on others and must acquire the knowledge needed to protect themselves.

There are four groups of patients at high risk of acquiring and carrying the hepatitis B virus. Patients born in the underdeveloped nations, especially in Asia or Africa are in the first group of high-risk patients because of the high endemicity of hepatitis B in that part of the world. Patients with health-related risks are in the second group, which includes patients with hepatoma, who are usually born in third world countries; hemophiliacs and others who have had multiple blood transfusions; patients on chronic hemodialysis who have, in the past, also been at high risk but whose prevalence of hepatitis B virus carriage is declining; and residents in mental institutions who are at risk because they tend to bite or otherwise practice poor hygiene. The third risk category (Table 5-4) is that which relates to high-risk behavior or life-styles, such as intravenous drug abuse and homosexual activity in males, which includes prison inmates and anyone who is also in a high-risk category for human immunodeficiency virus infection. In the last group are nurses, physicians, and others who have frequent contact with

---

Table 5-4 High-Risk Populations for Hepatitis B Virus Acquisition, Asymptomatic Carriage, or Hepatitis B Virus Infection

Behavior Related	*Country of Origin*
Intravenous drug abuse (27%)*	Especially Asia and Africa
Sexual transmission	Patient with hepatoma, mainly from Asia
Heterosexual (24%)*	
Homosexual activity (males 9%)*	
Prison inmates	
Health Related	*Health Care Workers*
Hemophiliacs	Staff in mental institutions
Recipients of multiple blood transfusions	Surgeons, all specialties
Hemodialysis patients (<1%)	Pathologists
Residents of mental institutions	Emergency department and intensive
Household contacts of hepatitis B virus	care unit nurses
carriers	Blood bank personnel
	Others having frequent contact with blood (1%)*

*MMWR 1988; 37:429–437.

blood, including 1% to 3% of dentists and oral surgeons, obstetricians and gynecologists, blood bank personnel, and nurses in emergency department and critical care units who may be chronic carriers of HBsAg.[15] The blood and body fluids of anyone admitted, for whatever reason, to a health care facility who falls into one of these categories must be handled with great care. Such a warning should be unnecessary in this day and age when *all* patients should be cared for with Universal Precautions, but, unfortunately, nurses become careless at times and need to be reminded that many patients could be potentially infected with the hepatitis B virus.

TRANSMISSION

Most persons are not aware of how they acquired hepatitis B. However, routes of transmission are well established. Both the hepatitis B and delta viruses can be acquired percutaneously and permucosally, which includes sexual and perinatal transmission. These modes will be discussed separately and are listed in Table 5-5.

Percutaneous Transmission

In the past, the major mode of hepatitis B virus transmission was by contaminated blood and its derivatives, as well as by transplanted organs. Donor blood

---

Table 5-5 Modes of Acquisition and Transmission of the Hepatitis B Virus

Percutaneous

1. Blood: blood byproducts or derivatives
2. Needles
    Intravenous drug abuse
    Accidental injury by sharp objects or needles
    Tattooing, acupuncture, ear piercing
3. Contaminated medical instruments
4. Shared razors
5. Blood and body fluid contamination of nonintact skin surfaces

Permucosal

1. Shared eating utensils, toothbrushes
2. Kissing (with damaged oral mucosa)
3. Blood and body fluid spatters to mucosal surfaces (eye, mouth, nose)
4. Sexual contact
5. Vertical transmission
    Intrauterine
    Perinatal
    Postnatal
      Breast milk
      Permucosal, percutaneous

testing for HBsAg has greatly reduced this mode of transmission, and less than 5% of post-transfusion hepatitis is now due to the hepatitis B virus. This rate will decline even further when donor testing for anti-HBc becomes standard procedure. The greatest beneficiaries of this rate decline will be hemophiliacs and others who receive blood products derived from hundreds of units of pooled blood. Percutaneous penetration by needles or instruments contaminated with blood containing hepatitis B virus is also an efficient mechanism for transmission. Intravenous drug abusers are at greatest risk. Health care workers who sustain accidental needlesticks with contaminated blood would face a risk of approximately 20% for contracting hepatitis B if they were not immune and did not receive prophylaxis. The virus is extremely infectious, and only very small quantities are required to cause infection. An excellent example of this is illustrated by descriptions of outbreaks among Scandinavian track finders. This cross-country sport, also called orienteering, was responsible for more than 600 cases of hepatitis B in Sweden and an equally large number elsewhere. These races, through wooded areas, take place in the warm months of the year. Shorts and short-sleeved shirts are standard clothing, and scratches are commonly acquired from trees and underbrush. The competitors usually cool down by bathing in ponds or stagnant tubs of water at the end of the race. The abrasions of the skin provided a ready portal of entry to the hepatitis B virus, which was transmitted by the shared, contaminated water. The epidemic was interrupted when new rules were enacted requiring use of long sleeves and pants. When these rules were ignored after the outbreak had been terminated, a large number of new cases appeared once again.[16] This is an excellent example of the risk to persons with abraded or otherwise damaged skin.

A respiratory therapist who acquired hepatitis B from a patient in a large suburban hospital was, in turn, responsible for causing five cases of nosocomial hepatitis in her patients. She had exudative lesions on her hands from chronic dermatitis, which were obviously the vehicle of transmission. Thus, both nurses and patients are potentially at risk when nurses do not wear gloves while performing invasive procedures or tasks that involve contact with body fluids.

Although contaminated medical equipment such as surgical instruments, respiratory therapy or anesthesia equipment, and endoscopes pose a greater risk to patients than to personnel, nurses must be aware of this risk, especially those responsible for decontamination and sterilization of such instruments.

Permucosal Transmission

The most efficient permucosal transmission of hepatitis B virus occurs between sexual partners. Both homosexual and heterosexual activity has been implicated. Although this is not of direct concern in the intensive care setting, the presence of hepatitis B infection in a spouse or other sexual partner, or in a family member, increases the likelihood that a patient may be acutely or chronically infected. Therefore, a family history should include a question on hepatitis B virus infection.

The presence of hepatitis B virus or delta virus in saliva is an established high-risk factor for transmission. Not only has quantitative analysis of hepatitis B virus DNA in saliva of chronically infected patients shown that high titers can be present (10^5–10^7 virions/mL), but also intrafamilial, nonsexual spread has been reported when sharing of saliva-contaminated articles is common.[17] In one study, chewing gum shared among children was implicated as the vehicle of transmission.[18] In another study of a large extended family, ten members were HBsAg carriers and all had HBeAg- or anti-HBe–positive blood. Shared toothbrushes and other articles and self-administered tattoos were probably the vehicles of transmission in this family.[19]

Vertical Transmission

Vertical transmission occurs transplacentally or during the perinatal period between a pregnant woman and her infant. Its discussion is, therefore, somewhat irrelevant in this book because it is the infant rather than the nurse who is at risk. However, it is one of the most efficient modes of transmission of hepatitis B and no chapter on this type of infection can be complete without its inclusion. It is an important topic for two other reasons. First, infection of the infant from vertical transmission is preventable. Nurses should, therefore, be aware of the recommendations for prophylaxis of these infants to ensure its timely administration. In addition there is a slight chance that an infected nurse may be pregnant and would need to know of the implications to her infant. For all these reasons, vertical transmission has been included in this book.

Hepatitis B does not pose a greater risk to the mother during pregnancy than otherwise. There is also no evidence that it produces congenital malformations in the fetus, but it may induce some premature births.[20] However, mother-to-infant spread is one of the most efficient modes of hepatitis transmission and may result in severe, long-term sequelae for the infant. If hepatitis B develops during the first and second trimesters, the risk to the infant is minimal. However, infants born to mothers positive for HBsAg, and there are 16,500 such births annually in the United States, face a 60% risk of chronic carriage. Of these women, 4,500 are also HBeAg positive, and the infant's chance of becoming infected is then 70% to 90%. The chronic carrier state, under these circumstances, occurs in 85% to 90% of the infected infants. Estimates are that 25% of these carriers will die of primary liver cancer in mid life. All this is preventable now that the hepatitis vaccine is available. Therefore, the recommendations of the

Immunization Practices Advisory Committee of the Centers for Disease Control is to perform prenatal screening of all pregnant women for hepatitis B markers, to administer HBIG at birth, and to begin the three-dose vaccine regimen within 12 hours.[21]

PRECAUTIONARY MEASURES

Vaccination

Unless nurses have already had hepatitis B and are thus immune, or there is a clinical contraindication such as allergy to yeast, all critical care nurses should be vaccinated against hepatitis B with the recombinant vaccine (Recombivax HB®, Merck Sharp & Dohme). In case of yeast allergy, the serum-derived vaccine (Heptavax-B®) is available and totally safe in persons who are not allergic to egg whites. Side effects are minor and may consist of soreness at the injection site or a brief period of a minor flulike illness. The vaccine, to be effective, must be given in the deltoid muscle, and three doses are required. A later booster may be indicated if hepatitis B virus antibody levels drop below a protective level[22,23] (Table 5-6).

Prevention of Acquisition

Prevention of acquisition during patient care is accomplished by following Universal (Blood and Body Fluid) Precautions.[24] In brief, covering cuts and wearing gloves for invasive procedures and when contact with a patient's blood or body fluids is anticipated is considered highly protective. Protective eye wear and masks, as well as gowning, is advised when the potential for spattering is present. Greater details are provided in Chapter 12. Gloves should be removed before leaving a patient's room to prevent contamination of the environment. Handwashing after removing the gloves is extremely important, and the face, eyes, nose, and mouth should never be touched with unwashed hands. The hepatitis B virus can survive for long periods in the environment and can be transferred to these areas by unwashed hands. Needles and sharp instruments should be handled with great care. Needles should not be recapped but deposited with the syringe in safe, puncture-resistant boxes near the area of use.

Blood spills should be wiped up immediately and the gloves and clean-up materials disposed of as infectious wastes. After cleaning the spill, the area should be decontaminated with any hospital-approved disinfectant. One of the most effective and inexpensive disinfectants is a 1:10 dilution of common household bleach (sodium hypochlorite 5.25%).

Table 5-6 Recommendations for Hepatitis B Prophylaxis Following Percutaneous Exposure

| | Exposed Person | |
Source (Patient)	Unvaccinated	Previously Vaccinated
Known HBsAg positive	Give HBIG × 1 immediately Initiate hepatitis B virus vaccine series	Test exposed person for anti-HBs If inadequate antibody, give HBIG immediately plus hepatitis B virus vaccine booster dose
Known source; high risk for HBsAg positive	Initiate hepatitis B virus vaccine series Test source for HBsAg; if positive, give HBIG × 1	Test source for HBsAg only if exposed is vaccine non-responder; if source is HBsAg positive, give HBIG × 1 immediately plus hepatitis B virus vaccine booster dose
Known source; low risk for HBsAg positive	Initiate hepatitis B virus vaccine series	Nothing required
Unknown source	Initiate hepatitis B virus vaccine series Immune serum globulin optional	Nothing required; immune serum globulin optional

Source: Adapted from *Morbidity and Mortality Weekly Report* (1985;34:313–324), 1980, US Centers for Disease Control.

Postexposure Prophylaxis

If an inadvertent exposure occurred via needlestick or blood and body fluid contact with a mucosal surface or an abraded or otherwise damaged area of skin, the following steps should be taken (see also the procedure for exposure to human immunodeficiency virus in Chapter 4):

1. The area should be washed with soap and water and well rinsed.
2. An antiseptic can be applied.
3. An incident report should be made out. Follow-up should be pursued as per hospital policy.

In many institutions, inadvertent exposures and incident reports are handled in the emergency department. Personal experience has shown that this often results in improper follow-up. If an institution has an employee health service, the exposed employee should be seen there, even if a weekend intervenes. If policy calls for reporting to the emergency department, follow-up should be by employee health or the infection control practitioner because repeat visits and counseling may be necessary. Regardless of who is responsible, if the exposed person is susceptible to hepatitis B (has not had hepatitis B or the vaccine series), the procedure outlined in Table 5-7 should be followed.

The hepatitis status of the source patient should be ascertained. If the patient is known to be HBsAg or anti-HBc IgM positive, and the exposed nurse is susceptible, HBIG should be administered and the vaccine series begun. In a previous vaccinee, antibody status (anti-HBs) should be ascertained. If antibody status is less than 1:100,000 by radioimmunoassay, protection may be inadequate and HBIG and a booster dose of the vaccine are indicated.

If the patient's hepatitis B status is not known, a hepatitis B virus screening test should be obtained. The susceptible exposed person should be given the first dose of vaccine immediately. If the patient's test result can be available within 7 days, HBIG need not be administered unless the test results indicate that the patient is infectious. If the patient is negative for HBsAg or anti-HBc IgM, no HBIG is required. Unfortunately, at times needlesticks occur because someone was careless and discarded a used needle in an inappropriate place, such as the garbage or with the laundry. In that case, the source patient is not known, there is no one to test, and the exposed person should be offered a one-time dose of immune serum globulin as well as the hepatitis vaccine.

Although prophylaxis of an infant born to an HBsAg-positive mother is not exactly within the intent and scope of this chapter, the recommendations for handling such an infant are shown in Table 5-7.

Questions are sometimes raised about the presence of human immuno-deficiency virus in immune globulins. The purification processes to which serum globulin are exposed have been shown to kill all known viruses, including the slow viruses and the retroviruses, which includes the human immunodeficiency virus. Batches of globulins are also tested for growth of viruses. Hundreds of thousands of doses of immune globulins have been administered and no outbreaks of hepatitis, AIDS, or other infections have resulted. The concerns originated because there have been reports of the antibody to human immunodeficiency virus in some lots of immune globulins.[25] Antibody, however, is *not* infectious, and, like the other antibodies contained in the immune serum globulins, the human immunodeficiency virus antibody will disappear from the recipient's blood within a few (usually 2 to 6) months. The only importance of the matter is that anyone who has received an injection of immune serum globulin who is then tested for human immunodeficiency virus antibody for whatever reason may test positive. This would, in reality, be a false-positive test result because it does not represent antibody produced by that person in response to his or her own

Table 5-7 Hepatitis B Virus Postexposure Recommendations

| Exposure | HBIG | | Vaccine | |
	Dose	Recommended Timing	Dose	Recommended Timing
Perinatal	0.5 mL intramuscularly	Within 12 hours	0.5 mL (10 μg) intramuscularly	Within 12 hours of birth* Repeat at 1 and 6 months
Sexual	0.06 mL/kg intramuscularly	Single dose within 14 days of sexual contact	†	

*The first dose can be given at the same time as the HBIG dose but at a different site.
†Vaccine is recommended for homosexual men and for regular sexual contacts of hepatitis B virus carriers and is optional in initial treatment of heterosexual contacts of persons with acute hepatitis B.

Source: Adapted from *Morbidity and Mortality Weekly Report* (1985;34:329), 1985, US Centers for Disease Control.

infection with the virus. Such a finding would undoubtedly cause great concern. Therefore, anyone to whom globulins are administered must be made aware of this possibility.

CONCLUSIONS

Infection with the hepatitis B virus is usually mild and self-limited. However, there can be serious, life-threatening complications and sequelae. Vaccination is available and safe, and every critical care nurse who is not already immune should take advantage of the protection it provides. Most institutions offer the vaccine without charge to its high-risk employees; otherwise a vial of three doses costs about $105.

For susceptible nurses and others who sustain accidental exposures, postexposure prophylaxis is also available and safe, and it offers reasonable protection against acquisition of hepatitis B.

Everyone can protect themselves against exposure to hepatitis B by knowing the type of patient who may be in a high-risk group for having acute or chronic hepatitis. By following the universally recommended precautions, nurses can provide themselves with a wide margin of safety against acquisition of hepatitis B and other bloodborne infections.

REFERENCES

1. Brechot C, Lugassy E, Dejean A, et al. Hepatitis B virus DNA in infected human tissues. In Nyas G, Dienstag JL, Hoofnagle JH (eds). Viral Hepatitis and Liver Diseases. New York: Grune & Stratton, 1984.

2. Summers J. Replication of hepatitis B viruses. In Nyas G, Dienstag JL, Hoofnagle JH (eds). Viral Hepatitis and Liver Diseases. New York: Grune & Stratton, 1984.

3. Gross P. Viral hepatitis. In Gurevich I, Tafuro P, Cunha BA (eds). The Theory and Practice of Infection Control. Philadelphia: Praeger-Greenwood Press, 1984.

4. Krogsgaard K, Wantzin P, Aldershvile, et al. Hepatitis B virus DNA in hepatitis B surface antigen positive blood donors: Relationship to the hepatitis B e system and outcome in recipients. J Infect Dis 1986;153:298–303.

5. Lieberman HM, LaBrecque DR, Kew MC, et al. Detection of hepatitis B virus DNA directly in human serum by a simplified molecular hybridization test: Comparison to HBeAg/anti-HBe status in HBsAg carriers. Hepatology 1983;3:285–291.

6. Dienstag JL, Wands JR, Koff RS. Acute hepatitis. In Petersdorf RG, Adams RD, Braunwald E, et al. (eds). Harrison's Principles of Internal Medicine. New York: McGraw-Hill, 1983.

7. Dienstag JL. Concurrent hepatitis B surface antigen and antibody and the clonal selection theory of antibody diversity. Gastroenterology 1987;93:899–902.

8. Shiels MT, Taswell HF, Czaja AJ, et al. Frequency and significance of concurrent hepatitis B surface antigen and antibody in acute and chronic hepatitis. Gastroenterology 1987;93:675–680.

9. Chatzinoff M, Friedman LS. Delta agent hepatitis. Infect Dis Clin North Am 1987;1:529–545.

10. Smedile A, Farci P, Verme G, et al. Influence of delta infection on severity of hepatitis B. Lancet 1982;2:945–947.

11. Lettan LA, McCarthy JG, Smith MH, et al. Outbreak of severe hepatitis due to delta and hepatitis B viruses in parenteral drug abusers and their contacts. N Engl J Med 1987;317:1256–1262.

12. Szmuness W, Harley EJ, Ikran H, et al. Sociodemographic aspects of the epidemiology of hepatitis B. In Vyas GN, Cohen SN, Schmid R (eds). Viral Hepatitis. Philadelphia: Franklin Institute Press, 1978.

13. Beasley RP, Hwang LY. Epidemiology of hepatocellular carcinoma. In Vyas GN, Dienstag JL, Hoofnagle JH (eds). Viral Hepatitis and Liver Disease. New York: Grune & Stratton, 1984.

14. Liaw YF, Tai DI, Chu CM, et al. Acute exacerbation in chronic type B hepatitis: Comparison between HBeAg and antibody-positive patients. Hepatology 1987;7:20–23.

15. Cooper BW, Klimek JJ. The pathogenesis and prevention of hepatitis B infection. Inf Med 1988;5:111–142.

16. Skoff R. Viral Hepatitis. New York: John Wiley & Sons, 1978.

17. Jenison SA, Lemon SM, Baker LN, et al. Quantitative analysis of hepatitis B virus DNA in saliva and semen of chronically infected homosexual men. J Infect Dis 1987;156:299–307.

18. Leichtner AM, LeClair J, Goldman DA, et al. Horizontal nonparenteral spread of hepatitis among children. Ann Intern Med 1981;94:346–349.

19. Centers for Disease Control. Hepatitis B in an extended family—Alabama. MMWR 1987;36(4S):744–746.

20. Shalev E, Bassan HM. Viral hepatitis during pregnancy in Israel. Int J Gynecol Obstet 1982;20:73–78.

21. Snydman DR. Hepatitis in pregnancy. N Engl J Med 1985;313:1398–1401.

22. Centers for Disease Control. Recommendations for protection against viral hepatitis. MMWR 1985;34:313–335.

23. Stevens CE, Taylor PE, Tong MJ, et al. Yeast-recombinant hepatitis B vaccine. JAMA 1987;257:2612–2616.

24. Centers for Disease Control. Recommendations for prevention of HIV transmission in health-care settings. MMWR 1987;36(3S):3–18.

25. Gocke DJ, Raska K, Pollack W, et al. HTLV-III antibody in commercial immunoglobulin. Lancet 1986;1:37–38.

CHAPTER REVIEW QUESTIONS

1. A particularly high-risk group of hepatitis B virus carriers are patients who have
   a. American Indian ancestry
   b. Anti-HBs
   c. Primary liver cancer

2. The serologic markers of a patient are as follows:
   HBsAg negative
   Anti-HBc positive
   Anti-HBs negative
   What test would you need to tell you if the patient is infectious?
   a. Anti-HBe
   b. HBc IgM
   c. Delta antibody

3. What statement(s) may be correct about the patient with the above markers. The patient is
   a. Immune to hepatitis B
   b. In the window phase
   c. Has chronic active hepatitis
   d. All of the above

4. A nurse has anti-HBc and anti-HBs. Can he or she acquire delta hepatitis from a patient?
   a. Yes
   b. No

5. The hepatitis B vaccine should be administered into which muscle?
   a. Deltoid
   b. Gluteal
   c. Either a or b

Answers are provided in Appendix B.

Chapter 6

Hepatitis A and Hepatitis Non-A, Non-B

HEPATITIS A

Strictly speaking, hepatitis A is not a problem in critical care. However, it is important to differentiate hepatitis A from hepatitis B because they require different precautionary measures. Measures for the prevention of hepatitis A also apply to other gastrointestinal infections and can thus be helpful in preventing diarrheal disease.

The hepatitis A virus is an RNA picornavirus in the same enterovirus group as coxsackieviruses and polioviruses. There are three major strains of the virus, which cause single cases of the disease but are often responsible for large food-borne outbreaks. Hepatitis A is a worldwide problem. Its frequency is related to an inverse relationship of socioeconomic levels and personal or community-related hygienic practices. Thus, in developing nations with crowded living conditions, poor hygiene, and inadequate sewage disposal mechanisms, infection is endemic. By 10 years of age, 90% to 100% of the population has been infected. In the United States, 100,000 cases a year are reported, but there are many more unreported or unrecognized cases. Antibody studies in the United States show a prevalence of about 24% in 10-year olds and 45% in adults.[1]

Hepatitis A has been studied somewhat less extensively than hepatitis B for several reasons. The disease is milder and has no serious sequelae, and there are very few animal models for experimental studies. Only chimpanzees and marmosets are susceptible for hepatitis A virus. However, much is known about the virus and molecular cloning is producing additional information, especially toward vaccine development, for which there is a worldwide need.

Clinical Manifestations

The incubation period of hepatitis A is short. Two to 6 weeks after exposure, adult patients report varying degrees of fatigue, malaise, anorexia, abdominal fullness, nausea, and vomiting. Onset is more abrupt than in hepatitis B. In fact, patients can often be quite specific about the day their symptoms began. Other than that, the clinical picture is indistinguishable from hepatitis B or hepatitis non-A, non-B. Jaundice is uncommon in children, but in adults it is preceded by 5 days of dark urine (bilirubinuria) and clay-colored stools.

Although the virus is hepatotropic, some extrahepatic manifestations have been reported, comprising arthritis, arthralgias, and, less frequently, cutaneous vasculitis in the form of an erythematous papular purpuric rash.[2] In most instances, patients recover completely within 2 to 6 months, although a small percentage of cases take up to 2 years to resolve. There are no chronic carriers of hepatitis A virus beyond that period. Clinical relapse is not common but has been reported.[3] Fulminant hepatitis develops in less than 0.5% of patients, and death is rare.

Diagnosis

Nonspecific Laboratory Tests

As in other types of viral hepatitis, neutropenia and lymphopenia may precede lymphocytosis. Liver enzyme levels elevate and decline more abruptly than in hepatitis B, and elevations are of shorter duration. Alanine aminotransferase elevations should be significantly higher than those of alkaline phosphatase, which may be normal or slightly elevated, and this finding is used to differentiate obstructive jaundice from jaundice related to hepatocellular injury. As in hepatitis B, aspartate aminotransferase elevations signify only nonspecific cellular damage and are not of help in ascribing damage to any specific organ.

Serodiagnosis

IgM-specific antibody to hepatitis A virus (anti-HAV IgM) is the first antibody to appear early in the acute phase (Figure 6-1). It is usually detectable while the patient is jaundiced but disappears fairly rapidly. IgM has been known to persist for up to 2 or more years in some patients. IgG anti-HAV appears within 2 weeks of IgM and persists for years, probably for life. IgG antibody positivity thus denotes past infection at an unspecified time and immunity to future hepatitis A virus infection (Table 6-1).

High-Risk Populations

Until recently there has been no specific group of persons at any special risk of developing hepatitis A. Since there is no chronic disease or carriage, only

Antibody Response in Hepatitis A

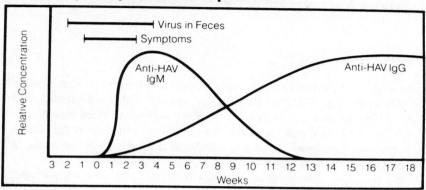

Figure 6-1 Antibody response in hepatitis A and its relationship to infectivity and symptoms. *Source:* Reproduced with permission from Abbott Laboratories, North Chicago, Illinois.

patients in the incubation period or with acute disease are infectious. The only predictable high-risk patient is one who reports having been exposed to someone with hepatitis A or having eaten hepatitis A virus–contaminated food within the previous 2 to 6 weeks (28 days mean). Recently, however, a new risk category has been emerging, that of young children in day-care centers and their care-takers.[4] This is not surprising, since hygiene among the very young is poor, objects are shared and mouthed, and, judging by the number of adults in that setting who acquire hepatitis A, handwashing is not always scrupulously observed. Thus outbreaks are common and nurses in pediatric intensive care units

Table 6-1 Serodiagnosis of Hepatitis A

ANTI-HAV		INTERPRETATION	INFECTIONS
IgM	*IgG*		
−	−	Never had hepatitis A Person is susceptible	No
+	±	Acute or recent infection or convalescent phase	Yes, from 2 weeks before to about 3 weeks after symptoms appear
−	+	Hepatitis A infection in past Person is immune	No

need to wash hands carefully, even when wearing gloves for changing diapers or otherwise cleaning children who attend day-care centers.

Transmission

As with other enteroviruses and gastrointestinal pathogens, transmission is by the oral-fecal route. Whether the virus is ingested with contaminated food or drinks or spread person to person, sexually, or via contaminated shared objects, virus-containing fecal material is the vehicle and poor hygiene is the culprit. In underdeveloped nations, poor sewage disposal is usually to blame in the large outbreaks seen in those areas.

Until recently, viremic spread was not believed to be an epidemiologically important mode of spread because the period of viremia is very short, probably less than 5 days. This belief was borne out by the absence of endemic hepatitis A virus infections in hemodialysis patients, in whom hepatitis B and probably hepatitis non-A, non-B have a much higher prevalence.[5] However, a number of viremically acquired cases have been described.

An outbreak of secondary nosocomial hepatitis A has occurred in 15 nurses and in the mother of one infant in an intensive care nursery. A unit of blood administered to two infants in this nursery contained the virus. The two infants developed hepatitis A, which was subsequently acquired by some of their caretakers.[6] In another instance, 11 infants were infected from a single shared unit of blood.[7]

Prevention

Precautionary Measures

Prevention of hepatitis A is based on an understanding of its mode of spread. First and foremost is handwashing after defecation and before food preparation. Nurses can protect themselves in the workplace by never touching their mouths before washing their hands. Nurses also must refrain from putting pens, pencils, and syringe caps into their mouths, since these can be contaminated with hepatitis A virus and a number of other organisms that may have been transferred there by others.

Patients are most infectious 2 to 3 weeks prior to appearance of the clinical manifestations of hepatitis A. This is the late incubation period. This is also the time in which the highest titers of hepatitis A virus are detectable in stool (10^7–10^9 infectious dose per milliliter) and serum (10^3–10^5) (Figure 6-1). Urine, semen, and saliva have very low titers, usually less than or equal to 10.[8] After about a week into the symptomatic period, patients' stool titers decline drastically and patients are probably noninfectious by that time. However, there are no absolutes in medicine and this is also true for hepatitis A. The virus has survived experimentally in dried and stored feces for 1 month.[9]

Patients with hepatitis A pose little danger to health care personnel if precautionary measures are observed. However, other patients may be at some risk for the short period during which the infected patient sheds the virus. Therefore, in many hospitals enteric precautions or contact isolation is maintained for patients admitted for hepatitis A.[10] Patients can share rooms, but preferably not bathrooms. Both patients must be reminded to practice careful hygiene and turn off faucets with paper towels after handwashing. Children should be in a private room because they tend to share belongings and cannot be relied on to maintain satisfactory standards of hygiene.

Pre-exposure Prophylaxis and Vaccine

Several vaccines for hepatitis A are under investigation but not yet available for use in humans. It is not known whether the hepatitis A virus itself causes damage to the liver or whether this damage is the result of the host's immune response. Therefore, a live attenuated virus vaccine, although it may be the most effective type of vaccine, may not be the ultimate choice.[8] At present, pre-exposure prophylaxis consists of administration of immune serum globulin for those who are susceptible and intend to travel to areas of high endemicity.

Postexposure Prophylaxis

Immune serum globulin, 0.02 mL/kg intramuscularly, is recommended for high-risk exposures.[11] This does not include health care personnel, since gloving and handwashing for handling infectious material (e.g., stool) is protective. Recommendations for non–health care–related exposures are given in Table 6-2. There is a 5% to 10% failure rate with immune globulins, but while infection may not be prevented the disease may be attenuated.

HEPATITIS NON-A, NON-B

As the name implies, hepatitis non-A, non-B is a diagnosis of exclusion when the origin of the viral disease cannot be ascribed to hepatitis B or hepatitis A or to other common causes of hepatitis, such as cytomegalovirus and Epstein-Barr virus. There are at least three hepatitis non-A, non-B viruses. None has been reliably or reproducibly identified in the laboratory. Their existence has been confirmed on epidemiologic grounds, on the occurrence of different clinical syndromes and multiple infections in humans, and experimentally in chimpan-

Table 6-2 Immune Globulin for Postexposure Prophylaxis of Hepatitis A and Hepatitis Non-A, Non-B

Exposure	Dose
Low Risk	
Health care–related exposure	Not applicable
High Risk	
Prior to anticipated exposure and after known exposure	
Foodborne outbreaks	0.02 mL/kg intramuscularly within 2 weeks of food ingestion
Staff of day-care centers	As above, within 2 weeks of exposure
Close contact with known case(s)	
Staff and residents in custodial care institutions with known cases	

Source: Morbidity and Mortality Weekly Report (1985;34:313–314), Copyright © 1985, US Centers for Disease Control.

---

zees.[12] At least one of the hepatitis non-A, non-B viruses has a short incubation, and two others have a long incubation.

Short-Incubation Hepatitis Non-A, Non-B

Since 1980, several outbreaks of a waterborne hepatitis A–like syndrome have been reported. The first documented cases occurred in India, but others have since been identified in Pakistan, Mexico, and East Africa.[13,14] All of these outbreaks were related to fecally contaminated water supplies, and large numbers of the population were involved.

In these outbreaks, acute disease ranged from mild to severe but was self-limiting with no chronic sequelae. However, among pregnant women, enterically transmitted hepatitis non-A, non-B tends to become fulminant with a significantly increased mortality rate.[13] This type of outbreak is unlikely to occur in the hospital setting and is of little danger to critical care nurses.

Long-Incubation Hepatitis Non-A, Non-B

Clinical Manifestations

In 75% of cases, hepatitis non-A, non-B is usually mild and anicteric and manifestations are indistinguishable from hepatitis B or hepatitis A. However, severe fulminant disease has been reported. It appears that liver cell injury is due to the cytopathic effect of the virus, as in delta hepatitis, rather than immunologically mediated as in hepatitis B.[15] The incubation period ranges between 2 weeks and 6 months, probably depending on the dose and type of virus transmitted.

Chronic hepatitis occurs with a higher frequency than in hepatitis B. In a National Institutes of Health study, 68% of patients developed chronic persistent and chronic active hepatitis, and these rates do not differ substantially from those of other studies.[16] Evidence of cirrhosis was found in biopsy specimens of 22% of patients. In general, cirrhosis is believed to be somewhat indolent, but there is no consensus.

Diagnosis

Nonspecific Tests. The only diagnostic tests available at this time are liver enzyme determinations. Patients with hepatitis non-A, non-B show an unusual but typical pattern of fluctuation of aminotransferases. Relapsing patterns occur in acute disease, but they are strikingly evident in the chronic state. Variations of as much as 500 to 1,000 IU/L have been observed. Although the magnitude of the elevations declines as acute infection progresses to the chronic state, low-level fluctuations persist.[16] These fluctuations, the clinical picture, and the absence of markers for acute hepatitis A or B can establish a diagnosis with some certainty.

Transmission and High-Risk Patients

In order to identify high-risk patient groups, the modes of transmission must be understood. They parallel those of hepatitis B but are predominantly related to blood transfusion and to intravenous replacement therapies (i.e., factor IX complex, antihemophiliac factor, and others).[15] Thus, 85% of post-transferase hepatitis is believed to be due to hepatitis non-A, non-B viruses.

Other modes of transmission include intravenous drug abuse, health care–related infections, and direct patient contact or work in hospital laboratories. Personal contact of a nonsexual nature in the community has been reported in about 16% of persons.[15] The virus can also be transmitted sexually and vertically from mother to child.[17]

High-risk populations closely parallel those groups with hepatitis B (see Chapter 5) but include a higher number of blood-transfusion recipients. Also included are patients in hemodialysis units, where hepatitis B has greatly declined.

Precautions and Prevention

Knowing the high-risk population and maintaining universal precautions by wearing gloves for blood and body fluid contact, handwashing after glove removal, covering damaged areas of skin, and avoiding needlesticks and splashing of blood onto mucous membranes should be totally protective in the workplace.[18]

Administration of immune globulin has not proved to be effective in preventing hepatitis non-A, non-B. In some instances, prolongation of the incubation period has been demonstrated.

Since there is empiric evidence that pregnant women with acute hepatitis non-A, non-B in the third trimester may transmit the infection to the neonate, administration of immune globulin should not be ruled out. An intramuscular injection of immune globulin, 0.5 mL, can be given within 24 hours after birth and repeated 28 days later.[19] This recommendation has not been made elsewhere.

If post-transfusion hepatitis non-A, non-B is to be reduced, a method for screening of donated units is mandatory. The main approach, until more precise diagnostic markers can be discovered, is to test the donor blood for aminotransferase elevations. It is believed that the presence of ALT in amounts greater than 45 IU/L indicates a hepatitis non-A, non-B virus. In most centers, such blood is now being rejected for donations. This screening promises to be the most effective method at present for excluding blood that is positive for hepatitis non-A, non-B from the donor pool.

REFERENCES

1. Gust ID. Comparison of the epidemiology of hepatitis A and B. In Szmuness W, Alter HJ, Maynard JE (eds). Viral Hepatitis. Philadelphia: The Franklin Institute, 1982.

2. Inman RD, Hodge M, Johnston MEA. Arthritis, vasculitis, and cryoglobulinemia associated with relapsing hepatitis A infection. Ann Intern Med 1986;105:700–703.

3. Sjogren MH, Tanno H, Fay O, et al. Hepatitis A virus in stool during clinical relapse. Ann Intern Med 1987;106:221–226.

4. Brunell PA. Infections in day care centers. Am J Dis Child 1987;141:404–405.

5. Szmuness W, Dienstag JL, Purcell RH, et al. Hepatitis type A and hemodialysis: A seroepidemiologic study in 15 U.S. centers. Ann Intern Med 1977;87:80–85.

6. Azimi PH, Robertson RR, Guralnik J, et al. Transfusion-acquired hepatitis A in a premature infant with secondary nosocomial spread in an intensive care nursery. Am J Dis Child 1986;140:23–27.

7. Noble RC, Kane MA, Reeves SA, et al. Post-transfusion hepatitis A in a neonatal intensive care unit. JAMA 1984;252:2711–2715.

8. Purcell RH, Feinstone SM, Ticehurst JR, et al. Hepatitis A virus. In Vyas GN, Dienstag JL, Hoofnagle JH (eds). Viral Hepatitis and Liver Disease. New York: Grune & Stratton, 1984.

9. McCaustland KA, Bond WW, Bradley DW, et al. Survival of hepatitis A virus in feces after drying and storage for one month. J Clin Microbiol 1982;16:957–960.

10. Garner JS, Simmons BP. CDC Guidelines for isolation precautions in hospitals. Infect Control 1983;4:249–323.

11. Centers for Disease Control. Recommendations for protection against viral hepatitis. MMWR 1985;34:313–334.

12. Bradley DW, Maynard JE, Cook EH, et al. Non-A/non-B hepatitis in experimentally infected chimpanzees: Cross challenge and electron microscope studies. J Med Virol 1980;6:185–201.

13. Tandon BN, Joski JK, Jain SK, et al. An epidemic of non-A, non-B hepatitis in northern India. India J Med Res 1982;75:739–744.

14. Centers for Disease Control. Enterically transmitted non-A, non-B hepatitis—Mexico. MMWR 1987;36:597–662.

15. Gerety RJ, Tabor E, Schaff Z, et al. Non-A, non-B hepatitis agents. In Vyas GN, Dienstag JL, Hoofnagle JH (eds). Viral Hepatitis and Liver Disease. New York: Grune & Stratton, 1984.

16. Alter H, Hoofnagle JH. Non-A, non-B: Observations on the first decade. In Vyas GN, Dienstag JL, Hoofnagle JH (eds). Viral Hepatitis and Liver Disease. New York: Grune & Stratton, 1984.

17. Tong M, Thursky M, Rakela J, et al. Studies on the maternal-infant transmission of the viruses which cause acute hepatitis. Gastroenterology 1980;80:999–1004.

18. Centers for Disease Control. Recommendations for prevention of HIV transmission in health care settings. MMWR 1987;36(2S):3S–18S.

19. Seef LB, Hoofnagle JH. Immunoprophylaxis of viral hepatitis. Gastroenterology 1979;77:161–182.

CHAPTER REVIEW QUESTIONS

1. In viral hepatitis which of the following is true?
   a. Alkaline phosphatase level will be highly elevated.
   b. AST (SGOT) will be less elevated than ALT (SGPT).
   c. AST (SGOT) will be more elevated than ALT (SGPT).

2. Hepatitis A is spread primarily by
   a. The fecal-oral route
   b. Blood and body fluids
   c. Both a and b

3. Patients are infectious
   a. Before clinical illness appears
   b. Two to 4 weeks after jaundice appears
   c. While they are hepatitis A IgG positive
   d. a and b
   e. All of the above

4. Which marker of hepatitis A lasts for life and denotes past infection?
   a. Hepatitis A IgM
   b. Hepatitis A IgG

5. Hepatitis non-A, non-B can be transmitted by
   a. Blood transfusion
   b. Water
   c. Both a and b

6. Most patients with hepatitis A are infectious until their aminotransferase levels begin to decline.
   a. True
   b. False

7. Which antibody denotes recovery from and immunity to hepatitis A?
   a. IgG
   b. IgM

8. The hepatitis non-A, non-B virus causes congenital infection in 15% of infants if the mother is infected in the first trimester.
   a. True
   b. False
   c. Unknown

9. In jaundice due to viral hepatitis (as opposed to obstructive jaundice), the following is usually true:
   a. ALT (SGPT) value is highly elevated; alkaline phosphatase value is minimally elevated or normal.
   b. Alkaline phosphatase elevation is higher than ALT (SGPT) elevation.
   c. Both are equally elevated.
   d. None of the above.

10. At least two hepatitis non-A, non-B viruses are transmitted like
   a. Epstein-Barr (mononucleosis) hepatitis
   b. Hepatitis B
   c. Hepatitis A
   d. None of the above

Answers are provided in Appendix B.

Chapter 7

Pulmonary Tuberculosis

Tuberculosis, once a killer of thousands, is now not only curable but also preventable. Until the mid-1980s, it had been estimated that pulmonary tuberculosis would maintain a steady 2% to 5% annual rate of decline and that it would be eliminated by the year 2100.[1] Unfortunately, with the appearance of AIDS, that estimate will have to be revised dramatically because the human immunodeficiency virus destroys the T lymphocytes that normally help to keep tuberculosis under control. Tuberculosis is one of the most frequent opportunistic infections that occurs in patients with AIDS, accounting for a dramatic increase in cases and the slowing of the downward trend of the disease. Many of these patients will be cared for in intensive care units because of the critical nature of the pulmonary infections.

There are other reasons why patients with tuberculosis will continue to be seen in critical care units. First, the age of hospitalized patients is increasing, and in an older patient population reactivation of long dormant disease is more likely to occur. Second, iatrogenically induced immunosuppression is more frequent, and, third, there is increasing exposure from third world immigrants. Added to the hazard is the fact that the steady decline in tuberculosis has decreased our expectation of it, thus one must have a high index of suspicion to look for tuberculosis. Tuberculosis can appear as an acute but easily recognized pulmonary infection, but it can also be present in a chronic, smoldering state in patients who are admitted for reasons not related to their tuberculosis. Dormant infections can be reactivated by a variety of stimuli and mistaken for noninfectious conditions such as sarcoidosis or lung tumors.

It is, therefore, important that critical care nurses become knowledgeable about tuberculosis and familiar with the populations at risk of developing or harboring tuberculosis. They must also know appropriate precautionary measures and their own susceptibility status; and in case an exposure occurs, they must be aware of the availability and risks of postexposure prophylaxis.

119

THE PATHOGEN: *MYCOBACTERIUM TUBERCULOSIS*

There are more than 20 species of mycobacteria. Since they all retain dye after acid washes or staining, they are called acid-fast bacilli (AFB). Some of these mycobacteria have not been implicated in human disease; others are clinically significant but cause only localized infections. Since the latter are not usually transmitted from person to person, they will not be included in the discussion, but some of the better-known ones are listed in Table 7-1.

Mycobacterium tuberculosis (tubercle bacillus) is the main human mycobacterial pathogen and is of concern to hospital personnel because of its airborne transmission. There are four types of *M. tuberculosis*. Type A is responsible for 70% of infections. It is a slow-growing organism that multiplies once every 18 to 24 hours, whereas other bacteria can multiply every 20 minutes. The importance of its slow growth will become apparent during the discussion on identification, prophylaxis, and treatment. The size of the tubercle bacillus is 1 to 5 μm, making it small enough to easily penetrate the alveoli. The organism is highly aerobic, which explains its preference for the lung, where oxygen content is high. It also requires a body temperature of 98.6°F (37°C) for its reproduction. *M. tuberculosis* does not survive for long outside the body and is not a hazard in the environment, other than in air.

DEFINITIONS: INFECTION VERSUS DISEASE

It is important to differentiate between tuberculous infection and disease. Infection means that a pathogen has entered the body and has begun to multiply.

Table 7-1 Other Mycobacteria That May Cause Disease in Humans

Organism	Comment
*M. avium** and *M. intracellulare**	Pulmonary and disseminated disease; probably spread by contaminated pulmonary equipment
M. bovis	Pulmonary disease; found in unpasteurized milk
M. fortuitum and *M. chelonei*	Wound and soft tissue infections; found in soil and water and can contaminate invasive medical devices and implants
M. kansasii	Pulmonary and other organ infections
M. scrofulaceum	Lymphadenitis, "scrofula"
M. leprae	Leprosy
M. marinum	Granulomas; found in salt water and swimming pools

*These nontuberculous (atypical) mycobacteria are found with increasing frequency in patients with AIDS.

Infection does not always lead to disease because the body's defense mechanisms and/or antimicrobial agents may destroy the organisms before they are able to cause manifestations of disease or clinical illness. The American Thoracic Society has divided tuberculosis into five classes (Table 7-2), which further clarifies the concept.[2]

When a person inhales a tubercle bacillus, several things may happen:

1. The organism may be stopped in the upper respiratory passages by mucociliary action and swallowed or expectorated with the mucus.
2. The organism may reach the lower respiratory tract and eventually attach and implant itself within a bronchiole or alveolus, where it begins to multiply and cause a primary infection.
3. The primary infection is contained and no disease develops at this time.
4. If the primary infection is not contained or localized, disseminated disease or miliary tuberculosis may develop.
5. Tuberculous disease may appear after a period of time at any originally (or primarily) infected site. This is known as reactivation.

Table 7-2 Classification of Tuberculosis

Classification	Description
No tuberculosis exposure, not infected	No history of exposure, reaction to tuberculin skin test not significant
Tuberculosis exposure, no evidence of infection	History of exposure; reaction to tuberculin skin test not significant
Tuberculous infection, no disease	Significant reaction to tuberculin skin test; negative bacteriologic studies (if done); no clinical or roentgenographic evidence of tuberculosis
Tuberculosis: current disease	*Mycobacterium tuberculosis* cultured (if done); otherwise *both* a significant reaction to tuberculin skin test *and* clinical and/or roentgenographic evidence of current disease
Tuberculosis: no current disease	History of previous episode(s) of tuberculosis or abnormal stable roentgenographic findings in a person with a significant reaction to tuberculin skin test; negative bacteriologic studies (if done); no clinical and/or roentgenographic evidence of current disease
Tuberculosis suspect	Diagnosis pending

Source: Adapted with permission from *American Review of Respiratory Disease* (1981;123(3)), Copyright © 1981, American Lung Association.

TRANSMISSION

Pulmonary tuberculosis is transmitted in two ways: (1) directly, person to person, to someone within 3 feet of the patient, and (2) indirectly, by droplet nuclei, which are coughed, sneezed, or talked out from a patient. These droplet nuclei carry the *M. tuberculosis* with them, and because they are so small (1– 5 μm) and light they can remain airborne for some time and travel over considerable distances. They are also small enough to be inhaled by a susceptible person and can find their way into the bronchioles and alveoli. Bacilli attached or contained in larger mucous particles and those that drop onto tables, clothing, or dishes do not become airborne again, are not inhaled, and are therefore of no concern. Patients may also swallow tubercle-containing mucus, but this also poses no risk, since it cannot be inhaled by others.

Tuberculosis is not very infectious. Prolonged contact is required for infection to develop. Family members who have lived together for some time are at greatest risk. In an experimental exposure of guinea pigs to air containing tubercle bacilli, it took 2 years to infect 51 of 63 animals, which is equal to 130 patient exposures. However, it may take only one tubercle bacillus to cause an infection in the right circumstances.[3] Obviously, not all patients are equally infectious. Patients who are coughing are more infectious than patients who are not. Patients with cavitary disease, especially if there is communication between the cavity and the bronchi, are highly infectious because the cavities contain large numbers of bacilli. Pharyngeal involvement also increases infectivity but is rarely encountered.

Primary Infection

After successful implantation of the tubercle bacillus within the primary site of infection, multiplication progresses slowly. At first there may be attempts by polymorphonuclear neutrophils to phagocytose the pathogen. These attempts will be unsuccessful. Phagocytosis by the next line of defense, the mononuclear macrophages, will be equally unsuccessful at first because *M. tuberculosis* is able to survive and even to multiply within these cells. This is true for a variety of other pathogens as well, and these organisms are, therefore, classified as intracellular pathogens. It takes 2 to 3 weeks before a competent cell-mediated immune system, whose chief component is the T lymphocyte, begins to marshall an effective defense. The T lymphocyte interacts with the macrophages, which are then "activated" and begin a more effective destruction of the tubercle bacillus.

During the 2 to 3 weeks it takes to marshall effective body defenses, the organism may have begun to disseminate via lymphatic drainage to regional lymph nodes in the hilum or the mediastinum and to more distant areas via the bloodstream. *M. tuberculosis* prefers a highly oxygenated environment, and although subsequent multiplication can take place in any seeded body site the upper lobes of the lung, the kidney, the liver, and the brain are favored over bone, ovary, and testes. In 90% of patients the activated macrophages either kill the organisms or contain them by walling them off. Localized tissue necrosis changes to a cheeselike material (caseation), which may later become calcified. In lymph nodes this is called the Ghon complex; in the lung a scar may result. Tubercle bacilli may persist within these walled-off areas for years without multiplying, but they provide a focus for possible reactivation at a later time.

In children with competent immune systems there are usually no clinical manifestations during the early process of infection and during containment. In adults, there may be some mild "flulike" symptoms, which soon resolve. In 10% of both infected children and adults there may be progression of the infection because of the inability of the cell-mediated immune system to contain the organisms. Signs and symptoms of tuberculous disease are usually slow to develop and can occur at any body site that was infected. In pulmonary tuberculosis, the most transmissible type of tuberculosis, there is usually a very slow progression of increasing fatigue, anorexia and resultant weight loss, and low-grade fever. Tuberculosis may go unrecognized in these patients, but they are potentially infectious. There may be a finding of unilateral hilar or mediastinal adenopathy, and nurses should always read the chest roentgenographic report of their patients, regardless of the reason for the patient's admission.

The occasional cough may at first be ignored, but as it increases in frequency over a period of weeks or months it may become productive. Children rarely cough and are, therefore, much less likely to be infectious. Late afternoon fevers may persist, and because patients defervesce during sleep the typical night sweats may be reported. Pulmonary symptoms may progress to aching pain or tightness in the chest. Hemoptysis is common, and by this time the diagnosis is usually already suspected. In others, the disease can progress more rapidly with signs similar to severe influenza or pneumonia, including myalgia and dyspnea. Patients with tuberculous "pneumonia" are less toxic in appearance than those with other bacterial pneumonias, and they show fewer disturbances of arterial blood gases.

Chest roentgenograms are not necessarily helpful in the diagnosis of tuberculosis, but, as mentioned before, unilateral hilar or mediastinal lymphadenopathy nodules measuring less than 2 cm, calcifications, and cavitation, especially thick-walled cavities, should alert the staff to the possibility of tuberculosis. An exudative type of pleural effusion can accompany pulmonary disease, and it may in time progress to empyema. Pleural effusion should always raise the index of suspicion for the presence of pulmonary tuberculosis.[4]

Another presentation of disease is miliary tuberculosis, which can develop into a medical emergency. It represents a dissemination of the disease at any stage by embolization via blood or lymphatics to any organ, but most often to the lung or the liver. Fever, weight loss, and, if the disease is untreated, prostration may progress to disseminated intravascular coagulation and acute respiratory failure.[4] The chest roentgenogram may be normal or show a millet seed–like pattern. The sputum may contain no organisms, and transbronchial biopsy is often required to establish a diagnosis of miliary tuberculosis.

Reactivation

Reactivation or recrudescence implies that a dormant focus of tubercle bacilli from a previous infection is the source of the new disease process. Reinfection would be defined as a new exogenous infection in a patient who has already had a previous infection with or without a previous disease process. Exogenous reinfection is probably very rare and does not require separate discussion. Reactivation of tuberculosis can occur at any time within 3 months after the initial infection or many years later, but the risk is greatest in the first year.[4] It is usually precipitated by some event that compromises the immune system such as AIDS, administration of corticosteroids, malignancy or chemotherapy, Hodgkin's disease, protein deficiency, alcohol abuse, and so on. The aging process decreases the efficacy of the cell-mediated immune system, and this is believed to add to the risk of tuberculosis in the aging person.[5]

However, there is another mechanism that is likely to increase the risk of recrudescence in the elderly. During the normal process of decalcification in advancing years, old, pre-existent calcified lesions in which viable tubercle bacilli may have been walled off for many years will lose their calcium, thus allowing the organisms to escape and resume multiplication. Reactivation may occur in any previously infected site, but the pulmonary site is the most common and most infectious.

Whatever the cause of reactivation, the clinical presentation is often subacute and slow to progress, or it may present as an acute process such as pneumonia. Indeed, it is often mistaken for pneumonia, which, however, does not resolve with the usual antimicrobial treatment. By the time it is suspected and diagnosed, many family members, other patients, and personnel may have been exposed.

HIGH-RISK POPULATIONS

It is important that critical care nurses are familiar with patients at risk of pulmonary tuberculosis and that they maintain a high index of suspicion. At highest risk are persons with depressed or incompetent cell-mediated immunity, most specifically those with T-lymphocyte problems. This includes patients with

AIDS, patients with Hodgkin's disease or non-Hodgkin's lymphoma, those on corticosteroid therapy, and patients who are asplenic, either from splenectomy or through a poorly functioning organ, as in sickle cell disease. Many physicians consider AIDS, Hodgkin's disease, and corticosteroids to be such high-risk factors that they will put these patients on rifampin prophylaxis during certain periods of extra high risk. Also in a high-risk group are immigrants from underdeveloped nations, including South America and Portugal, and malnourished persons in general. Postgastrectomy patients also face some increased danger, as do the elderly. A complete listing of those patients at risk is given in Table 7-3.

Nurses should read their patients' history, which may reveal other risk factors, and the x-ray reports. Any patient with exposure to a family member with tuberculosis should be evaluated carefully. A patient who has a past history of

---

Table 7-3 Populations at High Risk for Tuberculosis

 I. Immunosuppressed
   A. AIDS
   B. Hodgkin's disease
   C. Corticosteroid therapy (long term)
   D. Chronic renal failure
   E. Old age

 II. Asplenia
   A. Splenectomy
   B. Sickle cell disease

 III. History of Pulmonary Tuberculosis
   A. In the family
   B. In the patient
      1. Untreated
      2. Treated
         a. Prior to 1960s
         b. Noncompliant patient
         c. Drug-resistant organism

 IV. Immigrants from Underdeveloped Nations (Asia, Africa, Haiti), South America, and Portugal

 V. Economically Disadvantaged
   A. Homeless
   B. Malnourished
   C. Alcoholic
   D. Drug abuser

 VI. Gastrectomy and Cancer Patients

tuberculosis may still be infectious, even after treatment, if the organism is resistant to the antibiotics used or if the patient did not comply with the prescribed regimen. Resistant tuberculosis is on the increase and must be considered when a treated patient is admitted because of a lower respiratory tract infection. Any patient who was "treated" for pulmonary tuberculosis before the discovery of antituberculous drugs, that is, before the 1950s, is still potentially infectious, even if a pneumonectomy was done on the affected side. There is no guarantee that the remaining lung was not involved. The risk is greater if the patient has a lower respiratory tract infection, but asymptomatic disease should also be ruled out in a critically ill patient from a high-risk group.

Nurses should be suspicious of any patient with recurrent or persistent pneumonia who is resistant to treatment with antibiotics. Roentgenograms of such patients should be read and suspicious findings discussed with the patient's physician. Suspicion is warranted in any patient with an abnormality in the apical region, in the posterior segment of an upper lobe, or in the superior segment of the lower lobe. Tuberculosis should always be suspected in cavitary disease, especially in the above regions, since it can be superimposed on malignant lesions. Old tuberculous cavities are usually thick walled. Patients with pleural effusions and clinical manifestations compatible with tuberculosis such as cough, weight loss, and night sweats should be suspected of having active disease until proven otherwise.

SKIN TESTS AND DIAGNOSIS

Skin Tests

Although a definitive diagnosis of tuberculosis in any site can only be made by identification of *M. tuberculosis* on culture, many adjunct tests are available that can permit a presumptive diagnosis. One of these is the purified protein derivative (PPD, Mantoux) skin test. A positive skin test is one in which the intradermal injection of PPD produces a measurable area of induration after 48 to 72 hours. This induration is produced by a delayed hypersensitivity reaction of the cell-mediated immune system in persons who have had a previous exposure to or infection with *M. tuberculosis*. It takes from 2 to 10 weeks (usually around 8 weeks) for a positive skin test to develop in response to an infection, but the T lymphocytes remain sensitized for life as long as the cell-mediated immune system remains intact, although the reaction to the test may wane with age. The test should be read on the second or third day after placement. Induration is measured transversely to the long axis of the forearm and should be recorded in millimeters of induration, not simply as positive (reactive) or negative (nonreactive), for accurate interpretation.

Not all reactions are due to the tubercle bacillus. Some may represent infection or cross-reaction with other mycobacteria or with BCG vaccination. Absence of any reaction (negative reactor) also does not necessarily signify noninfection. Many considerations go into interpretation of the test, and the description that follows must be adjusted to the patient being evaluated.[6]

A negative reaction may mean that

1. The test was administered incorrectly.
2. The patient is not infected with *M. tuberculosis*.
3. The patient was infected very recently (less than 10 weeks) and has not developed delayed hypersensitivity.
4. Temporary suppression of delayed hypersensitivity may exist due to
   a. Concurrent infection with other pathogens, especially viruses
   b. Recent vaccination with live virus (within 1 month)
   c. Neoplastic disease
   d. Sarcoidosis
   e. Immunosuppressive therapy
5. The patient is anergic—the immune system is unable to "remember" a previous infection. Anergy should be confirmed by an additional panel of challenge tests to antigens commonly present in any population (e.g., *Candida*, mumps, and others). If these tests are also negative, anergy is most likely the cause. If they are positive, the patient is not anergic and explanations 1 through 3 are probably correct.

A positive reaction of less than 10 mm duration may mean that

1. Infection is probably not due to *M. tuberculosis* but may represent cross-reaction to other mycobacteria.
2. The patient may have received BCG vaccination in the past. Previous BCG vaccination is not a contraindication to PPD testing, and the test should be interpreted, as in any other patient, according to the clinical presentation.[7]
3. Delayed hypersensitivity may wane with age. Retesting within 7 to 10 days may elicit an increased response. If the increase is more than 6 mm of induration or increases from less than 10 mm to more than 10 mm, this "boost" should be considered to be the true result. Two-step testing in this manner, within 2 weeks, reduces the likelihood that a simple "boost" could be falsely interpreted as a conversion on subsequent tests of patients or employees who are tested once a year or every 2 years. The repeat test does not sensitize a person to tuberculin. It simply stimulates immunologic recall. If the person has never been exposed or infected with *M. tuberculosis*, there will be no "boosting" effect.[8,9]

A positive reaction greater than 10 mm is significant and is likely to represent infection with *M. tuberculosis*.

Sputum Examination

Although clinical manifestations, x-ray findings, and skin tests can provide a presumptive diagnosis of tuberculosis, a final diagnosis requires confirmation by identification of the organism on culture. In the case of pulmonary tuberculosis, a sputum specimen, bronchial washings or brushings, a tissue biopsy, or aspirated fluid from a pleural effusion is required. Three specimens of expectorated sputum, not saliva, should be submitted, preferably on 3 consecutive days. Specimens obtained during the early morning are most likely to contain the largest number of organisms. Aerosol induction may be required for patients unable to produce a spontaneous specimen. Nurses can speed up the diagnosis by making sure the patient understands the need for a ''good'' specimen and for obtaining the specimens as soon as possible. In children, gastric washings obtained very early in the morning may be the method of choice for at least one specimen.

Detection of acid-fast bacilli on stained and microscopically examined specimens should not be taken as a diagnosis of tuberculosis. There are several other mycobacteria that may be found in sputum. Although the acid-fast smear takes less than an hour, culture results will take 4 and up to 8 weeks, because of the slow growth habits of *M. tuberculosis*.

A negative smear does not rule out a diagnosis of tuberculosis. It may just mean that there were no acid-fast organisms in the portion of sputum examined, which usually indicates that the number of organisms was small. It does mean that the patient is probably not very infectious, since he or she is not coughing up large numbers of tubercle bacilli. If the first sputum specimen is reported as being positive with acid-fast organisms, it is not necessary to send further specimens just because three were ordered. On the other hand, if three sputum specimens are negative, three more should probably be sent, or a bronchoscopic examination may be used to obtain another specimen.

As in other infectious diseases, the organism must be transmitted and must find a suitable portal of entry into another person and, in order to cause a new infection, the other person must be susceptible to the disease. Thus, it is unlikely that someone previously infected with *M. tuberculosis* would be infected again with a new organism. Since very little is absolute in medicine, there may occasionally be an exception, even though it has not been established that a second infection can occur. Therefore, hospital personnel and others who have a nonreactive or negative PPD test are at a greater risk of acquiring tuberculosis from a patient or other contact than positive reactors (those with a positive PPD), if their reaction is due to the tubercle bacillus. Unfortunately the origin of the reaction is difficult to establish unless the person had previously diagnosed tuberculosis.

A reminder is in order that tuberculosis can also be acquired from drinking unpasteurized milk, and both patients and personnel should abstain from such ingestion.

PREVENTION

The concern in critical care is confined to inhaled organisms. It is, therefore, obvious that measures aimed at preventing the dissemination and inhalation of tubercle bacilli will also prevent acquisition of this infection (Table 7-4).[4]

Isolation of the Patient

When the physician or nurse admits a patient with suspected or previously diagnosed tuberculosis, AFB or Respiratory Isolation should be instituted at once.[10,11] This is also true if a patient in one of the high-risk categories is admitted for other reasons but has any manifestations of a possible tuberculous disease, such as cough, night sweats, and so on, that cannot definitely be ascribed to a nontransmissible cause. Children do not cough and are not considered infectious. A private room may, therefore, not be required.

Table 7-4 Measures That Can Prevent the Spread of Pulmonary Tuberculosis

1. Know high-risk groups of patients.
   a. Teach the patient preventive measures.
   b. Provide tissues at all times.

2. Maintain a high index of suspicion.
   a. Place suspect patients in a well-ventilated room.
   b. Institute AFB or Respiratory Isolation.

3. Wear a mask if
   a. You are susceptible to the disease (a negative PPD test result)
   b. The patient cannot comply with the appropriate use of tissues (i.e., a patient on a respirator)

4. If inadvertent exposure occurred
   a. Those with previously negative PPD should be retested at once and again at 8 to 10 weeks.
   b. Those with a previously positive PPD test result need not be retested, only followed if clinical disease develops.
   c. Converters should consider taking isoniazid prophylaxis.

Because of the airborne spread of the organism, a private room is required for an adult patient until infectivity has been ruled out. Patients who are able to cooperate should be provided with tissues at all times, even during transport to other areas for diagnostic studies or other reasons. Personnel in these other areas should be notified that the patient is in isolation. Patients should be instructed to always cover their mouth and nose when sneezing, coughing, or laughing. The tissues should be deposited in a plastic or other sturdy bag by the patient. Patients should *not* wear masks at any time. Masks do not prevent spread of organisms coughed or sneezed out, and patients may already have compromised pulmonary function without further obstruction.[12] Masks, however, can be worn by personnel who are susceptible to the disease (negative reactors). Of greater importance is adequate ventilation of the patient's room. The patient's room should be under negative pressure, so that the room air is vented to the outside via a central air control system or by using a window exhaust fan. Failing that, the window should be open as much as possible and the door always kept closed. Clothing is not implicated in the spread of pulmonary tuberculosis, nor are dishes and other articles.[11] (This does not pertain to pulmonary medical devices.)

Discontinuation of Isolation

The question often arises regarding the length of time a patient on antitubercular therapy remains infectious and how long Respiratory Isolation is required. The hospital's infection control practitioner should be consulted and guidelines established. Opinions vary.[13] Usually, patients should be evaluated after about 2 weeks. If their tuberculosis-related clinical condition is improving and the cough is decreasing, it can be presumed that therapy is effective. A repeat sputum sample for acid-fast stains should be sent for analysis at that time, and if the number of organisms has greatly diminished or no more acid-fast bacilli are seen, isolation can probably be discontinued. It must be remembered that there are drug-resistant strains of mycobacteria, especially in patients born in countries where antibiotics can be bought without prescription. Previously treated patients who are readmitted with tuberculosis are also more likely to harbor a resistant strain. An arbitrary presumption of noninfectivity cannot be made at any set time.

Chemotherapy for tuberculosis is physician directed and will not be discussed here. However, patient education is a nursing responsibility, and it is important that patients be made to understand that therapy will continue for at least 6 months. It may help to explain that the antibiotics work best on tubercle bacilli during the proliferative stage (when they are dividing). Since the bacilli proliferate slowly, it takes a long time to destroy them all.

POSTEXPOSURE TESTING AND PROPHYLAXIS

It is not at all unusual for a diagnosis of tuberculosis to be made several days after a patient's admission. As described earlier, the disease may have been unsuspected or just been one of several possible diagnoses. The suspicion may, therefore, not have been communicated to the staff by the patient's physician, or it may not have occurred to anyone to institute Respiratory or AFB Isolation, especially if the patient is not coughing. Whatever the reason, other patients sharing such a patient's room for more than a few hours, visitors if they were exposed, and health care workers should be followed for possibly newly acquired tuberculous infection. Since an investigation of all contacts must be undertaken, the infection control practitioner should be notified at once. The first step for previously negative reactors is to have a PPD test done as soon as possible, certainly within 2 weeks of exposure. Anyone whose PPD test result is still nonreactive should be retested in 8 to 10 weeks. Those whose result remains negative are considered not infected, and, unless they are immunosuppressed or anergic, require no further follow-up. Converters, those who had a negative result or had an induration of less than 5 mm on the first test and on the second test show more than 10 mm of induration, should be considered newly infected. It is here that the boosting phenomenon is of some importance, because in converters isoniazid therapy may be indicated. To differentiate boosting from true conversion, it is important that persons at high risk for "boosting" (i.e., the elderly) be tested 7 to 10 days after the first test. If they have not "boosted" at that time, an increase in induration of more than 6 mm or to greater than 10 mm at 10 weeks will be a true conversion.

The American Lung Association recommends that newly infected persons be offered prophylactic therapy with isoniazid regardless of age.[14] Others disagree because they believe that the benefit of preventive therapy does not outweigh its risk of isoniazid-induced hepatitis, even in young adults.[15]

PPD converters should discuss the benefit and the risk of isoniazid prophylaxis with their physician. If isoniazid is prescribed, it is wise to obtain a baseline liver enzyme test, and in those younger than 35 years of age to repeat it only if symptoms or adverse reactions occur. In those older than 35 years of age, aminotransferase measurements should be obtained at intervals throughout the course of therapy. If any of these tests exceed three to five times the upper limit of normal, isoniazid therapy should probably be discontinued. Slight amino-transferase elevations are not unusual, and they return to normal after therapy has been concluded. Other contraindications to isoniazid therapy are listed in Table 7-5.[14]

Prophylactic therapy consists of oral isoniazid, 300 mg/day for adults and 10 to 14 mg/kg/day for children, not to exceed the adult dose. Duration of therapy

Table 7-5 Possible Contraindications to Isoniazid Prophylactic Therapy

1. Previous and present history of liver disease of any etiology
2. History of adverse reactions to previous isoniazid therapy
3. Concurrent use of other medications that may cause drug interactions
4. Daily use of alcohol
5. Preexisting peripheral neuropathy or disease causing such neuropathy
6. Pregnancy. Delay until after delivery unless infection occurred very recently, then wait until after the first trimester.

Source: Adapted with permission from *American Review of Respiratory Disease* (1986;134:355–363), Copyright © 1986, American Lung Association.

varies between 6 and 9 months. In those with abnormal chest films, 12 months of therapy is indicated.[14]

CONCLUSIONS

Acquisition of pulmonary tuberculosis from infected patients is preventable. A high index of suspicion based on a knowledge of persons at risk, and on clinical manifestations suspicious for *M. tuberculosis*, can alert critical care nurses to the need for isolation of the patient until infectivity has been ruled out. All patients should be taught to cover their mouths and noses when coughing or sneezing. If patients are on ventilatory assistance, masks should be worn by those caring for the patient. Although tuberculosis is treatable, the course of therapy is long and is not without risks. Tuberculosis is rarely acquired in the workplace and usually not if precautionary measures are observed.

REFERENCES

1. Dall L, Grizt D. The changing patterns of tuberculosis: Risk, treatment and prevention. Infect Med 1987; July/August:280–284.

2. American Thoracic Society. Diagnostic standards and classification of tuberculosis and other mycobacterial diseases—1981. Am Rev Respir Dis 1981;123:343–358.

3. Epstein DM, Kline LR, Abelda SM, Miller WT. Tuberculous pleural effusions. Chest 1987;91:106–109.

4. Geppert EF, Leff A. The pathogenesis of pulmonary and miliary tuberculosis. Arch Intern Med 1979;139:1381–1383.

5. Stead WW. Does the risk of tuberculosis increase in old age? J Infect Dis 1983;147:951–955.

6. American Lung Association. The Tuberculin Skin Test. 1981.

7. Snider DE. Bacille Calmette-Guérin vaccinations and tuberculin skin tests. JAMA 1985;253:3438–3439.

8. Snider DE, Cauthen GM. Tuberculin skin testing of hospital employees: Infection, "boosting" and two-step testing. Am J Infect Control 1984;12:305–311.

9. Bass JB, Senior A. The use of repeat skin tests to eliminate the booster phenomenon in serial tuberculin testing. Am Rev Respir Dis 1981;123:394–396.

10. Garner JS, Simmons BP. Isolation precautions in hospitals. Infect Control 1983;4(S):245–349.

11. Centers for Disease Control. Guidelines for Prevention of Tuberculosis Transmission in Hospitals. HHS Publication no. (CDC) 82-8371. Atlanta: Centers for Disease Control Tuberculosis Division, 1982.

12. Ritter MA, Wiley AM, Schultz JK. Experts discuss value of various OR garments. Hosp Infect Control 1980;8:45–47.

13. Noble RC. Infectiousness of pulmonary tuberculosis after starting chemotherapy. Am J Infect Control 1981;9:6–10.

14. American Thoracic Society—American Lung Association. Treatment of tuberculosis and tuberculous infection in adults and children. Am Rev Respir Dis 1986;134:355–363.

15. Taylor WC, Aronson MD, Del Banto T. Should young adults with a positive tuberculin test take isoniazid? Ann Intern Med 1981;94:808–813.

CHAPTER REVIEW QUESTIONS

1. Which conditions are considered predisposing factors for pulmonary tuberculosis?
   a. High doses of corticosteroids
   b. Hodgkin's disease
   c. Gastrectomy
   d. Being born in an underdeveloped nation
   e. All of the above

2. Patients with active pulmonary tuberculosis are not considered infectious if they
   a. Have an unproductive cough
   b. Have been on antituberculous medications for 7 days
   c. Have a negative PPD test result
   d. None of the above

3. Once a person has a positive PPD test result, he or she will always test positive.
   a. True
   b. False

4. A patient with a negative PPD test result cannot have pulmonary tuberculosis.
   a. True
   b. False

5. On X-ray, reactivation of pulmonary tuberculosis is often seen
   a. In the hilar region
   b. In the anterior upper lobe
   c. In the posterior upper lobe

Answers are provided in Appendix B.

Chapter 8

The Herpesviruses: Epstein-Barr Virus and Cytomegalovirus

The group of viruses known collectively as the herpesviruses are among the oldest known pathogens to afflict humans. Included in this group are (1) varicella-zoster virus, which is the cause of chickenpox and shingles; (2) Epstein-Barr virus (EBV), which is the cause of mononucleosis and certain malignant tumors and now suspected as the agent of chronic EBV disease; (3) cytomegalovirus (CMV), whose spectrum of disease encompasses a single mononucleosis–like illness, infections of the central nervous system and other body organs, severe malformations and neurologic problems in those who are congenitally infected, and the postperfusion and post-transplant syndromes; and (4) the two herpes simplex viruses types 1 and 2, long known as the etiologic agents of herpes encephalitis and oral and genital infections (Table 8-1). A sixth herpesvirus, discovered in 1988, is being studied.

Because of these old and newly recognized manifestations that are of great clinical importance in the young and old alike, the herpesviruses have been studied extensively. These studies have resulted in the development of two of the first successful antiviral agents: vidarabine and acyclovir. There are similarities as well as differences among the members of this group of viruses. The most important and unique similarity is the ability of all of them to cause persistent infections. This means that part of the virus remains within the host in a viable state for long periods of time. Each of the viruses has a certain preference or specificity for different cells of the human host. For example, the herpes simplex and varicella-zoster viruses persist in nerve cells, EBV persists in the B lymphocytes, while CMV is less selective and affects most tissues and cells. In addition to this shared persistence, after the first active infection, the latency periods are interrupted by episodes of viral replication that then manifest as recurrent infections. Some of these recurrences present as different clinical manifestations than the primary infection; an example is herpes zoster or shingles, which is usually a localized eruption, whereas varicella, the original manifestation, is a disseminated, multisystemic infection.

Another similarity is the presumption, which is almost a certainty, that at the very least these viruses play a contributing role in the development of certain types of malignancies. The only exception is possibly the varicella-zoster virus.[1]

Similar to other viruses, the herpesvirus group penetrates the host cell and induces it to replicate the virus. The newly produced viruses then leave the host cell and are free to enter and infect new cells. Part of the viral genome may be preserved in the host cell where it can remain in a latent stage with the potential for later reactivation and in some cases causing malignant transformation of the host cells. Varicella-zoster and herpes simplex viruses are highly neurotropic, which explains their unique reactivation patterns along a specific dermatome. CMV and EBV infect peripheral leukocytes, with the B lymphocyte being the target for EBV.[2]

Although an infection with any of the four viruses produces virus-specific antibodies, these are not totally protective against reinfection or reactivation. However, in most cases a second infection will be less severe.

The similarities of the herpesviruses are far outnumbered by their differences. There are differences in the way they manifest themselves, in the different types of populations they affect, and even in the different ways they are transmitted. Each virus has its own high-risk population group in whom it may be hiding, and therefore there are differences in the way nurses and others can protect themselves against acquiring these viruses. Because of the large amount of

Table 8-1 Members of the Herpesvirus Group and Their Most Common Manifestations

Virus	Manifestations
Epstein-Barr virus (EBV)	Infectious mononucleosis (heterophil positive) ? Chronic EBV ("yuppie disease") Tumors (see Figure 8-1)
Cytomegalovirus (CMV)	Mononucleosis-like syndrome (heterophil negative) Central nervous system involvement Congenital malformations and central nervous system deficits Postperfusion and post-transfusion syndrome Pneumonia, hepatitis, and other organ involvement
Varicella-zoster	Chickenpox Shingles Pneumonia
Herpes simplex types 1 and 2	Central nervous system infections Herpetic whitlow (in health care personnel) Neonatal infections Oral and genital herpes
Human Herpes 6	Unknown

information known about the herpesviruses, the discussion is divided into two chapters. EBV and CMV are discussed in the rest of this chapter, whereas Chapter 9 is devoted to the herpes simplex and varicella-zoster viruses.

THE EPSTEIN-BARR VIRUS

The EBV is found worldwide and in all types of populations. In the United States it infects 45% of children younger than 15 years of age. In this age group, the infection is generally asymptomatic, but in those children with primary immune deficiencies, the infection can be fatal or become chronic. The clinical entity known as infectious mononucleosis does not appear in children but instead occurs in adolescents and young adults between 15 and 24 years of age. In adults, the prevalence of EBV antibodies is 90% or more, which demonstrates its widespread presence in the population. Most likely, the virus enters via the mouth, multiplies, and persists in the salivary glands of the host for a few days to weeks. Eventually, it infects the B lymphocytes, which in turn are attacked by the T lymphocytes, which try to destroy the virus-containing B lymphocytes. It is this immune response, as in other diseases, that causes the typical signs and symptoms of mononucleosis. The incubation period is 2 to 3 weeks, during which time the person is asymptomatic but is shedding the virus.[3]

In the immunocompetent host, which includes most health care workers, the disease is self-limiting, and such patients are not seen in intensive care. However, patients who are immunosuppressed may continue to shed the virus for months, even though they have no obvious clinical manifestations.

Complications, such as splenic rupture, are rare but dramatic. Another infrequent occurrence in about 1% of cases is EBV encephalitis and aseptic meningitis. There is a strong suspicion that EBV has oncogenic potential. Burkitt's lymphoma, which is a B-cell tumor found in African children, and anaplastic nasopharyngeal carcinoma in China are closely linked to the virus. Another type of B-cell lymphoma is being reported in young adults and in patients with kidney or bone marrow transplants.[4] Many other potentially EBV virus–associated problems are being investigated, among them EBV in genital ulcers, multiple sclerosis, and fetal infections.[5-7] In recent years, there are increasing reports that the virus may be the etiologic agent in a complex set of chronic symptoms whose main features are fatigue, loss of appetite, and depression. Although EBV antibody is present in these patients, the cause and effect relationship has not been established with any certainty, and these patients are not usually hospitalized.[8] Investigations are taking place into the possibility that one of the human T-cell lymphotropic viruses may be involved in this wasting and fatigue syndrome. Other EBV-associated diseases, some proven, some suspect, are shown in Figure 8-1.

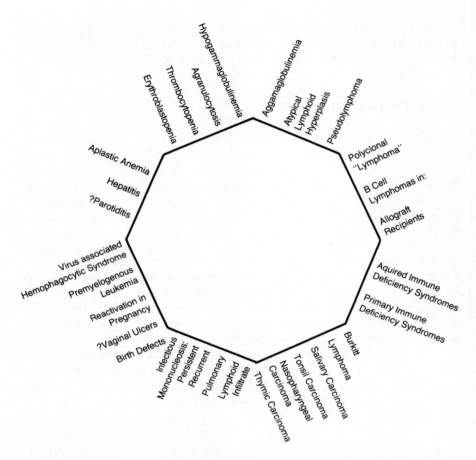

Figure 8-1 Spectrum of EBV-associated diseases. *Source:* Reprinted with permission from *Southern Medical Journal* (1987;80:944), Copyright © 1987, Southern Medical Association.

The diagnosis of EBV mononucleosis is made on clinical grounds and the finding of a heterophil antibody. In about 90% of cases this antibody is transient and may not develop for about 3 weeks or more after the first symptoms of infection appear. EBV-specific antibodies of the IgG type persist for life. Virus may also be cultured from oropharyngeal washings or from circulating lymphocytes, but the finding of virus is of little clinical use.[9,10]

High-Risk Populations

As previously stated, acute EBV mononucleosis is rarely severe enough to require admission to an intensive care unit. However, staff may be exposed by

Incubation
Period
14-21

Place of rash
Origin

SKIN

350

2339

2330 - 233

Back, chest

SKIN Lesion
macule, papule, vesicle
crust, lesions
at dif stages

Communicable Disease

Infectious Disease

301
302
2402
2403
2338
2329

2317
2357

IMPORTANT MESSAGE

FOR _____

DATE _____ TIME _____ A.M. / P.M.

M _____

OF _____

PHONE _____
    AREA CODE   NUMBER   EXTENSION

☐ FAX

☐ MOBILE _____
    AREA CODE   NUMBER   TIME TO CALL

TELEPHONED		PLEASE CALL	
CAME TO SEE YOU		WILL CALL AGAIN	
WANTS TO SEE YOU		RUSH	
RETURNED YOUR CALL		WILL FAX TO YOU	

MESSAGE _____

_____

_____

_____

_____

SIGNED

patients who are admitted for other problems, who had heterophil-positive mononucleosis within the previous 3 months, and who are still shedding the virus. Five to 20% of patients may excrete virus for more than 3 months, and immunosuppressed patients may shed the virus for even longer periods. It is, therefore, advisable to include a specific question about recent mononucleosis-like illnesses when a history is obtained, especially in young adults. High excretion rates can be expected in patients during an acute phase of lymphocytic leukemia, in renal homograft patients from the 3rd to 12th month after the transplant, and in patients who are in generally poor health.[11]

Other immunosuppressive states such as AIDS and lymphoma may cause indefinite shedding. A case of genital ulcers has been described in a patient with acute Epstein-Barr mononucleosis. Herpes simplex, chancroid, and syphilis were not found, but EBV was isolated from the lesions.[5]

Transmission and Precautions

Seronegative persons, meaning those who are susceptible, usually acquire viruses of the herpesvirus group through mucous membrane contact with the infected secretions. As in most infections, the portal of exit of the EBV (and most other pathogens) from the infectious source is the same as the portal of entry into a new host. The EBV is a good example. The vehicle of transmission is saliva. The virus in saliva leaves the infected person via the mouth, which is its portal of exit, and must enter the new host via the same portal, the host's mouth. For that very reason, mononucleosis has long been called the kissing disease.

Therefore, nurses can prevent acquisition of EBV from their patients by avoiding transfer of saliva to their own mouths. This is best accomplished by wearing gloves for contact with any patient's oral secretions, such as occurs during mouth care or suctioning, and always washing hands before touching their own mucous membranes, in this case the mouth. In general, the risk of EBV acquisition from patients is low, mainly because most nurses will have antibody from an earlier infection and will therefore be protected from a work-related reinfection.[10]

CYTOMEGALOVIRUS

Infection with CMV can be fairly innocuous in normally healthy, immunocompetent, nonpregnant persons, but it can cause serious and life-threatening disease in critically ill, immunosuppressed patients and in pregnant women and their infants. It is a typical herpesvirus in many ways. Studies show an inverse relationship of infection with socioeconomic standing, and in some populations 20% to 100% of infections occur early in life, and certainly by young adulthood.[12]

The virus can remain in a latent stage and become reactivated, and the presence of CMV antibody does not protect against reactivation. Even more serious is the fact that antibodies do not protect against reinfection.[2]

The majority of CMV infections, especially in children, are subclinical and inapparent. In some adults, CMV can cause a heterophil-negative mononucleosis-type of disease, which is usually mild and self-limiting. The virus may infect macrophages in salivary glands, but it is unusual to have a sore throat, whereas in EBV mononucleosis a sore throat is commonly experienced. CMV-induced morbidity and mortality is often the result of blood transfusion from a seropositive donor to a seronegative recipient. This is especially true for neonates. Even seropositive recipients may develop serious disease due to reactivation or reinfection, as evidenced by a fourfold rise in antibody titer.[13] The first evidence of CMV blood transfusion–related problems was recognized in what is now called the postperfusion syndrome, 4 to 6 weeks after open-heart surgery. A high temperature is often the first sign, followed by malaise, atypical lymphocytosis, and a variety of other complications. These complications are listed in Table 8-2, which also contrasts the features of postperfusion syndrome to those of noninfectious postcardiotomy syndrome.

The spectrum of CMV-induced diseases is wider and the risk greater in patients who are immunosuppressed, but even in the "normal" host, hepatitis, retinitis, pneumonitis, and central nervous system infections can occur. Virus has been implicated in diseases causing widespread ulcerations of the gastrointestinal tract. It may even play a role in schizophrenia and nonfebrile seizures in children, and these children may well be seen in pediatric intensive care units.[14,15]

CMV is also a potent immunosuppressor of the cell-mediated response, and at one time it was believed to be a precursor or co-factor of AIDS.

Congenital Infection

Perhaps the most worrisome aspect of CMV is the role it plays in congenital infections. Intrauterine infection occurs in 1% to 2% of infants. If the mother has a primary infection, there is a greater likelihood that the infant will be symptomatic at birth. The most familiar presentations are microcephaly, intracranial calcifications, and congenital heart disease (Table 8-3). In reactivated infection, the infant may develop a series of subtle manifestations later in life, all related to damage of the central nervous system. These features consist of a low IQ, which leads to learning and behavioral difficulty, of deficits in hearing and visual acuity, and of other neurologically induced problems.[16] Perinatal infections can occur during passage through a virus-shedding cervix, and postnatal infection is acquired from breast milk of the mother.[17] Later a seronegative newborn can also be infected by blood transfusions or organ transplants from

Table 8-2 Differential Diagnosis Between Cytomegalovirus-Induced Postperfusion Syndrome and the Noninfectious Postcardiotomy Syndrome

	Postperfusion Syndrome	*Postcardiotomy Syndrome*
Etiology	Transfusion-related CMV	? Autoimmune disease ? Inflammatory response to pericardial injury (i.e., trauma, surgery, or myocardial infarction)
Onset	Sudden or gradual onset 30 to 40 days after extracorporeal circulation, transfusion, or transplant	Sudden onset in 2 to 3 weeks
Clinical Presentation	Mononucleosis-like syndrome Malaise Chills and fever to 104°F (40.0°C) 4 weeks post operation Pharyngitis, 10%; splenomegaly, 30%; general lymphadenopathy, 20%	Fever, 101°F–104°F (38.3°C–40.0°C); no chills Chest pain (precordial or retrosternal), intensified by swallowing, deep breathing, recumbency Cough, dyspnea Splinter hemorrhages Pleural or pericardial effusion
Laboratory Findings and Diagnosis	Leukopenia, early acute phase Lymphocytosis after 2 weeks Atypical lymphocytes, 90%–100% Slight elevation of erythrocyte sedimentation rate Mildly elevated LFTs	Electrocardiographic abnormalities X-ray abnormalities Highly elevated erythrocyte sedimentation rate

Source: Reprinted with permission from *Heart and Lung Surgery* (1984;13:472), Copyright © 1984, The CV Mosby Company.

seropositive donors, from CMV in donated or stored human milk, and from the infected mother or caretaker.[18] Probable nosocomial transmission in an intensive care nursery between infants was first reported in 1981 and later confirmed in another study using restriction-endonuclease analysis.[19,20] Postnatal infection in the neonate most often results in pneumonitis or hepatitis and can be fatal.

The oncogenic role of CMV in mice and in Kaposi's sarcoma was postulated long before, as well as after, the appearance of AIDS.[21]

Table 8-3 The Range of Sequelae of Intrauterine Cytomegalovirus Infection

Central Nervous System
  Deafness
  Optic involvement—atrophy
  Choreoretinitis
  Microcephaly
  Cerebral calcifications
  Organomegaly
    Splenic
    Hepatic
      Hepatitis
      Fatty liver
      Hyperbilirubinemia
Vascular
  Thrombocytopenia—petechiae
Cardiac malformations
Limb atrophy and malformations

High-Risk Populations

Patients may be admitted with a primary or reactivated CMV infection, or they may still be shedding virus from an old persistent infection. They may be totally asymptomatic or may be suffering from all or any of the previously described manifestations of their infection. Primary CMV infections may be acquired in the hospital by transfusions or transplants, and these may also cause reinfection with a new virus. Additionally, the stress of serious illness and immunosuppressive conditions or therapies can cause reactivation. Because of the high incidence of CMV-specific antibody of the IgG class, serologic testing of patients is not routinely performed. The presence of CMV IgM or IgG does not necessarily denote present infection or shedding of the virus. As with the other herpesviruses, the antibody is not protective.

Therefore, almost any patient admitted to an intensive care unit can be excreting the virus. Patients who are most likely to become newly infected or suffer reactivation have already been described, and all of these are considered high-risk patients (Table 8-4). Four additional risk groups merit special attention. There is some question about CMV involvement in the Guillain-Barré syndrome, and virus is frequently isolated from patients with chronic gastrointestinal problems such as peptic ulcers, regional enteritis, and colitis. Until these questions are answered, such patients should be considered at high risk for shedding CMV. Some studies, although inconclusive, have been done on hemodialysis patients,[22] but highest on any list for risk factors should be patients with AIDS, who are commonly known to shed the virus and to suffer from CMV-induced infections of the lung, brain, and other organs.[23]

Table 8-4 Some of the Conditions That Can Produce Extensive Shedding of Cytomegalovirus

1. Congenital infection—prolonged shedding

2. Primary infection
   a. In children, especially those attending day-care centers
   b. In adults
      - With mononucleosis-like syndrome or CMV hepatitis, pneumonitis, central nervous system involvement
      - Blood transfusion
      - Organ transplant
      - Sexual transmission

3. Reinfection, most likely to occur in adults
   - Blood transfusion
   - Organ transplant
   - ? Sexual transmission

4. Reactivation, most likely to occur in adults
   - Physical stress (e.g., severe illness)
   - Pregnancy, especially in the third trimester
   - Open-heart surgery, postperfusion syndrome
   - Hemodialysis
   - Immunosuppression, acquired by disease state (AIDS, leukemia) or iatrogenically induced (corticosteroids, chemotherapy, radiation therapy)

5. Chronic gastrointestinal disease
   - Crohn's disease
   - Regional enteritis
   - Gastric ulcers

6. Kaposi's sarcoma

Transmission and Precautions

In hospital workers, acquisition of CMV would occur through mucous membrane contact with the virus. CMV is found in blood, but like the other herpesviruses it is not known to be transmitted via needlestick, other than during administration of transfused blood. It is present in semen and vaginal secretions and is therefore a sexually transmitted disease in the community setting. However, women may shed the virus during pregnancy and for 3 to 12 months thereafter.[18] Therefore, the vaginal secretions of all women should be considered infectious since there is no way of knowing who is shedding the virus. The virus is present in the urine of infected persons and in chronic shedders. This may include any immunosuppressed patient and congenitally or perinatally infected infants. There may be no obvious signs of infection; therefore, all urine should be suspect. Gloves should be worn when diapering infants, and careful handwashing is essential. This is also important in pediatric intensive care units, and especially with children who attend day-care centers. Because of their poor hygienic practices and close proximity, these children have a high prevalence of CMV infection.

Most commonly, CMV is present in saliva, and almost any patient who is critically ill is suspect; however, CMV can also be found in tears, breast milk, feces, and respiratory secretions and possibly on environmental surfaces.[24,25]

Donor tissue may also harbor the CMV, and recipients of bone marrow, kidneys, or other organs are at high risk of acquiring a CMV infection. The incidence of infection appears to be related to the number of donors, the volume of blood received, and the degree of immunosuppression of transplant and transfusion recipients. Prevention of this type of transmission in seronegative recipients can only be achieved if the seronegative recipient is able to receive donations from seronegative donors.[13] The American Association of Blood Banks ascribes some of the CMV post-transfusion hepatitis cases to the use of large volumes of fresh blood, which is more likely to transmit CMV than blood that is more than 5 days old.[26]

Transmission from staff to patients, between patients, and from patient to nurse can easily be prevented. Handwashing before touching any mucous membrane of the patient or oneself is most effective. Pregnant nurses, if they follow gloving and good handwashing technique, are at no greater risk than the general population.[27-29] Everyone must remember that wearing gloves does not reduce the need for handwashing after the gloves have been removed.

REFERENCES

1. Scully C. Viruses and cancer: Herpesviruses and tumors of the head and neck. Oral Surg 1983;56:285–292.

2. Jordan MC (moderator). Latent herpesviruses of humans. (Davis Conference). Ann Intern Med 1984;100:866–880.

3. Pochedly C. Etiology of infectious mononucleosis: Solving the riddle. NY State J Med 1987;87:352–358.

4. Purtilo DT. Epstein Barr virus: The spectrum of its manifestations in human beings. S. Med J 1987;80:943–946.

5. Portnoy J, Ahronheim GA, Ghibu F, et al. Recovery of Epstein-Barr virus from genital ulcers. N Engl J Med 1984;311:966–968.

6. Sumaya CV, Myers LW, Ellison GW, et al. Increased prevalence and titers of Epstein-Barr virus antibodies in patients with multiple sclerosis. N Engl J Med 1985;313:1720–1774.

7. Stagno S, Whitley RJ. Herpesvirus infection in pregnancy: I. N Engl J Med 1985;313:1270–1274.

8. Centers for Disease Control. Chronic fatigue possibly related to Epstein-Barr virus—Nevada. MMWR 1986;35:350–352.

9. Schooley RT, Dolin R. Epstein-Barr virus. In Mandel GL, Douglas RG, Bennett JE (eds). Principles and Practice of Infectious Disease, 2nd ed. New York: John Wiley & Sons, 1985.

10. Sumaya CV. Epstein-Barr virus serologic testing: Diagnostic indications and interpretations. Pediatr Infect Dis 1986;5:337–341.

11. Chang RS, Lewis JC, Reynolds RD, et al. Oropharyngeal excretion of Epstein-Barr virus by patients with lymphoproliferative disorders and by recipients of renal homografts. Ann Intern Med 1978;88:34–40.

12. Ho M. Cytomegalovirus: Biology and infection. New York: Plenum Books, 1982.

13. Adler SP. Transfusion-associated cytomegalovirus infections. Rev Infect Dis 1983;5:977–993.

14. Tomey EF, Yoken RH, Winfrey CJ. Cytomegalovirus antibody in cerebrospinal fluid of schizophrenic patients detected by enzyme immunoassay. Science 1982;216:892–894.

15. Iannetti P, Fiorilli MC, Paria A, et al. Nonfebrile seizures after febrile convulsions: Possible role of chronic cytomegalovirus infection. J. Pediatr 1982;101:27–31.

16. Hanshaw J. Cytomegalovirus. In Remington J, Klein J (eds). Infectious Diseases of the Fetus and Newborn Infant, 2nd ed. Philadelphia: W. B. Saunders, 1983.

17. LaRussa P. Perinatal herpesvirus infections. Pediatr Ann 1984;13:659–670.

18. Pass RF, Stagno S, Dworsky ME, et al. Excretion of cytomegalovirus in mothers: Observations after delivery of congenitally infected and normal infants. J Infect Dis 1982;146:1–6.

19. Gurevich I, Cunha BA. Nonparenteral transmission of cytomegalovirus in a neonatal intensive care unit. Lancet 1981;2:222–224.

20. Spector SA. Transmission of cytomegalovirus among infants in hospital documented by restriction-endonuclease-digestion analyses. Lancet 1983;1:378–381.

21. Giraldo G, Beth E. Antibody patterns to herpesvirus in Kaposi's sarcoma: II. Serologic association of American Kaposi's sarcoma with cytomegalovirus. Int J Cancer 1978;22:126–131.

22. Hardiman AE. Cytomegalovirus infection in dialysis patients. Clin Nephrol 1985;13:12–17.

23. Masur H, Macher AM. Acquired immune deficiency syndrome. In Mandell GL, Douglas RG, Bennett J (eds). Principles and Practice of Infectious Disease, 2nd ed. New York: John Wiley & Sons, 1985.

24. Centers for Disease Control. Guidelines for Infection Control in Hospital Personnel. Atlanta, 1983.

25. Faix RG. Survival of cytomegalovirus on environmental surfaces. J Pediatr 1985;106:649–652.

26. American Association of Blood Banks. Hepatitis. 1983.

27. Lipscomb JA, Linneman CC, Hurst PF, et al. Prevalence of cytomegalovirus antibody in nursing personnel. Infect Control 1984;5:513–518.

28. Dworsky ME, Welch K, Cassady G, et al. Occupational risk for primary cytomegalovirus infections among pediatric health care workers. N Engl J Med 1983;309:950–953.

29. Pomeroy C, Englund JA. Cytomegalovirus: Epidemiology and infection control. Am J Infect Control 1987;15:107–119.

CHAPTER REVIEW QUESTIONS

1. Which of the following are part of the group of viruses called human herpesviruses?
   a. Varicella-zoster
   b. Epstein-Barr
   c. Cytomegalovirus
   d. Herpes simplex types 1 and 2
   e. All of the above

2. Which of the herpesviruses are neurotropic?
   a. Varicella-zoster and herpes simplex
   b. Epstein-Barr virus and cytomegalovirus
   c. All of the above

3. The Epstein-Barr virus has been clearly established as the etiologic agent of a chronic infection called chronic fatigue syndrome or "yuppie disease."
   a. True
   b. False

4. Nurses in adult and pediatric intensive care units have a higher risk for CMV infection than other nurses.
   a. True
   b. False

5. Which of these measures are recommended for protection against cytomegalovirus in the workplace?
   a. Handwashing
   b. Wearing of gloves
   c. Wearing of gowns
   d. All of the above

Answers are provided in Appendix B.

Chapter 9

The Herpesviruses: Herpes Simplex and Varicella-Zoster—The Neurotropic Herpesviruses

In addition to their potential for latency and reactivation, which is shared by all the herpesviruses, the herpes simplex viruses (HSV) and the varicella-zoster virus (VZV) have another common aspect. They are neurotropic viruses, which means that in their latent state they remain in the nerve cells or ganglia of the host and when reactivation occurs the distribution of the resulting disease follows the dermatome whose root harbored the virus.[1]

THE HERPES SIMPLEX VIRUSES

There are two herpes simplex viruses: HSV type 1 and HSV type 2. The viruses vary somewhat in their epidemiology and their antigenic properties but are similar in their clinical manifestations and cause a wide spectrum of disease. HSV type 1 most frequently causes infection in the very young. About 35% of children already have antibody to the virus at age 5; at age 35, 98% of adults have antibody to HSV type 1. In contrast, HSV type 2 is extremely rare before 14 years of age (Table 9-1). There is an inverse relationship with the socioeconomic status of those infected with HSV type 1 because crowding and poor hygiene assist in the spread of the infection. HSV type 2 affects a much higher income group. HSV type 1 is isolated predominantly from oropharyngeal infections and only about 15% of genital herpes is due to HSV type 1, whereas HSV type 2 predominates in genital infections and to a much lesser extent in those of the oral mucosa.[2] Both viruses can infect the central nervous system, eyes, lungs, and liver, as well as the skin and mucous membranes of any part of the body.

Definitions

In order to clarify the terminology used in this chapter, a few definitions are in order. The term *primary infection* refers to the first infection with HSV that

Table 9-1 The Differences Between Herpes Simplex Viruses Types 1 and 2

	HSV 1	HSV 2
Ages Affected	1–5 years: ~35% Adults: ~98%	<14 years: 0 14–35 years: ~35%
Socioeconomic Class	Inverse relationship	Middle and upper class most frequently affected
Incidence *(New Cases)*	Not a reportable disease, number not known	~600,000 per year but may be much higher
Predominance	Oral: 85% Genital: 15%	Genital: ~90% Oral: ~10%
Recurrence	Mostly oral, 14% genital	60% genital, less recurrence of oral herpes

a person has encountered. *Reinfection* describes a second infection with the same type of HSV but at a new or different site. For example, if a patient has oral herpes as the initial or very first infection with an HSV and then spreads it to another part of the body (e.g., the eye, a finger, or chest), the infection at this second site would be called reinfection. Another example can be used to describe a patient who has penile herpes. If the patient later suffers a new infection around the anus or the mouth, this would be reinfection if the same HSV type (1 or 2) is involved. Since it is usually not necessary to establish which of the two types is the infecting agent, it is possible that a second and new infection at a different or even the same site could be due to the second of the two virus types. Knowing which is the infectious agent would not affect the diagnosis, the transmission, or the treatment and is therefore of academic concern only. It is important to remember, however, that both viruses can cause the same clinical manifestations even though they do have preferential sites.

After the initial or primary infection, any recurrence at the same (previously affected site) is called *reactivation* or *recurrent infection*.

Herpes Simplex Type 1 Infections

The spectrum of clinical manifestations varies according to the site, age, and immune status of the patient. The most common childhood infection is oral-facial, but ocular and digital HSV infections are not uncommon. These infections are usually self-limiting and do not require hospitalization unless they become disseminated (Figure 9-1). Ocular herpes can become a very serious infection and can be greatly exacerbated by the use of topical corticosteroids in the form

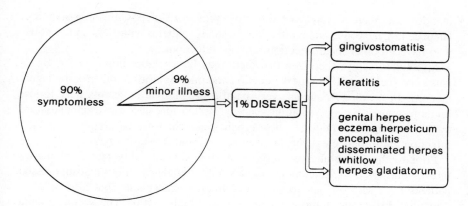

Figure 9-1 Diagrammatic representation of the spectrum of clinical disease resulting from primary infection with herpes simplex virus type 1. *Source*: Reprinted from *An Introduction to Herpes Infections* (p 24) by GOW McKendrick and S Sutherland with permission of Wellcome Foundation Ltd, © 1983.

of eye drops. These agents should not be used indiscriminantly but only after a viral etiology for the ocular infection or irritation has been ruled out. Herpetic whitlow is an occupational disease for health care workers and is discussed under transmission and prevention in this chapter.

Usually, adult patients are admitted to intensive care units because of HSV infection of the central nervous system or with pulmonary involvement. Neonates with any type of herpesvirus infection will require intensive care. However, almost any critically ill patient, regardless of the reason for admission to an intensive care unit, may experience recurrence of a previous HSV infection and may thus present a risk to health care personnel.

Prior to the availability of effective antiviral agents, the mortality from disseminated herpesvirus infections was extremely high. By far the most lethal expression of HSV type 1 infection was encephalitis. Two of three patients died within 2 weeks of onset, and 60% to 80% of those who survived were left with sequelae of varying degrees, ranging from mild to very severe. The prognosis has greatly improved with the available therapies, but even with intravenous therapy with acyclovir, neurologic sequelae are not infrequent.

Herpes encephalitis can be due to a primary infection or manifest after a recurrent episode. The virus is believed to reach the brain either by viremic spread from a distant site or by direct extension along the trigeminal or other neurotropic pathway. Most adults have evidence of mucocutaneous HSV infection prior to onset of encephalitis, but some studies have demonstrated different strains in the brain from those found at a mucocutaneous site. The theory is that in those cases there may be reactivation of a previous, and possibly long-standing, latent central nervous system infection.[3] Usually, patients with HSV encephalitis who have no other local infection are not infectious.

Investigators have theorized that there may be a relationship between Bell's palsy and recurrent HSV type 1 infection and other injuries to the oroesophageal mucosa. In oncology patients, very painful orogingival stomatitis may follow immunosuppressive or radiation therapy. Extension into the esophagus and tracheobronchial tree may present as esophagitis, which can be similar to candidal infection and produce dysphagia, weight loss, and substernal pain.

Prior to the availability of antiviral agents, the mortality rate from herpes pneumonia was 80%. Pneumonia occurs most frequently in immunosuppressed patients such as those undergoing bone marrow transplants, but also in other critically ill patients. In those patients it is still highly lethal. Herpes pneumonia may present as focal necrosis or diffuse interstitial pneumonia. Endotracheal or nasogastric intubation may predispose to direct dissemination into those areas from oral lesions. Viremia can spread the virus to any body system, includng the colon and liver, and the central nervous system can be involved both in the immunocompetent or immunosuppressed host.[4]

Herpes Infections in the Neonate

Because their immature immune system is unable to prevent dissemination of the viruses, morbidity and mortality rates are even higher among infected infants, even with treatment, than among adults. Outbreaks of HSV type 1 infections in neonatal and pediatric intensive care units have been reported.[5,6] Infections in these settings may originate from any of the infant's caretakers and can be transmitted between infants, nurses, physicians, and parents. As in adults, any of the aforementioned sites can become involved, as well as the liver, kidney, pancreas, intestine, and bone marrow.

Herpes Simplex Virus Type 2

HSV type 2 is still the virus most frequently responsible for genital herpes infections. Although it preferentially infects patients "below the waist," the virus can also be isolated from the pharynx (13% of women and 28% in men in one study) and other body sites. Because of the larger mucosal area involved, women usually suffer more extensive disease and may occasionally require hospitalization for intravenous therapy and for urinary drainage. In the study mentioned previously, aseptic meningitis occurred in 8% of women during primary infection and systemic symptoms such as fever and malaise are present in about two thirds of women.[7] Because genital herpes is a sexually transmitted disease, HSV type 2 infection rarely occurs prior to age 14, with two exceptions. One is neonatal herpes, and the other is in child abuse.

Mucocutaneous lesions in HSV types 1 and 2 are very painful. They begin as multiple papules, which quickly become vesicular and coalesce into an ulcerative lesion. Cervical and vaginal infections do not produce pain, but there will be a vaginal discharge. Herpetic lesions are not always easy to see on mucosal surfaces. When they are seen they must be differentiated from other infections. The quickest method is to deroof a vesicle and perform a Tzanck or Giemsa stain on the specimen, which will show the multinucleated giant inclusion cells typical for HSV types 1 and 2 but also for VZV. The virus can be grown in tissue culture, and a variety of serologic and other laboratory tests are available for diagnosis.[8]

Recurrent Herpes Simplex Infection

After a quiescent period in one of the sensory ganglia that were involved in a primary infection, a variety of stimuli can cause a latent infection to become reactive. This applies to both HSV types 1 and 2. Virus begins to multiply at its resting site and then migrates to the mucocutaneous site fed by the affected dermatome (Figure 9-2). In some instances recurrence is asymptomatic; in others there will be painful vesicular eruptions. In the immunocompetent host, recurrent infections are confined to one dermatome. They are less extensive and milder than primary infections and of shorter duration (7–10 days), but patients are no less infectious. Common stimuli for reactivation in the normal host are emotional or physical stresses such as fever (fever blisters), menstruation, or illness of any kind. It is, therefore, quite common to find that critically ill patients suffer a recurrence during their stay in intensive care units.

In immunocompromised hosts, especially those with suppression of T cells, which control cell-mediated immunity, the reactivated virus may disseminate via the bloodstream to any and all organs and sites.

High-Risk Populations

It is obvious from the discussion so far that any patient can be at high risk for developing an HSV infection. The infection can be acquired by the patient in the hospital from blood transfusion or bone marrow or other organ transplant, or it can be due to reactivation precipitated by the stress of illness.

Since neonates can be infectious from maternal herpes, a good history should always be available from the mother. Intrauterine infections are most likely to

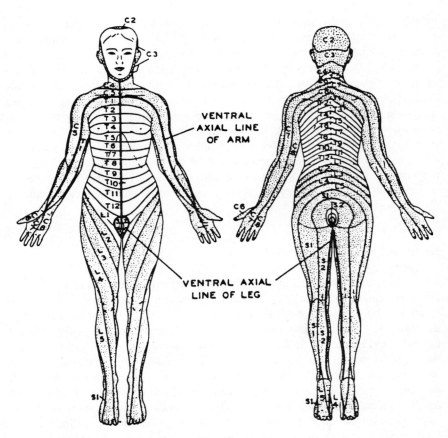

Figure 9-2 The segmental distribution of the cutaneous nerves in the limbs. *Source*: Reprinted with permission from *Anatomical Record* (1984;102:409), Copyright © 1984 Alan R Liss Inc.

occur during a primary infection when the possibility of viremia is greatest. However, recurrent infection can be transmitted to the infant during labor and delivery. The mother should be questioned about recurrent disease during the pregnancy, and it must be remembered that cervical or vaginal infections may be asymptomatic. There is no pain from herpes at these sites because the area is not enervated with pain-sensing nerves. Estimates of neonatal herpesvirus infection are approximately 1 in 7,500 live births, or about 500 cases annually.[3] Over 70% of infants with neonatal herpes have mothers without signs or symptoms of infection at delivery.[9]

Immunosuppressed patients are high-risk patients, especially those with AIDS, Hodgkin's disease, or leukemia. Nurses must remember that although reactivated disease usually causes pain, which could alert them to the presence of infection, critically ill patients present a special hazard. They may be confused, sedated, obtunded or comatose, or on ventilatory assistance and therefore unable to communicate their pain. Patients with herpes encephalitis or meningitis are usually not infectious by the time these complications develop.

Transmission and Precautions

Acquisition of HSV type 1 or 2 infection from mucocutaneous lesions occurs through direct contact of mucous membranes or abraded skin with the viruses. There is even the possibility that the virus can invade intact skin. There are three areas of concern in the health care setting:

1. Transmission *to* patients from an infected health care worker
2. Transmission *from* an infected patient to a health care worker
3. Autotransmission from one infected body site to a new site (of the same individual).

Regardless of who is infected, it is the vesicular fluid that contains the virus. Nurses and their patients should be careful not to transfer the virus from one body site to another when washing and wiping. Therefore, infected areas should be patted dry or left to air dry whenever possible. Nurses and other staff with herpes labialis should be reminded to avoid contact with their lesions and to wash hands well before patient care activities. The Centers for Disease Control recommend that nurses should

> where possible, not take care of patients at high risk of severe infection such as neonates, patients with severe malnutrition, severely burned patients, and patients in immunodeficient states. The potential of infection must be weighed against the possibility of compromising patient care by excluding personnel with oro-facial herpes.[10]

Virus has been found on the hands of infected nurses, and it survives in the environment for some hours.[11] Each hospital must provide its own policies in regard to infected personnel.[12] Such policies, however, cannot discriminate between physicians, nurses, and others. Unlike the lesions of varicella-zoster, herpetic lesions remain infectious until the scabs have fallen off. Scabs do not form on moist mucosal surfaces, and these areas are infectious until total re-epithelialization has taken place.

Herpetic Whitlow

The greatest risk, however, is not transmission of HSV from personnel to patients but from infected patients to personnel.

Herpetic whitlow is, unfortunately, an occupational disease, especially among critical care personnel whose patients may suffer from inapparent infections or who may not be able to discuss their infectious state with the nurse. Herpetic whitlow presents as vesiculation of a digit and "pulpitis." The pulp is usually less tense and swollen than in a bacterial infection. The vesicles, even before ulceration, may coalesce, and the turbid fluid may be mistaken for pus caused by bacterial infection. A clue to the etiology is that the pain is excruciating and far out of proportion to the appearance of the site. Primary herpetic whitlow can cause a temperature of up to 103°F (39.4°C), chills, malaise, myalgia, and lymphadenopathy. Dysesthesia, if present, may persist for weeks even after healing has taken place.[13] The greatest danger lies in the possibility of misdiagnosis and incision of the infected area, which could greatly extend the infection, the time of healing, and the duration of dysesthesia.

Because of the greater risk of transmitting an infection on the fingers to patients, personnel with herpetic whitlow should not have patient contact until the infection has healed, which could take 2 to 3 weeks with a primary infection and much longer if the area was incised.[10]

Prevention is obviously most important and requires two approaches. One is maintaining a high index of suspicion for symptomatic as well as asymptomatic HSV infection. Physicians or nurses who notice herpetic infection must so inform their co-workers. The second approach is to wear gloves for all contact with any patient's secretions and follow universal precautions as recommended by the Centers for Disease Control.[14] This pertains even when changing the tape holding an endotracheal tube in place, since the patient may drool onto the tape and onto the pillow. Damaged skin on the hands should be covered with a bandage or other cover, and nurses should not touch their own faces until their hands have been washed.

Treatment

Acyclovir is the treatment of choice for herpesvirus infections. Intravenous therapy is the most effective and is used for the more serious infections, while oral medications and topical applications are prescribed for nonhospitalized patients. Indications for therapy and other antiviral agents such as vidarabine are listed in Table 9-2.[3]

Table 9-2 Current Status of Antiviral Chemotherapy for Herpes Simplex Virus Infections

Type of Infection	Treatment and Benefits
Mucocutaneous HSV Infections	
Immunosuppressed patients	
Acute symptomatic first or recurrent	Intravenous or oral administration of acyclovir relieves pain and speeds healing; with localized external lesions, topical application of acyclovir may be beneficial.
Suppression of reactivation of disease	Daily intravenous or oral administration of acyclovir prevents recurrences during high-risk period (e.g., immediately after transplantation).
Immunocompetent patients	
First episodes of genital herpes	Oral therapy with acyclovir is preferred. Acyclovir may be administered intravenously if severe disease or neurologic complications are present; topical application of acyclovir may be beneficial in patients without cervical, urethral, or pharyngeal involvement.
Symptomatic recurrent genital herpes	Oral therapy with acyclovir has some benefits in shortening lesions and viral excretion time; routine use for all episodes is not recommended.
Suppression of recurrent genital herpes	Daily oral use of acyclovir prevents reactivation of symptomatic recurrences; at present it is limited to a 6-month course in patients with frequent recurrences.
First episodes of oral-labial HSV	Oral therapy with acyclovir has not yet been studied in this instance.
Recurrent episodes of oral-labial HSV	Topical use of acyclovir is of no clinical benefit; oral therapy with acyclovir has not been studied.
Herpetic whitlow	Studies of antiviral chemotherapy have not been performed.
HSV proctitis	Intravenous therapy with acyclovir appears to be beneficial in immunosuppressed patients; oral use of acyclovir is under investigation.
Herpetic eye infections (acute keratitis)	Topical use of trifluorothymidine, vidarabine, idoxuridine, acyclovir, and interferon; débridement may be required; topical corticosteroid therapy may worsen the disease.
HSV Infections of the Central Nervous System	
HSV encephalitis	Intravenous therapy with acyclovir or vidarabine decreases mortality; acyclovir is the preferred agent.
HSV aseptic meningitis	No studies of systemic antiviral chemotherapy have been performed.
Autonomic radiculopathy	No studies are available.

Table 9-2 continued

Type of Infection	Treatment and Benefits
Neonatal HSV Infection	Intravenous vidarabine or acyclovir therapy decreases mortality; a comparative trial is in progress.
Visceral HSV Infection	
HSV esophagitis	No controlled studies have been performed; systemic therapy with acyclovir or vidarabine should be considered.
HSV pneumonitis	No controlled studies have been performed; systemic therapy with acyclovir or vidarabine should be considered.
Disseminated HSV Infections	No controlled studies have been performed; systemic therapy with acyclovir or vidarabine should be tried; there is no definite evidence that therapy will decrease mortality.
HSV-Associated Erythema Multiforme	Controlled studies are under way; only anecdotal observations are available regarding the topical or oral use of acyclovir.

Source: Reprinted with permission from *New England Journal of Medicine* (1986;314:754), Copyright © 1986, Massachusetts Medical Society.

VARICELLA-ZOSTER

The second neurotropic member of the herpesvirus group is VZV. Varicella or chickenpox is a common childhood exanthem. The incubation period for varicella is 12 to 21 days. In the immunocompetent child it is a relatively benign disease, consisting of a vesicular rash with few systemic manifestations. The rash starts on the upper part of the head and body. New lesions spread downward centrifically for 4 to 5 days, even as the older lesions umbilicate and scabs form. Thus, there are lesions in various stages on the child.

The herpesviruses as a group are controlled by the cell-mediated immune system, even though the humoral system produces varicella-specific antibody. Therefore, in children and adults with cell-mediated immune deficiencies, the disease will present in a much more serious form. The lesions often persist without changing as new vesicles continue to erupt for days, even weeks. The patient's temperature will be high, around 105°F (40.6°C), and the virus can disseminate to the liver and central nervous system (neurotropism). Pneumonia occurs in about 10% of cases. The mortality rate is high. These children will often be seen in pediatric intensive care units.

Varicella in normal adults is a more serious disease than that in normal children. There is a higher incidence of varicella pneumonia that may require admission to intensive care units. And, as in children, immunosuppressed adults may face a devastating course of visceral involvement in the form of central nervous system problems, hepatitis, and pancreatitis.

The risk in pregnancy involves both the fetus and the mother, depending on the stage of pregnancy. The data gathered by several authors are based on small numbers because varicella is not a common disease of adults. Nevertheless, there is evidence to suggest that transplacental virus transmission during maternal varicella, but not zoster, does occur and that there may be a 10% incidence of fetal abnormalities, premature delivery, and abortion.

The risk to the pregnant woman is also greater than for nonpregnant adults. According to one report, it appears that varicella pneumonia is not only more common but also more severe in pregnancy. Two of four women in that study required ventilatory assistance for their pneumonia, and one of the two died.[15]

Infants are at greatest risk of developing neonatal varicella if they are born 5 days before or 48 hours after onset of the maternal varicella rash, presumably because a sufficient amount of maternal antibody cannot be produced and transferred to protect the infant before birth.[16]

Reactivation of Herpes Zoster

As with the neurotropic HSV, after the primary infection the varicella virus retreats to one or more contiguous sensory nerves and ganglia from the mucocutaneous sites and it enters a resting or latent state. A variety of stimuli, but especially a suppression of cell-mediated immunity and physical and emotional stresses, can induce the virus to resume replication. The virus then travels along the path of the affected nerve, causing the skin eruption known as herpes zoster or shingles. Zoster is thus the result of a previous varicella virus infection and can occur at any age.[17]

The herpes zoster virus very often announces its impending eruption by producing irritation of the nerve along which it travels before reaching the mucocutaneous site. Most patients ignore the itching, burning, or pain, if it is not too severe, or they ascribe it to a variety of causes. Thus, zoster in its preeruptive state has been mistaken for cholecystitis, sciatica, tooth decay, and other conditions depending on the involved area. The most frequently involved sites are the thoracic and upper cervical dermatomes. The lumbar, sacral, or facial areas are less often involved (see Figure 9-2). The full-blown shingles or herpes zoster becomes evident about 5 days after the first symptoms are felt. The zoster rash is characterized by a unilateral bandlike eruption and is considered to be localized if no more than one or two dermatomes are involved, and if they are adjacent to each other. Zoster is considered to be "disseminated" if more than two adjacent dermatomes are involved. The importance of that distinction will become apparent later.

The vesicles are small and closely grouped and usually appear on an erythematous base. The lesions may be confused with those of the recurrent HSV lesion, but the latter are not usually spread out along the whole length of the nerve. New vesicles may appear over a period of several days, but the numbness and even pain may persist long after all clinical signs have resolved. The lesions are infectious until they have crusted over and dried.

High-Risk Populations

Varicella has as its high-risk group all young children as well as susceptible adults. A history of all childhood diseases and/or vaccinations should be available on all children who are admitted to a hospital. In addition, the importance of reporting contact with a person with varicella by patients and health care workers to the infection control practitioner or the employee health service must be stressed. Persons who are incubating the disease are infectious 2 days prior to the eruption of the rash, and any susceptible employees should be furloughed from day 10 to day 21 after their exposure or they become at high risk for infection of co-workers and patients alike.[10] Other precautionary measures are discussed later in this chapter.

In order to prevent unnecessary exposures to herpes zoster, it is important for critical care personnel, especially those who are pregnant, to maintain a high index of suspicion with a wide range of patients in the critical care setting. Zoster may appear at any age, even in very young children who were infected with the varicella virus in utero. However, in the past, shingles has been mainly recognized as a disease of the elderly. It is now also recognized as a serious complication in patients who are immunosuppressed. Because of an increase in both these populations in intensive care units, and because zoster is frequently reactivated in the presence of stress, such as hospitalization for a serious illness, surgical procedures, irradiation, and trauma, all patients in this setting should be considered high-risk patients.

If all patients are in the high-risk category, then it is important that nurses and physicians have a high awareness of the early manifestations of zoster so that precautionary measures can be instituted. As already described, preceding the rash there may be a sensation of itching or burning along the dermatome. The pain may be severe enough to be mistaken for myocardial infarction, pleurisy, cholecystitis, and acute abdomen. In its early stages, the rash may also be mistaken for an allergic reaction such as drug fever or other eruption, and thus personnel may be exposed for some time before it is correctly identified. Patients who are sedated or intubated may not be able to communicate the prodromal manifestations, and a careful daily physical examination of the patient is essential.

Transmission and Prevention

Varicella and disseminated zoster are both highly contagious. The virus in these patients is transmitted by the airborne route from the infected respiratory tract and by direct contact with vesicular fluid, but transmission is somewhat less likely by indirect contact with articles contaminated with the virus. Patients are infectious up to 2 days before the rash appears and until the lesions have crusted. Localized herpes zoster is probably not airborne but is acquired by contact with vesicular fluid and inoculation into the nasopharyngeal mucosa of a susceptible person, such as the patient's nurse. It is, therefore, extremely important to place patients with varicella and disseminated zoster on strict isolation in a private room and to wear protective masks, gowns, and gloves.[18]

Patients with localized zoster can be cared for on Wound and Skin Precautions or Contact Isolation.[18] They should not share a room with an immunosuppressed patient. Patients with leukemia or other immunosuppressive conditions who have localized zoster but who are at considerable risk of developing disseminated disease should be placed in a private room on Strict Isolation as soon as even a localized rash appears. Any susceptible health care worker who was exposed to a case of varicella or disseminated zoster must be sent home, and a similar patient must be placed on Respiratory Isolation 2 days prior to and for the duration of the incubation period (10–21 days). Patients who develop signs and symptoms of the disease (varicella or disseminated zoster) must then be placed on Strict Isolation.[10]

Because there is prodromal infectivity as well as occasional delay in recognizing of the disease or in placing the patient on Strict Isolation, outbreaks of nosocomial varicella are not uncommon among patients or personnel.

Immune Status of Personnel

Therefore, the susceptibility or immunity of hospital personnel should be ascertained when the person is hired or as soon as possible thereafter. This includes persons who are not hospital employees but have contact with patients and may expose anyone in the hospital to VZV, such as medical and nursing students, attending physicians, volunteers, clergy, barbers, and others. The susceptibility status can be ascertained by a history of prior varicella or zoster or exposure to siblings or children who lived in the same household and had chickenpox. If a definite history cannot be established, susceptibility testing by enzyme-linked immunoabsorbent assay (ELISA) or fluorescent antibody to membrane antigen (FAMA) testing should be performed and the results kept on record.[19, 20] An intradermal skin test to establish immunity is also under investigation.[21]

Because of the severity of disease in adults, and keeping in mind the special risks in pregnancy, susceptible personnel, especially those who are pregnant, should not care for patients with varicella or zoster. Susceptible employees, male or female, who are exposed to varicella outside the hospital must report such exposures to the employee health service or to the infection control practitioner and must be furloughed from days 10 to 21 after their exposure, and if disease develops, until they are no longer infectious.[10] A history of all vaccinations and childhood diseases should always be obtained for children admitted to a pediatric intensive care unit, so that susceptible children can be watched carefully.

Postexposure Prophylaxis

Varicella-zoster immune globulin (VZIG) is available for postexposure prophylaxis of high-risk populations. Although it may not totally prevent the infection, it will ameliorate the disease in most cases. It is indicated for susceptible persons who are at risk of serious complications. Risks of administration are minimal, but the cost for an adult can reach $375. Hospital personnel should be considered for prophylaxis if they are immunosuppressed or have leukemia or lymphoma. Some experts have recommended VZIG for pregnant women, since there is a reportedly greater morbidity and mortality associated with pregnancy.[22] Indications for VZIG in patients are listed in Table 9-3. VZIG must be admin-

Table 9-3 Candidates for Whom Varicella-Zoster Immune Globulin (VZIG) is Indicated*

1. Susceptible to varicella-zoster
2. Significant exposure
3. Age younger than 15 years (administration to immunocompromised adolescents and adults and to other patients should be based on individual evaluations)
4. One of the following underlying illnesses or conditions
   a. Leukemia or lymphoma
   b. Congenital or acquired immunodeficiency
   c. Immunosuppressive treatment
   d. Newborn of mother who had onset of chickenpox within 5 days before delivery or within 48 hours after delivery.
   e. Premature infant ($\geq$28 weeks' gestation) whose mother lacks a prior history of chickenpox.
   f. Premature infants (<28 weeks' gestation or $\leq$1,000 g) regardless of maternal history.

*Patients should meet these four criteria for VZIG candidates.

Source: Reprinted from *Morbidity and Mortality Weekly Report* (1984;33:84–100), Copyright © 1984, US Centers for Disease Control.

istered within 96 hours (preferably sooner) and may prolong the incubation period to 28 days. Therefore, hospital personnel who have received VZIG should be furloughed for this length of time and the isolation period for patients should also be extended.

CONCLUSIONS

The varicella-zoster and herpes simplex viruses pose a variety of risks for patients as well as for personnel. Familiarity with high-risk patients, early manifestations of the diseases, and precautionary measures can greatly reduce the risk of disease transmission. In the case of varicella-zoster there is a special risk for pregnant health care workers and their fetuses, and avoidance of exposure to varicella and zoster is advisable.

REFERENCES

1. Overall JC. Persistent problems with persistent herpesviruses. N Engl J Med 1981;305:95–97.

2. Nahmias AJ, Roizman B. Infection with herpes simplex viruses 1 and 2. N Engl J Med 1983;289:667.

3. Corey L, Spear PG. Infections with herpes simplex viruses. N Engl J Med 1986;314:749–757.

4. Wong KK, Hirsch MS. Herpes virus infections in patients with neoplastic disease. Am J Med 1984;76:404–478.

5. Adams G, Stover BH, Keenlyside RA, et al. Nosocomial herpetic infections in a pediatric ICU. Am J Epidemiol 1981;113:126–132.

6. Hammerberg O, Watts J, Chernesky M, et al. An outbreak of herpes simplex type 1 in an intensive care nursery. Pediatr Infect Dis 1983;2:290–294.

7. Corey L, Adams HG, Brown ZA, et al. Genital herpes simplex virus infections: Clinical manifestations, course and complications. Ann Intern Med 1983;98:958–972.

8. Couch RB, et al. Grand rounds in critical care—genital herpes: An epidemic disease. Heart Lung 1983;12:320–324.

9. Whitley RJ, Nahmias AJ, Visintine AM, et al. Management of genital herpes simplex virus infection during pregnancy. Obstet Gynecol 1980;58:1–4.

10. Centers for Disease Control. Guidelines for Prevention of Nosocomial Infection: Personnel Health. Atlanta, 1983.

11. Turner R, Shehab Z, Osborne K, et al. Shedding and survival of herpes simplex virus from "fever blisters." Pediatrics 1982;70:547–549.

12. Crane LR, Haruka BT, Friedman C. Restriction of hospital employees with active herpes simplex virus. Infect Control 1982;3:359.

13. Greaves WL, Kaiser AB, Alford RH, et al. The problem of herpetic whitlow among hospital personnel. Infect Control 1980;1:381.

14. Centers for Disease Control. Recommendations for the prevention of HIV transmission in health care settings. MMWR 1987;36:3.

15. Panyani SG, Arvin AM. Intrauterine infection with varicella-zoster virus after maternal varicella. N Engl J Med 1986;314:1542–1546.

16. Centers for Disease Control. Varicella immune globulin for the prevention of chickenpox. MMWR 1984;33:84–100.

17. Adams HG. Herpes: A problem in older age groups. Geriatrics 1983;38:91–100.

18. Garner JS, Simmons BP. CDC Guidelines for Isolation Precautions in hospitals. Infect Control 1983;4:245–325.

19. Krasinski K, Holzman RS, LaCouture R, et al. Hospital experience with varicella-zoster virus. Infect Control 1986;7:312–316.

20. Gustafson TL, Lavely GB, Brawner ER, et al. An outbreak of airborne nosocomial varicella. Pediatrics 1982;70:550–556.

21. La Russa P, Steinberg SP, Seeman MD, et al. Determination of immunity to varicella-zoster virus by means of an intradermal skin test. J Infect Dis 1985;152:869–875.

22. Centers for Disease Control. Varicella zoster immune globulin for the prevention of chickenpox: Recommendations of the Immunization Practices Advisory Committee. Ann Intern Med 1984;100:859–865.

CHAPTER REVIEW QUESTIONS

1. Infection with herpes simplex virus type 2 provides immunity against reinfection with the same virus at another body site.
   a. True
   b. False

2. The cloudy fluid present in herpetic whitlow infections should be
   a. Almost never incised and drained
   b. Promptly incised and drained to relieve the pain

3. A neonate may become infected with herpes simplex virus during normal vaginal delivery from reactivated genital herpes of the mother
   a. If the mother has visible lesions of the cervix or vagina
   b. If the mother has symptomatic (painful) herpetic lesions of the genital tract
   c. Even if there are no visible cervical or vaginal lesions at the time of delivery
   d. a and b
   e. All of the above

4. If a susceptible nurse is exposed to a patient with shingles, the nurse can develop
   a. Varicella
   b. Herpes zoster
   c. Herpes labialis

5. A susceptible nurse is exposed to chickenpox. The nurse is pregnant and receives varicella-zoster immune globulin. If the incubation period of varicella (chickenpox) is usually 12 to 21 days, how soon after the exposure must this nurse be furloughed and for how long, even if no rash appears?
   a. From day 10 after exposure to day 21
   b. From day 12 after exposure to day 21
   c. From day 10 after exposure to day 28
   d. From day 12 after exposure to day 28

Answers are provided in Appendix B.

Chapter 10

Meningitis: Early Recognition and Prevention of Spread

Meningitis can be caused by a variety of organisms, but only two of these are considered contagious enough to warrant isolation of the patient. *Neisseria meningitidis* (the meningococcus) is one, and *Hemophilus influenzae* is the other.

Because the onset of meningitis can be very acute and disabling, patients are often brought directly to an emergency department. If the presentation is not typical, and especially if it does not include nuchal rigidity, the diagnosis may be missed at first and many emergency department or intensive care unit personnel may be exposed to the organisms before isolation is instituted. Even if meningitis is being considered, it is not always easy to distinguish between bacterial and viral causes on clinical grounds alone.

A third possibility for exposure exists when physicians and nurses are so concerned with the patient's needs for rapid therapy and vital support systems that their own protection is not considered in a timely fashion.

Meningitis is a frightening disease. When the diagnosis of meningococcal or *H. influenzae* meningitis is finally made, panic may ensue and postexposure prophylaxis may be administered indiscriminately, without awareness of certain risks connected with the medication itself. It is, therefore, important for clinicians to recognize the early clinical manifestations of bacterial meningitis and to know the precautionary measures that can protect them from acquiring the patient's infection. It is also important for exposed persons to know when rifampin prophylaxis is indicated and safe.

CASE HISTORY

Robert was a 17-year-old white male brought to the emergency department at noon on a Thursday with a complaint of fever, abdominal discomfort, nausea, and sleepiness. He was confused about what he had eaten the evening before and where he had eaten. His mother was notified of his illness by the school nurse and arrived at the hospital within minutes. She related that he had eaten lasagna at a restaurant the night before with other family members, none of whom was ill. In the emergency department, Robert's temperature was 102.8°F (39.3°C); he vomited twice and had diarrhea. A diagnosis of gastroenteritis was made, he was admitted to the teenage pediatric unit, and an intravenous drip was started to hydrate him. Therapy was started with trimethoprim-sulfame-thoxazole. According to the results of the history and physical examination, Robert was photophobic, irritable, and confused, and his mother confirmed his state of confusion. In spite of adequate hydration, his blood pressure and renal output declined within the next 4 hours. He complained of "head pain" and became increasingly lethargic. A spinal tap was done and showed 550 white blood cells/cu mm, of which 95% were polymorphonuclear neutrophils and 5% were lymphocytes; glucose level was 60 mg/dL, protein level was 160 mg/dL, and lactic acid value was 4.2 mg/dL. No organisms were seen on Gram stain. On transfer to the medical intensive care unit, with a diagnosis of meningitis, his systolic blood pressure fell to 88 mm Hg by palpation, he had an 8 mL/hr urinary output, and he became increasingly obtunded. After 6 hours, another lumbar puncture showed cloudy cerebrospinalfluid with 1,200 white blood cells/cu mm, 90% of which were polymorphonuclear neutrophils, and gram-negative diplococci were evident on Gram stain. Respiratory Isolation was instituted at 11 PM.[1] At the same time, the microbiology technician called the infection control practitioner to report the results of the lumbar puncture.

The infection control practitioner on call phoned the evening nursing supervisor to make sure that the patient was on Respiratory Isolation and to request that a listing of all personnel who had been exposed to the patient before he was put on isolation be left on her desk. Altogether, 21 persons, including a patient, were named.

CLINICAL MANIFESTATIONS

Most exposures to the meningococcus and *H. influenzae* are unnecessary and can be avoided. Physicians and nurses in emergency departments and intensive care units must be familiar with certain clues in adults that should raise their index of suspicion for meningitis before the unmistakable sign of a stiff neck is manifested.

Fever of 102°F (38.9°C) is present in 90% of patients with meningitis and may be accompanied by chills. Eighty to 90% of adult patients will complain of a generalized severe headache, which may be aggravated by movement and light (Table 10-1). Both of these manifestations were present in the patient in the case presented previously. However, the clue that was totally ignored was the change in mentation seen in this young adult. Meningitis should always be

Table 10-1 Clinical Manifestations Suggestive of Bacterial Meningitis

Finding	Relative Frequency (%)
Fever >102°F (38.9°C) ± chills	90
Headache (adults) and photophobia	90
Refusal to feed (infants and children)	90
Nausea and vomiting	80
Change in mentation	90
Irritability (children)	
Confusion, lethargy, obtundation, coma	
Nuchal rigidity	≥80
Myalgias	30–60
Focal neurologic signs	15
Seizures	25
Petechial rash (*Neisseria meningitidis*)	30–50

suspected in the presence of high fever with lethargy and a change of mentation such as agitation, confusion, or delirium.[2] In young children, refusal to eat and irritability with variable fever are common and often the only early signs. Seizures and coma may occur later in the disease in all age groups and would have serious prognostic implications. In the very young, seizures are most commonly seen in *H. influenzae* meningitis, possibly because febrile seizures and *H. influenzae* are both more frequent in those younger than 4 years old. Nausea and vomiting may also be present, and the gastrointestinal symptoms diverted attention from the fact that the adolescent in the case history, even if he had a food-related fever and gastrointestinal symptoms, should not have been irritable, photophobic, and confused.

Nuchal rigidity and other signs of meningeal irritation, such as Brudzinski's and Kernig's signs, are present in only about 50% of adult patients and much less so in young children. They cannot, therefore, be relied on to help establish an early diagnosis.

In the presence of these early symptoms a diagnosis of bacterial meningitis should be entertained. Viral meningitis should be considered in patients with a history of a nonspecific viral syndrome or a prodromal upper respiratory tract infection. Bacterial meningitis is occasionally accompanied by a petechial rash with a centrifugal distribution. These rashes occur in 30% to 50% of meningococcal meningitis but can also be seen in infection with *Streptococcus pneumoniae*, Rocky Mountain spotted fever, and, less frequently, some viral infections.

However, rashes may be missed if the patient is not totally undressed, because they often begin on the trunk or lower extremities where clothing may exert pressure. The early rash may also be missed unless a careful examination of mucosal surfaces, such as the palpebral conjunctiva, is performed.[3]

LABORATORY FINDINGS

The Gram stain is still the most valuable test for establishing the presence of bacteria in the cerebrospinal fluid. It is 80% reliable in untreated cases and can be done very quickly by house staff, if necessary. In some cases of bacterial meningitis a Gram stain obtained early in the infectious disease process might not show organisms because there may be too few of them to be detected. Another reason, especially in a partially treated patient, may be that multiplication of the organisms has been temporarily disrupted by the antibiotic, and their number may therefore be small. If the clinical manifestations remain compatible with bacterial meningitis, two strategies for improving the yield of the Gram stain can be used. The cerebrospinal fluid specimen should be incubated for 4 to 6 hours and then Gram stained again. If even one organism was present it will have had a chance to multiply within that period of time and will therefore improve the chance of discovery. The second alternative is to perform another spinal tap after 6 hours with the expectation that any organisms present within the cerebrospinal fluid of the patient will have had a chance to multiply in sufficient numbers to be more easily seen on Gram stain.

During the waiting period the patient will of course be treated because untreated meningococcal meningitis can be rapidly fatal in the majority of patients. In the case history presented earlier, the second Gram stain made the diagnosis.

A finding of gram-negative diplococci indicates *N. meningitidis*, while the presence of gram-negative rods establishes *H. influenzae* as the pathogen. In the continued absence of a positive Gram stain due to partial antimicrobial therapy, other data can help with establishing a differential diagnosis between viral and bacterial meningitis.[4] The opening cerebrospinal fluid pressure is normally between 65 and 195 nm H_2O. If the pressure is greater than 250 nm H_2O, bacterial infection is most likely. Normal cerebrospinal fluid is clear; turbidity occurs when more than 200 to 300 white blood cells/cu mm are present.[5] More than 400 red blood cells/cu mm in the cerebrospinal fluid will give it a pink appearance. In adults, the cell count normally consists of 1 polymorphonuclear neutrophil and 0 to 5 lymphocytes per cubic millimeter, and in infants there are less than or equal to 30 cells/cu mm with a predominance of lymphocytes. In bacterial nontuberculous meningitis, the count is usually elevated above 100 cells/cu mm. In viral infections the count is usually lower, but there can be great variation. More helpful than the actual count is the differential. In bacterial infection, there is polymorphonuclear neutrophil predominance throughout. A greater percentage of lymphocytes ($\geq 50\%$) usually indicates viral disease, except in the very early stages when polymorphonuclear neutrophils may predominate, but rarely in amounts greater than 80% (Table 10-2).[6]

Normal cerebrospinal fluid protein levels range from 15 to 45 mg/dL. Changes are nonspecific but may be elevated in bacterial meningitis. Elevation can rule

Table 10-2 Comparison of Normal Cerebrospinal Fluid Components with Bacterial and Viral Meningitis (*N. meningitidis* and *H. influenzae*)

	Normal	Bacterial	Viral
White Blood Cells	Adults: 1 polymorphonuclear–5 lymphocytes/cu mm Neonates: 0–30 lymphocytes/cu mm (>50% polymorphonuclear neutrophils)	≥ 90% polymorphonuclear neutrophils (100–10,000/cu mm)	Early: predominantly polymorphonuclear neutrophils, but no more than 80% Late: predominantly lymphocytes (5–300/cu mm)
Glucose	50% of serum glucose Neonates: variable (limited diagnostic value)	<40 mg/dL or <50% of serum Neonates: variable (limited diagnostic value)	Normal or decreased
Protein	15–45 mg/dL	Normal or elevated (nonspecific finding)	Normal or decreased (nonspecific finding)

in bacterial meningitis, but normal values cannot rule it out. The cerebrospinal fluid glucose value is reported to be normal within a range of 50 to 90 mg/dL or approximately 60% of the blood glucose level. In bacterial meningitis, the cerebrospinal fluid glucose level is often decreased; in viral disease, it may be normal or slightly decreased.[2] However, without a comparison with the serum glucose level, actual numbers are not helpful. Equilibration between serum and cerebrospinal fluid glucose levels takes about 2 hours, and if the patient is diabetic, ratios are different than in the normal person.[7] It is also important to remember that the stress of infection alone can increase blood sugar levels significantly (see Table 10-2).

There was one other clue present in the case history presented—the lactic acid level (Table 10-3). It has long been known that cerebrospinal fluid lactic acid concentrations are elevated in bacterial meningitis. Analytical methods have improved with the ready availability of enzymatic methods or gas–liquid chromatography.[5] As shown in Table 10-3, the lactic acid (pH) values can sometimes be of help in differentiating between bacterial meningitis (range, 2.2–15; pH, 7.15) and aseptic or viral meningitis (range, 0.5–2.5; pH, 7.30), as well as provide a clue to viral or partially treated bacterial infection. The lactic acid value in this case was clearly elevated and should have provided a clue to the bacterial origin of the patient's meningitis.

Table 10-3 Lactic Acid Variations in Cerebrospinal Fluid

	Lactic Acid (mg/dL)*	pH
Normal Control	0.5–2.2	7.30
Aseptic	≈ 0.5–2.5	7.30
Purulent	≈ 2.2–13.2	7.15
Purulent Meningitis		
Partially treated	≈ 2.2–7.0	7.25
Fully treated	≈ 2.2–3.5	7.35

*Range of lactic acid levels will vary depending on the laboratory used.

HIGH-RISK POPULATIONS

Because it is so important to institute Respiratory Isolation as soon as possible when meningococcal or *H. influenzae* meningitis is suspected, knowing the age groups in which these two infections occur can be very helpful. The mode of spread is the same for all age groups, directly from the respiratory tract to close contacts. Table 10-4 shows age–organism relationships for all major bacteria causing meningitis.[6] The age relationship to *H. influenzae* begins before birth when the fetus acquires protective maternal *H. influenzae* IgG (antibody).

At about 2 months after birth, maternal antibody protection begins to wane and the risk of *H. influenzae* meningitis increases dramatically because the infant's own immune system is immature and is not efficient at producing protective antibody. In unvaccinated children, this high risk persists until 4 to 6 years of age. *H. influenzae* group b vaccine is recommended at 24 months of age. Prior to that antibody production is insufficient for protection. *H. influenzae* normally colonizes 2% to 6% of the upper respiratory tracts of young children. Therefore, by age 6, most children will have come in contact with a sufficient number of organisms to produce their own protective antibody either in response to the normal, if intermittent, colonization, to natural infection, or to vaccination. Carriage of *H. influenzae* after contact with a patient with meningitis can vary between 20% in adults to 60% in children. In recent years, a few cases of *H. influenzae* meningitis have been reported in the elderly, possibly due to a waning of immunity in an aging population, and thus *H. influenzae* must also be suspected in this age group.

All age groups are at risk for meningococcal meningitis, but the highest numbers affected are adolescents and young adults (25% to 40%). Epidemics due to type A and C are most likely to occur in close living quarters, such as dormitories at colleges or in the armed forces. Meningococcus group B is responsible for most of the endemic cases, with an occasional group Y and W135

Table 10-4 The Relationship of Age to the Most Common Bacterial Pathogens in Meningitis

Age	Most Common Pathogen	Possible Origin
Birth– 2 months	Group B *Streptococcus* *Escherichia coli* *Listeria monocytogenes*	May be maternal flora Maternal flora
2 months– 5 years	*Hemophilus influenzae* *Neisseria meningitidis* *Streptococcus pneumoniae*	Look for otitis or pharyngitis Nasopharyngeal origin
5 years– young adults	*Hemophilus influenzae* *Neisseria meningitidis* *Streptococcus pneumoniae* Other organisms	Trauma or surgery
Adults to 60 years	*Streptococcus pneumoniae* *Neisseria meningitidis* Other organisms	Respiratory tract infection Trauma or surgery
60 years– older	*Streptococcus pneumoniae* *Listeria monocytogenes* *Hemophilus influenzae* Other gram-negative organisms	Waning immunity Rare, but being reported; waning immunity

strain. Children younger than 5 years of age account for 55% of all endemic cases, with an incidence of 20% to 30%. Intermittent nasopharyngeal carriage of the meningococcus is normal in approximately 6% of the general population.

TRANSMISSION AND PRECAUTIONS

All that is needed to protect emergency department, intensive care unit, and other health care workers from meningococcal and *H. influenzae* meningitis is a high index of suspicion and a face mask. If one adds a private room, all requirements for the Centers for Disease Control's category for Respiratory Isolation will have been met. If emergency department personnel had worn face masks as soon as it became apparent that the young patient in the case history was febrile as well as irritable and confused, all but two exposures, those of the first house officer and first nurse to care for the patient, could have been prevented. The same is true of patients of any age who present with fever and confusion. Meningitis has been mistaken for a cerebrovascular accident more than once. Patients in whom a cerebrovascular accident is suspected may be confused, but a high temperature should not be routinely present in the early stages and should alert physicians and nurses to the possibility of meningitis. Respiratory Isolation can be discontinued when meningococcal and *H. influenzae* meningitis has been ruled out and for those two types of meningitis after 24 hours of effective therapy.[1] This means that the organism is sensitive to the antibiotic being administered and that the patient is responding to the regimen.

POSTEXPOSURE PROPHYLAXIS

Rifampin is the drug of choice for high-risk exposures that occur when a person is in close (less than 3 feet) contact with a patient without wearing a mask. However, rifampin is not an innocuous drug and should be taken only when indicated. For *Neisseria meningitidis* meningitis, a high-risk exposure consists of the following:[8]

- Living in the same household or having had other close personal contact (e.g., kissing or sharing of food or beverages)
- Attending the same nursery or day-care class
- Performing mouth-to-mouth resuscitation on the patient
- Intubating or suctioning the patient
- Performing oral or fundoscopic examination
- Assisting a patient who was vomiting or coughing directly at a health care worker

The dosage of rifampin for adults is 600 mg orally twice daily for four doses.

For exposures to *H. influenzae* meningitis, prophylaxis is recommended with less certainty. There does seem to be agreement that health care workers exposed to patients with that type of meningitis fall into a low-risk category because of their age and do not require prophylaxis. When adults and children live in the same household as a patient and if there are other children younger than 4 years old in the household, prophylaxis should be offered to family members by their private physician. This also applies to all members of a preschool or day-care class. The dosage of rifampin for children is 20 mg/kg orally for 4 days.[9]

When an exposure such as that described for the patient in the case history occurs, the nursing supervisor on duty when the exposure is discovered is usually responsible for collecting the names of *all* exposed medical, nursing, and other personnel. These persons can then be instructed to check their type of exposure against the high- or low-risk list available in the institution's infection control manual, which is available on every nursing unit, and to indicate into which category they fall. The names of those with high-risk exposures are then given to the infection control practitioner, who requests prescriptions for rifampin from the employee health service physician or the infectious disease resident on call. The infection control practitioner reminds the hospital pharmacist to hand out a list of "warnings" provided by the infection control office with each filled prescription (Table 10-5).[10]

This approval procedure provides a safeguard for personnel who tend to panic when informed of an exposure to meningococcal meningitis. Previous to the implementation of such a procedure, it was not unusual to find 15 or more persons being given prescriptions by frightened house staff, many of whom had only a minimal exposure, such as bringing supplies into the patient's room.[11] In some instances, pregnant staff were given rifampin and other employees had to replace contact lenses that had turned permanently orange because they were not told to remove them before taking the drug.

Contacts who are not considered to have had high-risk exposures, or those who cannot or do not want to take rifampin, should be told to report at once to a physician or the employee health service if these signs or symptoms appear:

- Upper respiratory tract infection, including pharyngitis
- Fever
- Headache or malaise
- Nausea or vomiting
- Lethargy or confusion
- Stiff neck or petechiae

The 19 exposures that occurred in the case history are described in Table 10-6. Most of them could have been avoided if emergency department physicians and nurses had maintained a high index of suspicion for meningitis, in view of the fever and confusion manifested by the patient. All that would have been required at the time was the wearing of a mask. Avoiding exposures prevents unnecessary anxiety for personnel. Exposures require many hours of contact

---

Table 10-5 Warnings and Contraindications to Rifampin Prophylaxis

---

Pregnancy
Wearing of soft contact lenses (rifampin will discolor them)
Gastrointestinal discomfort
Efficacy of other medications
    Oral contraceptives (for whole month)
    Anticoagulants
    Others (consult personal physician)

Table 10-6 Number and Typical Exposures Sustained During Care of Patient Prior to Institution of Respiratory Isolation

Professional Category	Type of Exposure	Rifampin Indicated
Emergency Department		
1. Resident house officer #1	Examined patient, including fundoscopy	Yes
2. R.N. #1	Took blood pressure, temperature, and pulse and checked respiratory rate	Yes
3. Unit secretary	Placed wristband on patient	No
4. Pediatric resident #2	Started intravenous drip, took blood for culture and sensitivity, etc.	No
5. Orderly	Obtained urine specimen; transported patient to pediatrics	No
Pediatric Unit		
6. R.N. #1	Took blood pressure, assisted patient with nausea/vomiting, placed Swan-Ganz catheter	Yes
7. Private medical doctor	Talked to mother in room	No
8. Fellow in neurology	Performed spinal tap	No
9. Respiratory therapist	Applied Venti-mask	No
10. R.N. #2	Assisted first R.N., changed soiled linen, put up piggyback intravenous lines	No
11. Nurse's aide	Brought equipment into room	No
12. Phlebotomist	Took blood culture	No
13. Radiology technician #1	Took chest roentgenogram	No
14. Orderly	Transported patient to intensive care unit	No
15. Patient (roommate)	Was in room with patient for several hours	Yes
16. Maid	Cleaned room after patient was transported to intensive care unit	No
Intensive Care Unit		
17. R.N. #1 R.N. #2	Took blood pressure and monitored central venous pressure and arterial blood gases	Yes
18. Respiratory therapist	Administered oxygen	No
19. Medical resident #1	Performed spinal tap	No
20. Medical resident #2	Performed frequent physical examinations	Yes
21. Infectious disease fellow	Looked at patient	No

investigation by the infection control practitioner and are thus a waste of valuable time. In addition, rifampin is an expensive drug, and it is much more cost effective for personnel to wear a mask than to have to take the drug.

CONCLUSIONS

A significant number of intensive care personnel are exposed annually to bacterial meningitis because the condition may go unrecognized and precautionary measures are not taken. Although postexposure prophylaxis in the form of rifampin is available for meningococcal and *H. influenzae* meningitis, the drug is not innocuous and produces undesirable side effects. It is, therefore, important that physicians and nurses be familiar with the early manifestations of meningitis and maintain a high index of suspicion for the disease. It is equally important that simple protective measures, such as the use of masks, are instituted on suspicion, not after a diagnosis is made. When exposure has occurred, appropriate warnings must be issued along with the rifampin for prophylaxis.

REFERENCES

1. Centers for Disease Control. Guidelines for Isolation Precautions in Hospitals. Atlanta, 1983.

2. Oill PA, Yoshikawa TT, Yamauchi T. Infectious disease emergencies: I. Patients presenting with an altered state of consciousness in infectious disease emergencies. Teaching Conference, University of California. West J Med 1976;125:36.

3. Apicella MA. *Neisseria meningitidis*. In Mandell GL, Douglas RG, Bennett JE (eds). Principles and Practice of Infectious Disease, 2nd ed. New York: John Wiley & Sons, 1979.

4. Fishman RA. Cerebrospinal fluid. Diseases of the Nervous System. Philadelphia: W.B. Saunders, 1980.

5. Clayton MT, Scheld WM. The central nervous system: Infections with *Neisseria meningitidis* and *Haemophilus influenzae*. In Gurevich I, Tafuro P, Cunha BA (eds). The Theory and Practice of Infection Control. New York: Praeger Scientific, 1984.

6. Yoshikawa TT. Meningitis and encephalitis. In Yoshikawa TT, Chow AW, Guze LB (eds). Infectious Diseases, Diagnosis and Management. Boston: Houghton Mifflin, 1980.

7. Powers WJ. Cerebrospinal fluid to serum glucose ratios in diabetes mellitus and bacterial meningitis. Am J Med 1981;71:217.

8. Advisory Committee on Immunization Practices (ACIP). Meningococcal disease—United States. MMWR 1981;30:113–115.

9. Daum RS, Glode MP, Goldman DA, et al. Rifampin chemoprophylaxis for household contacts of patients with invasive *H. influenzae* type b. J Pediatr 1981;98:485.

10. ACIP. Update—Prevention of *Haemophilus influenzae* type b disease. MMWR 1986;35:172.

11. Gurevich I. Transmissible infections in critical care. Heart Lung 1988;17:331–334.

CHAPTER REVIEW QUESTIONS

1. Patients should be placed on Respiratory Isolation if they are suspected of having meningitis due to
    a. *Mycobacterium tuberculosis* or *Staphylococcus aureus*
    b. *Hemophilus influenzae* or *Neisseria meningitidis*
    c. Herpes simplex or *Cryptococcus*
    d. All of the above

2. A patient admitted with acute onset of confusion and a high temperature should be placed on Respiratory Isolation until one of the following has been ruled out
    a. Meningitis
    b. Cerebrovascular accident
    c. Varicella pneumonia
    d. Herpes encephalitis

3. The cerebrospinal fluid sample of a patient admitted with r/o meningitis shows the following:
    Opening pressure: 210 nm H_2O
    Clear fluid
    Protein: 40 mg/dL
    Glucose: 90 mg/dL
    White blood cells: 210/cu mm, 90% polymorphonuclear neutrophils
    Gram stain negative
    According to the above findings, the patient is most likely to have
    a. Cerebrovascular accident
    b. Viral meningitis
    c. Bacterial meningitis

4. The Gram stain in the list in question 3 may be negative because
    a. Viruses do not show up on Gram stain
    b. There may be too few organisms to be detected on Gram stain

5. Which type of meningitis is transmitted by air?
    a. Cryptococcal
    b. Viral
    c. Meningococcal
    d. All of the above

Answers are provided in Appendix B.

Part III

Special Aspects: Infection Control, Critical Care, and the Pregnant Nurse

Pregnant nurses and their special concerns are discussed in Chapter 11. The infections discussed include not only those that can be acquired in the workplace but also those that are more likely to originate in the home or community. Toxoplasmosis, listeriosis, and fifth disease are three examples.

In Chapter 12 the special relationship between critical care nurses and infection control practitioners is examined. Precautionary measures and various approaches to isolation of infectious patients are compared and related to the epidemiologic aspects of infectious diseases.

Chapter 11

Pregnancy and the Risk of Infection

The degree of risk pregnant nurses face when caring for patients with infection is the cause of some controversy. Infection control personnel are often consulted when a nurse declines an assignment to care for patients with tuberculosis, meningitis, hepatitis, AIDS, and gastrointestinal or wound infections. Administrators seek justification for such refusals in view of the fact that physicians continue their practice during pregnancy. They are also concerned about the significant impact repeated reassignment of pregnant nurses may have on non-pregnant staff.

In order to enable employers and employees to resolve these issues, three questions must be examined.

1. Does pregnancy itself heighten a woman's susceptibility to infection?
2. Can precautionary measures adequately protect pregnant nurses, and their fetuses, from a patient's infection?
3. If an inadvertent exposure should occur, is postexposure prophylaxis effective and safe during pregnancy?

It is impossible to guarantee that any physician or nurse can be totally protected from exposure to infection in the hospital. Such exposures are inherent in the health care setting. Therefore, any woman who has made the decision to continue with her work during pregnancy may have to accept that risk. Most nurses are willing to accept a certain amount of risk for themselves but are understandably less willing to accept the potential of an adverse effect for their fetuses.

Maternal infections may manifest in several ways and can have a variety of outcomes. They may

- Be asymptomatic and inapparent with no discernible effect on mother or fetus

- Be asymptomatic or have an insignificant effect on the mother but have an adverse effect on the fetus or newborn
- Produce significantly greater morbidity or mortality in a woman during pregnancy, with or without adverse outcome for the fetus

In addition, therapeutic interventions for maternal infection may also have detrimental effects on the fetus. Nurses may, of course, transfer to an area that they consider "safer" within the hospital, but infections that affect the fetus can also be encountered in the community. As a matter of fact, some of the most serious congenital infections are not likely to be transmitted nosocomially at all. Toxoplasmosis is one example; listeriosis is another. In addition, many perinatal infections are caused by the mother's own flora, which become opportunistic pathogens during pregnancy and delivery. Common maternal infections and their likely source of acquisition are listed in Table 11-1.

The second question of whether pregnant health care personnel can protect themselves from their patient's infection cannot be answered with a yes or no. Precautionary measures are intended to interrupt transmission of infections, and the pathogens involved do not change their mode of spread to pregnant women. After all, if precautions are not effective for pregnant women, the implication would be that they are not effective for others. The difference lies in the human factor. Nurses and physicians become careless at times, and a few occasionally acquire infections from their patients. A pregnant nurse or physician cannot afford to ever become careless because not only may she suffer more serious consequences during pregnancy but the infection may also adversely affect the fetus. Therefore, a woman must know herself and honestly assess the likelihood that she will always follow all prescribed precautions. Otherwise, she has no place in patient care during her pregnancy.

PREGNANCY AS A RISK FACTOR

The answer to the question whether pregnancy increases the risk of infection for the mother is yes and no. Pregnancy itself does not make it more likely that a woman will acquire an infection from a patient if she takes the appropriate precautionary measures. However, if a woman is immune to an infection because she had the disease or the disease-specific vaccine, she is no more likely to get it again than any other immune person. There are other differences however. One difference is the degree of effect infections have during pregnancy, and the other is the potential effect on the fetus. These differences were already well known in the days before vaccines were discovered. Smallpox, polio, and influenza did not affect a greater number of pregnant women, but when a woman became infected during pregnancy these infections were more serious and the

Table 11-1 Organisms of Concern During Pregnancy and the Most Likely Setting for Their Acquisition

Organisms	Nosocomial Acquisition	Community Acquired	Normal Flora
Bacteria other than those listed individually	Rare		X
Candida			X
Chlamydia		X	
Coxsackievirus A and B	Rare	X	
Cytomegalovirus	Rare	X	Reactivated
Echovirus	Possible	X	
Enterovirus	Possible	X	
Escherichia coli and other Enterobacteriaceae	Unlikely		X
Group B hemolytic *Streptococcus*			X
Hepatitis A, B, non-A, non-B viruses	Rare	X	
Herpes simplex virus	Rare	X	Reactivated
Human immunodeficiency virus (AIDS)	Rare	X	
Influenza virus	Possible	X	
Listeria		X	X
Measles, mumps viruses	Possible	X	
Meningitis: meningococcal, *Hemophilus influenzae*	Rare	X	
Mycobacterium tuberculosis (pulmonary infection)	X	X	Reactivated
Neisseria gonorrhoeae		X	
Parvovirus B19 (fifth disease)	Unlikely	X	
Pneumocystis carinii		X	Reactivated
Rubella virus	X	X	
Toxoplasma		X	Reactivated
Treponema pallidum (syphilis)		X	
Varicella-zoster virus	X	X	Reactivated (shingles)

mortality rates were higher in pregnant than in nonpregnant women.[1-3] There may be many other examples. And in the past few years, evidence has emerged showing that pregnancy, itself, may indeed increase the risk of acquisition for some infections. One example is listeriosis, which rarely causes infections in nonpregnant young women but increasingly affects those who are pregnant.

As far as the second difference is concerned, many infections are recognized as having the potential for causing serious congenital infections, even though the effect on the mother may be minimal. Toxoplasmosis, cytomegalovirus, and hepatitis B are the most frequent of these.

These problematic infections will all be discussed, but first of all it is important to understand why a pregnant woman is more susceptible to certain infections, and this in turn requires reexamination of the human immune system.

PREGNANCY AND THE MATERNAL IMMUNE SYSTEM

Of the three broad components of the immune system, two are not known to be affected by pregnancy. They are the phagocytic-inflammatory response and the humoral or B-lymphocyte–mediated systems. For example, a woman who has had chickenpox will remain immune during pregnancy, as will a pregnant woman who had measles or rubella vaccine. In addition, this type of antibody-dependent maternal immunity will be transferred to, and protective for, the fetus in the form of IgG.

The story is different for the third component, the cell-mediated immune system that is controlled by the T lymphocytes. As discussed in detail in Chapter 2, this system is responsible for detecting and destroying "foreign" or nonself antigens within the body. Cell-mediated immunity is also responsible for mounting delayed hypersensitivity reactions to some previously encountered substances (e.g., *M. tuberculosis*). Foreign antigens include not only bacteria, viruses and fungi, but also tumor cells and "nonself" allografts.

At pregnancy, the immune system encounters such an allograft in the form of a fetus, which contains paternal "antigens" that are "foreign" to the mother's T cells. The question arises why this foreign substance is not rejected by the mother's cell-mediated immune system as other allografts would be. Studies seem to confirm that tolerance of the fetal allograft may be mediated by a variety of factors that suppress the maternal immune response, especially the T-cell–mediated immune system.[4] Among the factors studied were decreases in the number of helper T cells, production of IgG antibody against HLA-D/DR antigens, ability of certain hormones to become immunosuppressive, and release of fetal lymphocyte inhibiting factors.

Many of the infections listed in Table 11-1 may be encountered more frequently during pregnancy and other immunosuppressive states, while others may increase the morbidity or mortality rate during pregnancy or may increase the risk of intrauterine or perinatal infection for the fetus. Also shown in the table are the most likely sources of the pathogens, whether nosocomial, in the community, or from the woman's own "normal flora."

An example of "normal flora" as a potential pathogen is the group B β-hemolytic *Streptococcus*. It does not cause maternal infections but can severely affect the infant. Another example of a mother's own organism-induced problem is reactivation of a latent cytomegalovirus infection. As pregnancy progresses, shedding of this virus becomes more common, ranging from 1.6% in the first trimester to 13.5% in the third trimester.[5] Reactivation is a likely result of the increasing suppression of cell-mediated immunity with advancing pregnancy. Therefore, the answer to the question of whether pregnancy itself heightens the risk of infection is yes, but only for certain infections.

IMMUNITY AND VACCINE SAFETY DURING PREGNANCY

The most protective of all measures is immunity against disease. All adults, but especially health care workers, should be vaccinated against vaccine-preventable infections. Prior to becoming pregnant, women should discuss their immune status with their private physician and update vaccinations and boosters as needed. Thus, no female critical care nurse or physician should be susceptible to rubella, diphtheria, mumps, measles, poliomyelitis, or tetanus. Hepatitis B vaccine is also available and safe, and, when possible, vaccination should be completed or at least begun prior to pregnancy.[6] Exposure to these infections should therefore present no problem, and discussion in this chapter is concerned mainly with infections listed in Table 11-1, for which there is no immunity and for which there may be nosocomial transmission. A list of safe and unsafe vaccines is presented in Table 11-2.

RISKS FROM PATIENT EXPOSURES

Cytomegalovirus

The prevalence of cytomegalovirus (CMV) antibody, denoting a previous infection in the adult population of the western world, is between 40% and 90%. This means that by the time a woman reaches childbearing age she may already have been infected with CMV. Most often this infection was asymptomatic, but occasionally it may have presented as mononucleosis-like symptoms. It is usually difficult to establish where such an infection was acquired,[7] but the virus is shed for prolonged periods of time in saliva, urine, and vaginal secretions. In congenitally infected infants and immunosuppressed patients, the virus may be shed for 2 years or more, even though the child or adult may be asymptomatic. It is almost impossible to prevent acquisition of the virus during a lifetime, but except during pregnancy or other periods of immunosuppression CMV infection is of little consequence. Unfortunately, CMV is the most common virus known to be transmitted in utero.[8] And when it is, it can be responsible for some of the most devastating of the congenital infections, involve every organ system, and cause profound central nervous system abnormalities (Table 11-3).[9]

Table 11-2 Vaccinations and Immunoglobulins During Pregnancy

Immunizing Agent	Risk from Disease to Pregnant Female	Risk from Disease to Fetus or Neonate	Type of Immunizing Agent	Risk from Immunizing Agent to Fetus	Indications for Immunizing during Pregnancy	Comments
Hepatitis B virus	Possible increased severity during third trimester	Possible increase in abortion rate and prematurity. Perinatal transmission may occur if mother is a chronic carrier or is acutely infected	Inactivated hepatitis B vaccine	None reported	Indications for prophylaxis not altered by pregnancy	Infants born to HBsAg-positive mothers should receive 0.5 mL HBIG as soon as possible after birth, plus 0.5 mL hepatitis B vaccine within 1 week of birth. Vaccine should be repeated at 1 and 6 months
			Hepatitis B immune globulin (HBIG)	None reported	Postexposure prophylaxis	
Hepatitis A virus	Possible increased severity during third trimester	Probable increase in abortion rate and prematurity; possible transmission to neonate at delivery if mother is incubating the virus or is acutely ill at that time	Pooled immune globulin (IG)	None reported	Postexposure prophylaxis	IG should be given as soon as possible and within 2 weeks of exposure. Infants born of mothers who are incubating the virus or are acutely ill at delivery should receive 1 dose of 0.5 mL as soon as possible after birth

Influenza virus	Possible increase in morbidity and mortality during epidemic or with new antigenic strain	Possible increased abortion rate; no malformations confirmed	Inactivated type A and type B virus vaccines	None confirmed	Usually recommended only for patients with serious underlying diseases; public health authorities to be consulted for current recommendation	Criteria for vaccination of pregnant women same as for all adults
Measles virus	Significant morbidity, low mortality; not altered by pregnancy	Significant increase in abortion rate; may cause malformations	Live, attenuated virus vaccine	None confirmed	Contraindicated	Vaccination of susceptible women should be part of postpartum care
			Pooled immune globulin (IG)	None reported	Postexposure prophylaxis	Unclear if it prevents abortion; must be given within 6 days of exposure
Meningococcus	No increased risk during pregnancy; no increase in severity of disease	Unknown	Killed-bacteria vaccine	No data available on use during pregnancy	Indications not altered by pregnancy; vaccination recommended only in unusual outbreak situations	

Table 11-2 continued

Immunizing Agent	Risk from Disease to Pregnant Female	Risk from Disease to Fetus or Neonate	Type of Immunizing Agent	Risk from Immunizing Agent to Fetus	Indications for Immunizing during Pregnancy	Comments
Mumps virus	Low morbidity and mortality; not altered by pregnancy	Possible increased rate of abortion in first trimester. Questionable association of fibroblastosis in neonates	Live, attenuated virus vaccine	None confirmed	Contraindicated	
Pneumococcus	No increased risk during pregnancy; no increase in severity of disease	Unknown	Polyvalent polysaccharide vaccine	No data available on use during pregnancy	Indications not altered by pregnancy; vaccine used only for high-risk populations	

| Poliovirus | No increased incidence in pregnancy, but may be more severe if it does occur | Anoxic fetal damage reported; 50% mortality in neonatal disease | Live attenuated virus (OPV) and inactivated (IPV) vaccine | None confirmed | Not routinely recommended for adults in United States, except persons at increased risk of exposure | Vaccine indicated (IPV) for susceptible pregnant women traveling in endemic areas or in other high-risk situations |
| Rubella virus | Low morbidity and mortality; not altered by pregnancy | High rate of abortion and congenital rubella syndrome | Live attenuated virus vaccine | None confirmed | Contraindicated | Teratogenicity of vaccine is theoretically not confirmed to date; vaccination of susceptible women should be part of postpartum care |

Source: Adapted from *Morbidity and Mortality Weekly Report* (1984;33(S)). September 1984, U.S. Centers for Disease Control.

Table 11-3 The Range of Manifestation for Congenital Cytomegalovirus Infection from Mild to Severe

Learning disabilities	Multiorgan, multisystem dysfunction
Hearing loss	Microcephaly
Delay in psychomotor development	Hydrocephaly
Chorioretinitis	Premature birth
Seizures, spasticity	Stillbirth
Cerebral calcification	

Studies show that the risk of congenital infection is greatest during a primary or first-time maternal infection. However, recurrent or reactivated disease can also cause fetal CMV infection and can do so in consecutive pregnancies of the same woman (Figure 11-1).[8,10,11]

One to 2% of all newborns are infected with CMV. They may be totally asymptomatic at birth, but virus may be present in tears, saliva, urine, and all

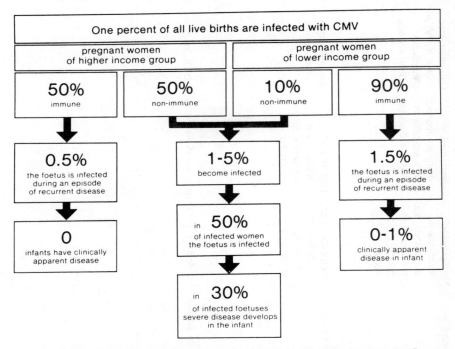

Figure 11-1 The effects of primary and reactivated cytomegalovirus infection in pregnancy. *Source:* Reprinted from *An Introduction to Herpes Infections* (p 44) by GOW McKendrick and S Sutherland with permission of The Wellcome Foundation Ltd, © 1983.

other body fluids. Shedding from urine and saliva may continue for years. Cytomegalic inclusion disease affects 0.5% to 0.1% of all newborns, and usually these infants are symptomatic at birth.

The risk of CMV acquisition in health care workers of childbearing age has been studied extensively. More recently, the frequency of CMV in the day-care center population and the risk of transmission to other children and the teachers has also been investigated as a source for bringing CMV into the home and thus infecting a pregnant mother.

A study of health care workers in high-risk settings such as the nursery and intensive care units reported CMV IgG antibody rates of 41% to 78% in the staff. The presence of CMV IgG denotes past infection, and as expected the higher rate of 78% was found in those 35 years of age and older. Age-adjusted prevalence rates were no higher for nurses in high-risk areas than in low-risk areas.[12]

The annual conversion rate from seronegative to seropositive, indicating primary CMV infection, was examined in another study. Results showed that the annual attack rate for medical students was 0.6%, that for house staff was 2.7%, and that for nurses was 3.3%. These rates were lower than those in young women in the community: 2.5% during pregnancy and 5.5% between pregnancies.[13] Other studies have supported these findings.[14] In studies of five day-care centers, the percentage of children who had CMV in their saliva or urine ranged from 9% to 49%, and their caretakers showed a 50% to 100% seropositivity. Therefore, mothers are at some risk of CMV acquisition from children who attend these centers.[15]

Prevention of Nosocomial Acquisition

There is no conclusive evidence that work-related CMV infection in hospitals occurs any more frequently than that of community-acquired infection.[16–18] In all the literature, in only one study were data presented that contradicted these findings.[19]

One approach would be for pregnant health care workers to be tested for CMV antibody at the beginning of pregnancy. Although this is not universally recommended, a woman who is seronegative and pregnant and who is working in a pediatric or neonatal intensive care unit might consider transfer to a setting where she will have no contact with children who may be shedding the virus. However, this does not ensure lack of acquisition from other persons who may be shedding CMV. Other sources could include her own children, relatives, friends, or spouse.

In view of all the foregoing discussion of possible sources and modes of CMV acquisition and reactivation there cannot be any foolproof method or recommendation about how to avoid infection with CMV. There is just no guarantee that hospital- or community-based contact with CMV can be avoided. There is, however, consensus among previously cited authors and the Centers for Disease Control that the wearing of gloves for contact with any patient's body fluids, especially urine (and contact with diapers) and saliva, and careful handwashing offer the best protection in the hospital setting and that a known shedder should be brought to the attention of pregnant staff.[20] An additional safeguard is to avoid touching one's own mucous membranes (eyes, nose, mouth) with unwashed hands because environmental contamination with CMV has been demonstrated.[21-23]

Although the virus is known to be present in the respiratory secretions of some patients, airborne spread has not been investigated, nor is it a likely mode of spread. In patients who require ventilatory assistance there is the theoretical possibility of virus transmission to someone who is intubating or suctioning such a patient and who may be spattered with the patient's saliva. Therefore, the observance of Universal Precautions, which includes protecting the eyes, nose, and mouth, is of great importance, especially during pregnancy, if contact with a patient's body fluids is a possibility.

Prophylaxis

Research into a vaccine against CMV infection is inconclusive.[24] As with all the herpes viruses, antibody is not protective against reinfection or reactivation and much work must still be done. There is no postexposure prophylaxis against CMV, and prevention in the workplace is the only modality of protection available.

Herpes Simplex

Although congenital herpes simplex infection is rare, perinatal infection can occur during labor, delivery, and thereafter if the parturient is shedding the virus at that time. Since genital herpes is not a nosocomially acquired infection, a reminder to wear gloves for contact with any patient's body fluids should be sufficient. Herpes simplex type 1 or type 2 can infect all parts of the body, and health care workers should never touch any part of themselves, especially their mucous membranes, with unwashed hands. Work restriction or transfer to "safer" areas is not advocated for the prevention of herpesvirus infections during pregnancy, and there is no postexposure prophylaxis.

Human Immunodeficiency Virus

The potential for intrauterine infection and perinatal acquisition of the virus(es) that cause AIDS (HIV-1 and HIV-2 and probably others yet to be identified) is well known. Nosocomial transmission of HIV-1 has occurred and is discussed in Chapter 4. There remains only the difficult task of presenting the data in perspective with the three questions asked at the beginning of this chapter.

Question 1: Does pregnancy itself heighten a woman's susceptibility to infection? Coincidentally, the T-cell–mediated immune system, which is already suppressed in pregnancy, is also the target of HIV. However, increased susceptibility itself does not heighten the risk for HIV infection. To become infected, a person must first come in contact with the virus, as with any pathogen, in such a way that it is able to find a portal of entry into the body. As far as HIV is concerned, once it has entered a body it does not discriminate between persons whose cell-mediated immune system is competent or incompetent. So, the answer to the question of whether pregnancy itself heightens a woman's susceptibility to HIV acquisition, is *no*.

Question 2: Can precautionary measures adequately protect pregnant women from nosocomial infection with the AIDS virus? Precautionary measures also do not discriminate between pregnant and nonpregnant personnel. If transfer to a safer environment were advisable, the implications would be (1) that there is a safer environment within a hospital and (2) that precautions are not adequate and that nonpregnant personnel are thus also not protected. Since any patient could be harboring the virus, any patient contact would be unsafe.

It is true, however, that outside the hospital the risk of acquiring HIV is lower if the person, pregnant or not, does not indulge in high-risk behavior. So, if a nurse decides to continue to care for patients, although the risk is low, it is still higher than for persons who do not have contact with any person's blood or body fluids and who are therefore not at risk for accidental needlesticks or other untoward exposures.

The Centers for Disease Control states that because of the special risk to the fetus, pregnant health care workers should be especially familiar with and strictly adhere to Universal Precautions to minimize the risk of HIV transmission.[25,26]

Meningitis

Acquisition and severity of meningitis does not differ in pregnant women from nonpregnant persons. Risk to the fetus is not known or described. There is no contraindication to caring for patients with meningococcal or *Hemophilus influenzae* meningitis if respiratory isolation precautions are observed. The early warning signs for meningitis, and patients who are at high risk for such infection, are discussed in Chapter 10, as are the precautionary measures. Meningitis is specially mentioned in this chapter only to warn health care workers that pregnancy is a contraindication to taking rifampin prophylaxis.[27] Should exposure occur, any upper respiratory tract symptoms as well as malaise, nausea, vomiting, headache, and fevers should be reported to a physician at once. These manifestations could occur up to 10 days after exposure. Waiting until more specific manifestations appear, such as nuchal rigidity or petechiae, is dangerous. It is then up to the physician to decide whether antimicrobial therapy is indicated.

Tuberculosis

A pregnant worker faces the same risks as her co-workers for acquiring nosocomial tuberculosis. There is some difference of opinion, however, about the effect pregnancy may have on the prognosis of already existing active disease. Because of the importance of cell-mediated immunity on containment of tuberculosis there is also controversy on the likelihood of reactivation of latent disease during pregnancy.[28] Neither of the above conditions is nosocomial and therefore not pertinent to this chapter. However, questions are asked occasionally about the safety of tuberculin skin tests during pregnancy. Pregnancy is not a contraindication to skin testing and has no bearing on past BCG vaccination.[29] There is also no evidence that the PPD test is any less accurate in pregnancy than otherwise, even though there is a well-documented decrease in cell-mediated immunity.[4] Any pregnant health care worker who has been exposed to pulmonary tuberculosis should therefore be tested if she is a previously negative reactor. Tuberculosis poses a possible risk to the fetus and a serious risk to the newborn and should be identified by all possible means.

Transmission and Prevention

Tuberculosis is an airborne disease, and the wearing of masks during patient care is protective. Both pregnant and nonpregnant personnel must be aware of patients who are at high risk for having or developing tuberculosis. They must maintain a high index of suspicion for early disease manifestations so that they can adequately protect themselves (see Chapter 7).

Although recent converters, or those who show an increase of more than 5 mm of induration after an exposure, are at greatest risk of developing active disease within the next 1 to 2 years, it may be advisable to delay prophylaxis with isoniazid until after delivery. The exception, according to the American Thoracic Society, is "for pregnant women who may have been recently infected: in that situation, isoniazid preventive therapy should begin when the infection is documented but after the first trimester."[30] The American Thoracic Society also recommends two- or three-drug treatment regimens if active tuberculosis has been diagnosed. Such therapy must be discussed with the patient's physician and obstetrician.

Varicella and Zoster

Chickenpox is generally a comparatively benign disease in immunocompetent children. In contrast, adults are often sicker and complications such as encephalitis and pneumonia are more severe. Pregnant women seem to be at greatest risk of varicella pneumonia. In one study, 4 of 43 pregnant women with varicella developed pneumonia. Two of these (50%) required ventilatory assistance, and one woman died.[31] Whether this increased risk of varicella pneumonia is due to depression of the cell-mediated immune system that accompanies pregnancy, decreased respiratory efficiency from the enlarged uterus, or other factors is not known. Women who smoke are at even higher risk for this complication. In addition, about 10% of infants develop congenital anomalies ranging from chorioretinitis to limb hypoplasia and cortical atrophy if the mother was infected in the first trimester.[31,32]

The risk for neonatal acquisition of maternal varicella is greatest when the maternal rash appears 5 days before delivery to 2 days after the infant is born, because maternal antibody has not had time to be transferred transplacentally to protect the neonate at that time.[33] Perinatal infection carries a fatality rate of about 31%. Frequently the cause of death is pneumonia or visceral involvement.[32,34]

Transmission and Prevention

Varicella and disseminated zoster are highly contagious. Both airborne spread and acquisition from vesicular fluid is likely. This is one infectious disease against which protective measures such as masks and gloves may not be effective. Even localized zoster, which is not usually airborne, may present a problem in the hospital setting. Aerosolization from uncovered lesions could occur especially during bedmaking. Therefore, all hospital personnel, but especially women who intend to become pregnant and who have not had chickenpox or shingles, should undergo serologic testing to determine their susceptibility status. Appropriate tests are fluorescent antibody to membrane antigen (FAMA), immune adherence hemagglutination (IAH), and enzyme-linked immunoabsorbent assay (ELISA). Those who are not immune should avoid contact with patients who have varicella-zoster.[20] It may even be advisable to transfer from a high-risk pediatric or adult intensive care or oncology unit for the duration of the pregnancy. A vaccine is being considered for licensure in the United States.

Postexposure Immunoglobulin Prophylaxis

Inadvertent exposure to varicella-zoster virus can occur both in the hospital and in the home or the community. It is important to remember that infectivity precedes the rash by 2 days. Varicella-zoster immune globulin (VZIG) is a readily available preparation for preventing, or at least modifying, varicella infections. Criteria for administering VZIG include pregnant women and newborns of mothers who had onset of chickenpox less than 5 to 6 days before or less than 2 days after delivery. It is important to administer the immune globulin within 96 hours of exposure.[35] A vial of VZIG costs about $75, and for an average-weight adult up to five vials may be required.

RISKS FROM COMMUNITY EXPOSURES

There are two other infections that although they are not nosocomially acquired, are of great risk during pregnancy and therefore deserve inclusion in this chapter. They are listeriosis and toxoplasmosis.

Listeriosis

Listeria monocytogenes is a gram-positive bacillus originally found in nature that has long been known to cause disease in animals and humans. However, it has become an important human pathogen in recent years. It is an intracellular pathogen, and as such it is most likely to cause severe disease, especially meningitis, in persons whose cell-mediated immune system is compromised. Over the years, the number of those who are immunosuppressed, including the elderly, has increased and so have *L. monocytogenes* carriage and infections. Among pregnant women a 20% to 30% intestinal carriage has been reported, whereas in the rest of the population carriage is about 5%.[36]

Since 1980, there has been increasing evidence that *L. monocytogenes* is a foodborne organism. Raw vegetables such as cabbage and celery have been implicated in outbreaks, but most foodborne outbreaks have been linked to milk and milk products, including ice cream and cheese. On several occasions, brie cheese, both domestic and imported, has been found to be contaminated.[37,38]

Maternal and Perinatal Infections

There is a well-documented association between *Listeria* infection and pregnancy. In the mother, the disease can be mild and manifest as gastrointestinal disease. Flulike symptoms, high fever with bacteremia, and genital tract infections have also been reported.[39] Congenitally acquired listeriosis may lead to stillbirth or an early-onset pneumonia within the first week of life. There may be widespread microabscesses, central nervous system disorders, and pustular skin eruptions. Mortality approaches 50%. In late-onset disease, probably acquired perinatally, meningitis may be present at 2 or 3 weeks of age.[37] Treatment of neonatal infection is often, but not always, successful.[40-42]

Prevention

Many obstetricians are advising their pregnant patients to avoid eating soft cheeses during pregnancy. The most important advice is to obtain prompt treatment for any febrile illness suggestive of listeriosis. Meconium of potentially infected neonates should be Gram stained and, if positive, cultured. Prophylactic antibiotics should be administered.[37] There is no documented person-to-person transmission except from mother to fetus or newborn, but handwashing prior to eating or preparing food is always advisable.

Toxoplasmosis

Toxoplasma gondii is a parasite that causes infections in animals and humans. Prevalence rates are about 30% in the United States and significantly higher in Europe and third world countries. In most adult immunocompetent hosts, the disease is asymptomatic or mild with occasional posterior cervical lymphadenopathy or mononucleosis-like manifestations. Only rarely is there involvement of the lungs, heart, liver, or central nervous system. Once infected, the parasite remains within the body for life, where it can reactivate during periods of immunosuppression, including pregnancy. In immunosuppressed persons toxoplasmosis causes increased morbidity and a higher mortality rate.

Pregnancy and Congenital Infection

Primary toxoplasmosis, like cytomegalovirus and other infections, can cause a wide range of congenital infections, even though maternal symptoms were absent or mild.[43] Of special interest are the findings that the severity of congenital involvement can be predicted with some certainty in relationship to the trimester of the mother's primary infection. The risk of congenital infection is greatest (65%) if maternal infection occurs in the third trimester. Stillbirth or perinatal death, however, occurs more frequently if maternal toxoplasmosis is acquired in the first trimester.[44]

Infected infants may be asymptomatic at birth and remain unaffected or may develop blindness, epilepsy, and mental retardation later in life. Those that are severely affected and survive (about 30%) will present with chorioretinitis, intracranial calcifications, and neurologic deficits.

Diagnosis is made by paired (acute and convalescent) titers in the mother (IgG) or by isolation of *Toxoplasma* from the placenta. In the infant, the second antibody test should be done after passively transferred maternal antibody titers have waned, to differentiate between maternal and infant antibody.

Transmission and Prevention

The parasite has a complicated life cycle. It is not transmitted person to person, except from mother to fetus, because it requires maturation in the gastrointestinal tract of the cat. Asymptomatic animals harbor the parasite, which may be ingested by a cat along with the infected bird, mouse, or other animal. The parasite multiplies within the cat's intestine and is then excreted for 10 or more days in the form of an oocyst. Cats usually do not shed these oocysts from repeat infections, only after primary encounters. Two to 4 days after excretion, the oocysts mature. They each contain eight sporozoites or infectious parasites. They can survive for months in soil and sand (sandboxes). If these sporozoites are ingested after hand-to-mouth transfer or via infested, undercooked meat from animals who themselves ingested the parasite, they penetrate the intestinal wall, disseminate through the vascular system, and multiply within penetrated tissue. Eventually, the body's immune system will cause encystation and these cysts will remain in the host for life.[45]

Prior to and during pregnancy, preventive measures include the following:

1. Indoor cats should be fed only well-cooked meats or cat food.
2. Close contact with an outdoor cat should be avoided just before and during pregnancy. (Testing a cat is not useful; a positive test may mean only that the cat has been infected at an indeterminate time.)
3. Pregnant women should not change cat litter boxes. Litter boxes should be changed daily because oocysts take 4 days to mature. The litter box should be filled with boiling water and left to stand for 5 minutes or more. *Note:* if a pregnant woman must change the litter, she should wear gloves. Handwashing is *always* recommended after handling a litter box or cat.
4. Gloves should be worn when working with soil in the garden, and home-grown foods should be washed well and thoroughly cooked.
5. Sandboxes should be covered when not in use.
6. Insects should be kept off food and cooking utensils.
7. Undercooked meat can infect humans; therefore, meat should be cooked thoroughly and utensils well cleaned, and hands should then be washed.

Treatment, if required, is available and should be promptly instituted.

Fifth Disease

Fifth disease is worth mentioning because of increasing evidence that it may cause intrauterine infection. The cause is parvovirus type B19, identified in 1975 as one of a group of viruses that are also responsible for infections in animals, such as feline panleukopenia and canine diseases. In immunocompetent humans it is a disease of early childhood. Ten percent of children younger than 5 years of age have antibodies denoting past infection, most of which will have been silent or inapparent or mild. By age 18 years, 35% have antibodies, and adults have a 50% prevalence rate.[46]

Clinical Manifestations

In immunocompetent persons, infection presents as a maculopapular rash that blanches on pressure. It begins on the face where the erythematous eruption gives a typical "slapped face" appearance. The rash usually spreads to the extremities but stops at the wrists and ankles. In children, the rash may be very faint and the infection a silent one. Patients may experience coryza and low-grade fever with the rash, which can take up to 80 days to fade. In adults, the rash may be less pronounced, but it often recurs with exertion, emotional stress, and temperature changes. In 60% to 80% of adults there is arthralgia or there is arthritis in the symmetrical joints of the hands, wrists, elbows, knees, or ankles, with intermittent swelling of the fingers. This, too, can recur for extended periods of time, from 4 to 28 days to 4 years in extreme cases.[47] The disease syndrome may mimic rheumatoid arthritis, and other less common manifestations have been reported.[48]

The data on intrauterine infection and its consequences are sparse. Abortions have been documented after acute parvovirus infection and the virus identified in all fetal organs and tissues, but an exact rate of risk has not yet been established.

Transmission and Precautions

In children, fifth disease is extremely contagious and outbreaks in schools and families are common. Adult cases usually occur more sporadically because many adults are already immune. Transmission occurs via the nasopharynx, probably with direct contact, and possibly the virus is airborne and in the urine. The virus was detected in pharyngeal secretions 7 to 10 days after experimental infection in volunteers, but shedding ceased just before the rash appeared, on days 17 and 18 after inoculation.[49] Since the infected person is most contagious during the prodromal period, avoiding contact with patients who have a rash is not necessary because they are no longer shedding the virus. Thus, there is no way to prevent acquisition of the disease in sporadic occurrences. In epidemic situations, avoidance of children who may be incubating the disease (who have not had a previous infection), may possibly be helpful during pregnancy. There is evidence of viremic transmission during the incubation period.

Black children with sickle cell disease who are suffering an aplastic crisis shed the virus at the onset of the rash and for about a week thereafter. It may be advisable for a pregnant woman who works with these children to be tested and to avoid contact with infectious children during pregnancy.

Miscellaneous Infections

Acquisition of other infections from patients with surgical wounds or gastrointestinal infections is preventable. The pathogens involved require a portal of entry into a new host, which can be denied to them by adhering to universally accepted precautionary measures. Wearing the required protective apparel can prevent carriage of these organisms out of the patient's environment.

CONCLUSIONS

Once a pregnant woman has made the decision to continue with her career in a health care setting with patient contact, it would be difficult to find a really "safe" environment into which to transfer. Therefore, she should

- Know her own susceptibility/immunity status
- Update her vaccinations
- Follow all applicable preventive measures
- Avail herself of available postexposure prophylaxis if it is safe to do so during pregnancy

In the final analysis, each woman must make her own decision whether to work and where.

REFERENCES

1. Ledger WJ. Community acquired obstetric infections. In Infection in the Female, 2nd ed. Philadelphia: Lea & Febiger, 1986.

2. Siegel M, Goldberg M. Incidence of poliomyelitis in pregnancy. N Engl J Med 1955;253:841–847.

3. Freeman DW, Barno A. Deaths from Asian influenza associated with pregnancy. Am J Obstet Gynecol 1959;78:1172–1175.

4. Lederman MM. Cell-mediated immunity and pregnancy. Chest 1984;86(3S):6S–9S.

5. Ho M. Cytomegalovirus. In Mandell GL, et al. (eds). Principles and Practice of Infectious Diseases. New York: John Wiley & Sons, 1985.

6. Advisory Committee on Immunization Practices (ACIP). Adult immunization. MMWR 1984;33 (suppl) September.

7. Chandler SH, Alexander ER, Holmes KK. Epidemiology of cytomegalovirus infection in a heterogeneous population of pregnant women. J Infect Dis 1985;152:249–256.

8. Stagno S, Whitley RJ. Herpesvirus infections of pregnancy: I. Cytomegalovirus and Epstein-Barr virus infections. N Engl J Med 1985;313:1270–1274.

9. Zaia JA, Lang DJ. Cytomegalovirus infection of the fetus and neonate. Neurol Clin 1984;2:387–410.

10. Hanshaw JB. Cytomegalovirus. In Remington JS, Klein JO (eds). Infectious Diseases of the Fetus and Newborn Infant. Philadelphia: W.B. Saunders, 1983.

11. Stagno S, Pass RF, Dworsky ME, et al. Congenital cytomegalovirus infection: The relative importance of primary and recurrent maternal infection. N Engl J Med 1982;306:945–949.

12. Lipscomb JA, Linnermann CC, Hurst PF, et al. Prevalence of cytomegalovirus antibody in nursing personnel. Infect Control 1984;5:513–518.

13. Dworsky ME, Welsh K, Cassady G, Stagno S. Occupational risk for primary cytomegalovirus infection among pediatric health care workers. N Engl J Med 1983;309:950–953.

14. Pomeroy C, Englund JA. Cytomegalovirus: Epidemiology and infection control. Am J Infect Control 1987;15:107–119.

15. Centers for Disease Control. Prevalence of CMV excretion from children in 5 day-care centers—Alabama. MMWR 1985;34(4):49–51.

16. Yaeger AS. Longitudinal, serological study of cytomegalovirus infection in nurses and in personnel without patient contact. J Clin Microbiol 1975;2:448–452.

17. Ahlfors K, Ivarsson SA, Johnsson T, Renmaker K. Risk of cytomegalovirus in nurses and congenital infection in their offspring. Acta Pediatr Scand 1981;70:819–823.

18. Adler SP. Nosocomial transmission of cytomegalovirus. Pediatr Infect Dis 1986;5:239–247.

19. Friedman HM, Lewis MR, Nemerofsky DM, Plotkin SA. Acquisition of cytomegalovirus infection among female employees at a pediatric hospital. Pediatr Infect Dis 1984;3:233–235.

20. Centers for Disease Control. Guidelines for infection control in hospital personnel. Infect Control 1983;4(S):326–349.

21. Spector SA. Transmission of cytomegalovirus among infants in hospital: Documented by restriction endonuclease-digestion analysis. Lancet 1983;1:378–381.

22. Faix RG. Survival of cytomegalovirus on environmental surfaces. J Pediatr 1985;106:649–652.

23. Hutto SC, Pass RF. Isolation of cytomegalovirus from toys and hands in a day-care center. Pediatr Res 1985;19:202–217.

24. Plotkin SN, Friedman HM, Fleisher GR, et al. Vaccine-induced prevention of cytomegalovirus disease after renal transplants. Lancet 1984;1:528–530.

25. Centers for Disease Control. Recommendations for assisting in the prevention of perinatal transmission of HIV. MMWR 1985;34:721–726, 731–732.

26. Centers for Disease Control. Recommendations for prevention of HIV transmission in health-care settings. MMWR 1987;36(S):3S–17S.

27. Huber GL. Tuberculosis. In Remington JS, Klein JO (eds). Infectious Diseases of the Fetus and Newborn Infant. Philadelphia: W.B. Saunders, 1983.

28. Snider D. Pregnancy and tuberculosis. Chest 1986;3(suppl):10S–19S.

29. Gillum MD, Maki DG. Brief report: Tuberculin testing, BCG in pregnancy. Infect Control Hosp Epidemiol 1988;9:119–121.

30. American Thoracic Society. Treatment of tuberculosis and tuberculosis infection in adults and children. Am Rev Respir Dis 1986;134:355–363.

31. Paryani SG, Arvin AM. Intrauterine infection with varicella-zoster virus after maternal varicella. N Engl J Med 1986;314:1542–1546.

32. Brunell PA. Fetal and neonatal varicella-zoster infection. Semin Perinatol 1983;7:47–56.

33. Myers JD. Congenital varicella in term infants: Risk considered. J Infect Dis 1974;129:215–218.

34. Preblud SR, Bregman DJ, Vernon LL. Deaths from varicella in infants. Pediatr Infect Dis 1985;4:503–507.

35. Strauss SE (moderator). Varicella-zoster virus infections. Ann Intern Med 1988;108:221–237.

36. Samra Y, Hertz M, Altman G. Adult listeriosis: A review of 18 cases. Postgrad Med J 1984;60:267–269.

37. New York State Department of Health. Listeriosis. In Epidemiology Notes, NY State Department of Health Newsletter 1986;11(1):1–2.

38. Food and Drug Administration. Research on *Listeria monocytogenes*. FDA Drug Bulletin 1987;October:28–29.

39. Brabin BJ. Epidemiology of infection in pregnancy. Rev Infect Dis 1985;7:570–603.

40. Lennon D, Lewis B, Markell C, et al. Epidemic perinatal listeriosis. Pediatr Infect Dis 1984;3:30–34.

41. Evans JR, Allan AC, Stinson DA, et al. Perinatal listeriosis: Report of an outbreak. Pediatr Infect Dis 1985;4:237–241.

42. Sen P, Louria DB. Human listeriosis. Infect Med 1987;4:204–215.

43. Remington JS, Desmonts G. Toxoplasmosis. In Remington JS, Klein JO (eds). Infectious Diseases of the Fetus and Newborn Infant. Philadelphia: W.B. Saunders, 1983.

44. Desmonts G, Couvreur J. Congenital toxoplasmosis: A prospective study of the offspring of 542 women who acquired toxoplasmosis during pregnancy. In Thalhammer O, Baumgarten K, Pollak A (eds). Perinatal Medicine. Stuttgart: Georg Thieme, 1979.

45. National Institutes of Health. Toxoplasmosis (pamphlet). Bethesda, MD: U.S. Department of Health and Human Services, 1983.

46. Anderson LJ. The role of human parvovirus in human disease. J Pediatr Infect Dis 1987;6:711–718.

47. Frickhofen N, Raghavachar A, Heit W, et al. Human parvovirus infection. N Engl J Med 1986;314:646–650.

48. Young N. Hematologic and hematopoietic consequences of B19 parvovirus infection. Semin Hematol 1988;25:159–172.

49. Anderson MJ, Higgins PG, Davis LR, et al. Experimental parvovirus infection in humans. J Infect Dis 1985;152:257–265.

CHAPTER REVIEW QUESTIONS

1. Pregnancy increases a woman's susceptibility to *all* infections.
   a. True
   b. False

2. Which of the following may produce significantly greater morbidity in pregnant women compared with nonpregnant women without affecting the fetus?
   a. *Listeria monocytogenes*
   b. Hepatitis B
   c. Cytomegalovirus
   d. Meningitis

3. Which of the following infections do not pose a greater risk for the pregnant woman but may have serious implications for the fetus?
   a. Varicella-zoster and meningococcal meningitis
   b. Toxoplasmosis and cytomegalovirus
   c. Hepatitis B and herpes simplex
   d. b and c
   e. All of the above

4. In order to prevent congenital infection, a pregnant woman should take rifampin after exposure to a patient with meningococcal meningitis.
   a. True
   b. False

5. Administration of varicella-zoster immune globulin (VZIG) to an exposed susceptible pregnant woman
   a. Is recommended to protect the fetus from intrauterine infection
   b. Is contraindicated during pregnancy
   c. Is intended to protect the mother from varicella pneumonia
   d. a and c

Answers are provided in Appendix B.

Chapter 12

The Infection Control Practitioner and the Critical Care Nurse: Collaboration for Safety in Patient Care

The previous chapters contained specific information related to the development, recognition, and transmission of some of the more serious infectious diseases encountered in critically ill patients. All these diseases had one common denominator—they could endanger the health of nurses and others who worked, or were cared for, in the critical care area.

The discussion of infectious diseases in this book is far from complete because no single book could possibly cover all potentially infectious conditions that nurses might encounter or could acquire. As a matter of fact, such a book might do a disservice to professional nurses. After all, if a new organism or infection that had not been included in such a book were to be discovered, nurses would not have learned to think for themselves about how to protect themselves and could therefore be at some risk.

In the past 2 decades several ''new'' infectious diseases have been discovered. Legionnaire's disease, Lyme disease, babesiosis, hepatitis non-A, non-B, AIDS, and toxic shock syndrome are just some examples. Many readers will have cared for patients with methicillin-resistant *Staphylococcus aureus*, another ''new'' agent. And, without doubt, other agents and diseases will be discovered in the future. The epidemiology of infectious disease transmission is, therefore, of significant concern to nurses.

THE CYCLE OF DISEASE TRANSMISSION

All infections have certain common denominators. When these are understood, the whole concept of infection prevention and control is demystified. The concept, simply put, can be compared with a circle or cycle. An even more descriptive name would be a vicious cycle.

As shown in Figure 12-1, there is always a reservoir or source of a potential pathogen; the organism must leave the source via a portal of exit, and in order

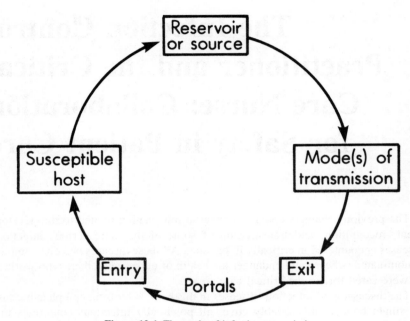

Figure 12-1 The cycle of infection transmission.

to cause a new infection the pathogen must be transmitted to a portal of entry in another person. However, the cycle does not end there. The new "victim" must be susceptible—a susceptible host. If all these events take place, the new host now becomes the reservoir or source of infection and the whole cycle can begin again.

The Reservoir or Source of Infection

Pathogens can originate in animate or inanimate reservoirs. An animate source could be a patient, visitor, or staff member, and even an animal or insect. Inanimate sources consist of the remote or immediate environment—the air, soil, water, food, and less frequently furniture and shared personal equipment or medical instruments.

There will always be reservoirs of infectious organisms. We carry billions of bacteria and fungi on our skin, on our mucous membranes, and in our gastrointestinal tract. Only medical instruments can or need be sterilized. We can only try to reduce other reservoirs by personal hygiene, by maintaining a clean environment, and by using aseptic techniques when applicable. However, animate or inanimate reservoirs cannot really be eliminated.

The Portals of Exit and Entry

The portal of exit for an organism is usually but not always the same as its portal of entry. For example, if a patient has a respiratory tract infection such as tuberculosis or influenza, the organisms exit via the respiratory tract of the source patient. Their portal of entry into the next person must also be that person's respiratory tract. An organism that causes gastroenteritis, such as *Salmonella*, would naturally exit the alimentary tract in feces. Its portal of entry to a new host would, therefore, have to be that person's alimentary tract via the mouth.

The requirement for the similar exit and entry points of many organisms is explained by their tropism or affinity for a specific organ or tissue. This is called *tissue specificity*. For example, the meningococcus cannot cause wound infections because it cannot bind to that type of tissue cell. It can adhere only to respiratory epithelium and cells of the meninges. Salmonellae do not cause urinary tract infections: they find the most effective binding sites in the intestinal mucosa. However, there are exceptions.

One such exception is the familiar *Staphylococcus aureus*. This organism is transiently present in the nares or on the skin of most persons without causing an infection. The same is true of the millions of enteric organisms that make up the normal flora of the intestinal tract. As long as they remain in their normal habitat, these normal flora or commensal organisms cause few problems. When they enter areas in which they do not belong, they may become pathogenic and are thus called opportunistic pathogens. A patient's "normal" *Escherichia coli* can exit the intestinal tract and cause a urinary tract infection or a wound infection if the patient has a surgical wound. A nurse's transient or permanently carried *Staphylococcus aureus* can be shed onto a neonate's skin and cause pustules or shed into a surgical wound and cause a postoperative wound infection. It can also contaminate the nurse's hands and be transferred to a patient's intravenous line, causing bacteremia.

The point of this discussion should be clear by now. To protect oneself from any infection, a portal of entry for a potential pathogen must not be provided.

Modes of Transmission

To get from the source to a portal of entry, organisms must be transmitted or spread. The modes of spread are listed in Table 12-1. Probably the least frequent mode, especially in hospitals, is airborne transmission, which can be direct or indirect. An example of direct person-to-person airborne spread occurs with the meningococcus. The organism must leave the source (the infected patient) by the portal of exit (the respiratory tract). It must be transmitted directly through the air to the portal of entry (the respiratory tract) of the new potential host. To

Table 12-1 Modes of Pathogen Transmission*

Vehicle	Organism / Infection
Air	
Direct (within 3 feet)	*Neisseria mningitidis*
	Hemophilus influenzae
	Influenza and cold viruses
	Mycobacterium tuberculosis
	Childhood exanthems
	? Fifth disease
Indirect (source can be in same room or in distant rooms or areas)	*Mycobacterium tuberculosis*
	Childhood exanthems (i.e., measles, chickenpox)
Contact	
Direct (person to person via touching, kissing, and being splashed by body fluids)	All "normal" flora of patient or nurse (via wound or urinary tract infection)
	Epstein-Barr virus, CMV, and mononucleosis
	Herpetic whitlow and herpes labialis
	Childhood exanthems
	Gastrointestinal infection
	Influenza, cold viruses
	Sexually transmitted diseases
Indirect (requires an intermediate vehicle or fomite)	Influenza and cold viruses
	Intravascular infections
	Bloodborne infections via needles, transfusions, instruments
	Any organism transmitted by a contaminated medical device (e.g., respiratory therapy tubing, endoscopes)
	Food and waterborne infections
Vectors (insects or animals)	Rickettsial diseases
	Malaria and babesiosis
	Certain types of encephalitis
	Lyme disease
	Toxoplasmosis

*Note: Organisms may be transmitted in more than one way

accomplish this, no more than 3 feet of space can intervene between the two. Another example of direct airborne spread is a *Staphylococcus aureus* wound infection from shedding of this organism from the nose of a surgeon or nurse.

Indirect airborne transmission requires an intervening "vehicle," the air, which can carry the organisms over greater distances to others who may not even be in the same room. Examples of infections that result are measles, chickenpox, and tuberculosis but *not* meningococcal or *Hemophilus influenzae* meningitis.

Obviously it is much more difficult to prevent acquisition of indirect airborne infection because air currents can carry organisms without anyone being aware that an infectious source is "downwind." Indirect airborne spread has caused outbreaks of rubella in office buildings and measles in the waiting rooms and offices of pediatricians.

Contact transmission is another way infections are spread. It can be direct, person to person, or indirect, by a vehicle or fomite. Epstein-Barr viral infection is acquired by direct contact with an infected person, and chickenpox is caused by contact with the vesicular fluid of a patient with varicella or zoster. Examples of indirect acquisition requiring an intermediary vehicle are the hepatitis B virus and the human immunodeficiency virus via shared drug paraphernalia or accidental needlesticks. Indirect transmission occurs in patients, too. A patient can get tuberculosis from a bronchoscope that was not sterilized between uses or bacteremia from a contaminated stopcock or transducer.

Colds and influenza can be acquired in three ways: (1) by air when the virus particles are sneezed or coughed at another person; (2) by direct contact person to person (e.g., kissing); or (3) by indirect contact from a telephone or pencil contaminated by the source person and used by another, who then transferred the virus to his or her own mouth, nose, or eyes.

Other types of indirect transmission occur when the vehicle is food or water and when an animal or insect vector is involved, as in Lyme disease or malaria and toxoplasmosis. None of these infections is usually transmitted within a critical care unit.

The Susceptible Host

The last prerequisite for becoming infected is that the new host is susceptible to the disease or infection. Nurses can avoid susceptibility to many diseases by being adequately vaccinated, as discussed in Chapter 2. They can also make themselves less susceptible to wound or skin infections by covering nonintact skin. Without a wound, they cannot acquire a patient's wound infection, but they can be an indirect vehicle for transmitting the organisms from one surgical patient to another via their own hands, clothes, or equipment. Patients, by virtue of their illnesses, therapeutic regimens, and invasive procedures, including indwelling vascular and urinary catheters, are much more susceptible than healthy nurses and physicians.

Finally, if the infection is acquired by the newly exposed person, that person then becomes the source or reservoir, and the whole cycle starts again. How then can this vicious cycle be interrupted? Since there will always be reservoirs of pathogens and they cannot be prevented from exiting the source, the only effective intervention is to prevent transmitting them and not to present a new entry point to the pathogens.

Barriers to Infection Transmission

There are two issues when one discusses prevention of infection. The first is the mandate physicians and nurses have not to do the patient harm. The type of harm at issue here is the acquisition of a nosocomial infection. These infections are usually caused by patients' own normal flora being allowed to enter areas where they do not belong because the intact physical defense mechanisms have been breached. When the skin is surgically incised or an intravascular line placed, the skin barrier is broken. When a patient is intubated, the normal upper respiratory filtering mechanism is bypassed. When a urinary catheter is placed in the bladder, a "highway" to external organisms is provided, leading straight to the bladder. Another mechanism of infection is the use of contaminated medical devices, and a third is the transmission of organisms from nurse to patient or patient to patient.

Critical care nurses and physicians know how to prevent these types of infections. And yet many breaches in sterile or aseptic techniques occur. Of the 35 million patients admitted to hospitals in the United States, about 2.5 million develop nosocomial infections annually. About 25% of these infections are considered preventable. The most significant numbers of all are the 80,000 to 100,000 patients a year who die of their hospital-acquired infections.

The second issue is the acquisition of nosocomial infections by critical care and other nurses. Health care workers are not going to acquire nosocomial urinary tract infections, bacteremias, pneumonias, or wound infections because they do not have the necessary risk factors in the workplace. However, they can acquire some infections from their patients, as has been shown. The most effective preventive approaches have also been discussed individually with each disease, including placement of patients on some type of Isolation or Precautions. There are a variety of systems in use in hospitals, and there is some controversy about which of these are most effective.

The next part of this chapter is, therefore, devoted to a comparison of Isolation and Precaution methods. Understanding why a particular system is selected, cumbersome though it may seem, will clarify the issues. It is hoped that by understanding the rationale, critical care nurses will be more willing to adhere to the policies and requirements of their hospitals and therefore better protect themselves and their patients from transmissible infections.

INFECTION CONTROL IN CRITICAL CARE

Although critical care nursing is a comparatively new discipline, infection prevention and control is not. Florence Nightingale was the first to recognize that safe food and water and a clean environment with aseptic technique could greatly decrease the infection-related morbidity and mortality rates in military hospitals during the Crimean War. She had to persistently fight a hostile military bureaucracy to protect her patients.[1]

There are many contacts between critical care nurses and infection control practitioners because critically ill patients are the most likely to develop or harbor infections. Both disciplines require specialized and extensive knowledge, and both can learn from each other. Critical care nurses know what knowledge is required for effective patient care. They may not know much about what infection control practitioners need to know. Over and above clinical expertise, infection control practitioners must know epidemiology, outbreak investigation and statistics, microbiology, infectious diseases, basic antibiotics, surveillance methods for nosocomial infections, research and its evaluation, rules of regulatory agencies, and Centers for Disease Control (CDC) guidelines. They must be able to evaluate the policies and procedures of every hospital department from medicine and nursing to dietary and housekeeping. Many infection control practitioners do research and publish on their special interests. They are required to ensure that isolation and precautions are carried out and that the health department is notified when patients with certain infectious diseases are admitted. They must also be effective communicators and teachers to all disciplines.

In most hospitals there is only one infection control practitioner: the suggested ratio is one practitioner per 250 beds. Therefore infection control practitioners, themselves, feel isolated and without a support group. Since they are considered the experts on surveillance, prevention, and control of infection, they have no one to ask for advice, and are called on to make many unpopular decisions. The responsibility of infection control practitioners is to protect the hospital and its administration from unfavorable citations from regulatory agencies. They must protect patients and staff from infections, and the measures required to do all this are not easy or popular. It is often tempting for infection control practitioners to ignore the breaks in technique or policies that they observe. However, in the long run, the consequences of such a lack of action could be costly to an institution and disastrous to patients and staff alike. Some of the consequences of ignoring applicable policies have been described in earlier chapters, and no doubt most critical care nurses could provide examples from their own experience.

Legal and Ethical Implications

There has been a significant increase in lawsuits against hospitals and physicians and nurses involving patients who develop nosocomial infections. Such infections are not always innocuous. Of the 35 to 40 million patients admitted annually to hospitals in the United States, 2 to 4 million will develop nosocomial infections. Some of these infections are unavoidable, but others may develop

because someone used poor judgment or placed convenience or other considerations above concern for others. This raises moral, ethical, legal, and cost-
related issues.[2]

In the 1970s, the cost of diagnosing and treating nosocomial infections was
estimated to be a billion dollars annually. Naturally, this figure has now increased
proportionally to the increase in hospital costs. But most significantly, 80,000
to 100,000 patients a year die of their hospital-associated infections.

Part of the responsibility of an infection control practitioner is to help nurses
avoid such problems by providing them with new infection control information
and occasionally reviewing and revising policies, procedures, and techniques in
the process. Indeed, infection control practitioners who do not correct problems
can be held liable for the consequences. Understandably, busy infection control
practitioners are required to direct most of their efforts to the protection of patients
rather than personnel. This can be frustrating and was the impetus for writing
this book about the needs of nurses instead of patients. However, it is the patients
who are most susceptible to nosocomial infections by virtue of their critical
illnesses, underlying immunosuppressive conditions, and chronic diseases. The
therapeutic regimens and invasive procedures to which they are subjected contribute to their susceptibility and risk. Nurses on the other hand are usually young
and healthy and as professionals must take responsibility for their actions toward
their patients and for themselves. This is illustrated in the following case.

A nurse in the newborn nursery reported to her supervisor what she thought
to be herpetic lesions on the neck of one of the neonates. Indeed, further lesions
developed and were cultured for herpesvirus. Shortly thereafter, the nurse developed a herpetic lesion near her right eye and later developed headache, fever,
and nausea. She was diagnosed as having herpes encephalitis and sued the infant's
pediatrician because he had not ordered the infant's isolation. The court ruled
that "the nurse was not a patient of the pediatrician, she was a health professional
trained to handle ill patients, and there was no evidence that room placement or
use of masks or gowns would have kept her face free from herpes."[3]

The interrelated responsibilities of critical care nurses and infection control
practitioners are listed below:

1. Critical care nurses should inform the infection control practitioner when
   a patient develops a nosocomial infection. The infection control practitioner
   in turn should alert critical care personnel to a potential transmissible
   infection and investigate the probable cause of infection.
   a. Unless the infection was caused by gross negligence or a pattern is
      discernible, no action will be taken other than reviewing measures with
      the staff that might have prevented the infection.
   b. If a pattern of infections is discernible, corrective action should be
      discussed with the critical care staff. Policies and procedures may need

to be revised, with the approval of the infection control committee. One example of this would be an increasing number of bacteremias related to the length of time centrally placed intravascular lines are left in place.

2. Critical care nurses should inform the infection control practitioner of transmissible infections in patients, whether these are present on admission or developed in the hospital. Patients should be placed on the appropriate category of precautions or isolation depending on the categories in use at each hospital. This will protect staff as well as other patients. The infection control practitioner should:

   a. Review the appropriateness of the category used.
   b. Report infections to the health department when required by law.
   c. Ensure that no one was exposed to the patient's infection before precautionary measures were instituted. This includes ambulance or emergency medical personnel if the patient was brought to the hospital with the infection. It also includes other patient care areas from which the patient may have been transferred and other staff members who had contact with the patient.
   d. Arrange for follow-up and/or postexposure prophylaxis, if indicated.
   e. Discuss discontinuation or change of precautionary measures when the infection resolves.

PRECAUTIONS AND ISOLATION

Early in this century, patients with infections were cared for in separate facilities, such as sanatoria for tuberculosis. In general, hospital isolation consisted of a private room for the patient and anyone entering that room had to wear a gown, mask, and gloves. This type of isolation garb was cumbersome, hot, and time consuming to put on. The staff avoided entering the patient's room whenever possible, and patients felt truly isolated and uncared for. When antibiotics and vaccines became available, the number of infectious diseases such as diphtheria, tuberculosis, measles, and others began to decrease. In the 1950s, new "plagues" arrived in hospital patients in the form of staphylococcal wound infections. Outbreaks of infections due to antibiotic-resistant organisms began to surface in the 1970s. These infections were not airborne however, and isolation as it was then practiced was believed to be excessive. Prevention of some infections was possible by improving handwashing and by the introduction of closed versus open urinary drainage systems. The new discipline of Infection Control evolved from these efforts in 1962. In the early 1970s, the CDC developed a new set of Guidelines for Isolation Techniques for Use in Hospitals.[4] The precautionary measures were categorized according to the mode of transmission of the organism. Categories were called Strict Isolation, Respiratory Isolation, and Protective or Reverse Isolation. These patients required private rooms as suggested by the word "isolation," meaning being set apart from others. Wound and Skin Precautions and Enteric Precautions allowed patients to share a room under certain conditions (Table 12-2). Color-coded cards were used, and a number of similarly transmitted diseases were grouped together under each category. The system was far from perfect, and in 1983 it was redesigned to give hospitals a choice between two approaches: category-specific or disease-specific isolation or precautions.[5]

Category-Specific Isolation Precautions

Category-specific isolation precautions use color-coded cards as before, but the names of most categories have been changed and the diseases regrouped and new ones added (see Table 12-2).

Although these new categories were adopted in many hospitals they have several disadvantages. The largest category is called Contact Isolation. Since isolation, by definition, means to "separate out," all patients in this category require a private room. Also the word "isolation" reminds physicians of the old method in which patients were neglected because everyone entering the room had to wear mask, gown, and gloves. Such terminology should be reserved only

Table 12-2 Categories of Precautions and Isolation Identified by Color-Coded Cards and Based on Mode of Spread

1974	1983
Strict Isolation	Strict Isolation
Respiratory Isolation	Respiratory Isolation and AFB* Isolation (for tuberculosis) and Contact Isolation
Reverse or Protective Isolation	Has been eliminated
Wound and Skin Precautions	Contact Isolation and Drainage-Secretion Precautions
—	
Enteric Precautions	Enteric Precautions
—	Blood and Body Fluid Precautions (new category)

Note: Added in 1988—Universal Precautions (for bloodborne infections): no card required; use for all patients—meant to replace the 1983 category of Blood and Body Fluid Precautions

*Acid-fast bacilli

(Front of Card)

Contact Isolation

Visitors—Report to Nurses' Station Before Entering Room

1. Masks are indicated for those who come close to patient.
2. Gowns are indicated if soiling is likely.
3. Gloves are indicated for touching infective material.
4. HANDS MUST BE WASHED AFTER TOUCHING THE PATIENT OR POTENTIALLY CONTAMINATED ARTICLES AND BEFORE TAKING CARE OF ANOTHER PATIENT.
5. Articles contaminated with infective material should be discarded or bagged and labeled before being sent for decontamination and reprocessing.

(Back of Card)

Diseases or Conditions Requiring Contact Isolation*

Acute respiratory infections in infants and young children, including croup, colds, bronchitis, and bronchiolitis caused by respiratory syncytial virus, adenovirus, coronavirus, influenza viruses, para-influenza viruses, and rhinovirus

Conjunctivitis, gonococcal, in newborns

Diphtheria, cutaneous

Endometritis, group A *Streptococcus*

Furunculosis, staphylococcal, in newborns

Herpes simplex, disseminated, severe primary or neonatal

Impetigo

Influenza, in infants and young children

Multiply-resistant bacteria, infection or colonization (any site) with any of the following:

1. Gram-negative bacilli resistant to all aminoglycosides that are tested. (In general, such organisms should be resistant to gentamicin, tobramycin, and amikacin for these special precautions to be indicated.)
2. *Staphylococcus aureus* resistant to methicillin (or nafcillin or oxacillin if they are used instead of methicillin for testing)

3. Pneumococcus resistant to penicillin
4. *Hemophilus influenzae* resistant to ampicillin (beta-lactamase positive) and chloramphenicol
5. Other resistant bacteria may be included in this isolation category if they are judged by the infection control team to be of special clinical and epidemiologic significance.

Pediculosis

Pharyngitis, infections, in infants and young children

Pneumonia, viral, in infants and young children

Pneumonia, *Staphylococcus aureus* or group A *Streptococcus*

Rabies

Rubella, congenital and other

Scabies

Scalded skin syndrome (Ritter's disease)

Skin, wound, or burn infection, major (draining and not covered by a dressing or dressing does not adequately contain the purulent material), including those infected with *Staphylococcus aureus* or group A *Streptococcus*

Vaccinia (generalized and progressive eczema vaccinatum)

---

*A private room is indicated for Contact Isolation: in general, however, patients infected with the same organisms may share a room. During outbreaks, infants and young children with the same respiratory clinical syndrome may share a room. See Guideline for Isolation Precautions in Hospitals for details and for how long to apply precautions.

Figure 12-2 Example of a category-specific designation. *Source:* Reprinted from *Morbidity and Mortality Weekly Report* (1983;4(S):245–325), 1983, U.S. Centers for Disease Control.

for airborne infections. Contact isolation, however, applies to a variety of infections that are not airborne, such as pediculosis, endometritis, and conjunctivitis in the newborn and requires masking for those who come "close" to the patient, which is very vague and an overreaction (Figure 12-2). The result is overisolation of certain patients, which is undesirable and may result in a loss of credibility and compliance.

This problem was recognized at the time the 1983 changes were made, and therefore an alternate system was included in the revised guidelines. Some readers may be familiar with this system.

Disease-Specific Isolation Precautions

Disease-specific isolation precautions require that a card with a checklist of protective apparel and requirements be placed at the patient's door. The appropriate protective measures have to be checked off by someone who knows how the infection is transmitted and what the applicable measures are (Figure 12-3). Such a knowledgeable person is not always available, and patients are often over- or under-"isolated," resulting in a loss of credibility and compliance with requirements.

Universal Precautions

With the emergence of AIDS, what had been quite obvious earlier with hepatitis B became an overriding concern: namely, that it was impossible to know which patients were carriers of either virus and were thus potentially infectious. In 1987, the CDC suggested that blood and body fluids of *all* patients be considered infectious and proposed observance of Universal Precautions in all health care institutions and for all patients.[6] The Occupational Safety and Health Administration (OSHA), a federal regulatory agency, established Universal Precautions as the law in health care–related patient contacts. Body fluids considered infectious by OSHA and the CDC, as well as those considered noninfectious, are listed in Table 12-3.[7]

At present the proposal is that OSHA inspectors will be empowered to observe health care personnel as they carry out patient care procedures, to ascertain whether the recommendations pertaining to Universal Precautions are being carried out. Employees will also be questioned to ascertain what they have been taught about these precautions. Employees who do not follow the mandated measures or cannot answer the question will cause a fine to be levied against the institution of between $1,000 and $10,000.[8]

Sample Instruction Card for Disease-Specific Isolation Precautions

(Front of Card)

Visitors—Report to Nurses' Station Before Entering Room

1. **Private room indicated?**   ____ No
                                        ____ Yes
2. **Masks indicated?**   ____ No
                                        ____ Yes for those close to patient
                                        ____ Yes for all persons entering room
3. **Gowns indicated?**   ____ No
                                        ____ Yes if soiling is likely
                                        ____ Yes for all persons entering room
4. **Gloves indicated?**   ____ No
                                        ____ Yes for touching infective material
                                        ____ Yes for all persons entering room
5. Special precautions   ____ No
   indicated for handling blood?   ____ Yes
6. **Hands must be washed after touching the patient or potentially contaminated articles and before taking care of another patient.**
7. Articles contaminated with _____ should be
                               infective material(s)
   discarded or bagged and labeled before being sent for decontamination and reprocessing.

(Back of Card)

Instructions

1. On Table B, Disease-Specific Precautions, locate the disease for which isolation precautions are indicated.
2. Write disease in blank space here: _____
3. Determine if a private room is indicated. In general, patients infected with the same organism may share a room. For some diseases or conditions, a private room is indicated if patient hygiene is poor. A patient with poor hygiene does not wash hands after touching infective material (feces, purulent drainage, or secretions), contaminates the environment with infective material, or shares contaminated articles with other patients.
4. Place a check mark beside the indicated precautions on front of card.
5. Cross through precautions that are *not* indicated.
6. Write infective material in blank space in item 7 on front of card.

Figure 12-3 Example of disease-specific isolation card to be checked off by knowledgeable person. *Source:* Reprinted from *Morbidity and Mortality Weekly Report* (1983;4(S):245–325), 1983, U.S. Centers for Disease Control.

Universal Precautions as written by the CDC are reproduced in their entirety in Appendix A. They require a physical barrier to separate the skin and mucous membranes of the health care provider from the blood and certain body fluids of all patients. This can be achieved by the wearing of gloves, eye and face protectors, and gowns when splashing or other body fluid contact is anticipated.

Table 12-3 Infectious and Noninfectious Body Fluids as Described by OSHA
and the CDC

Infectious		Noninfectious
OSHA	CDC	(unless visibly bloody)
Blood	Blood	Saliva
Blood products	Semen	Sputum
Semen	Vaginal secretions	Tears
Vaginal secretions	Fluids	Vomitus
	Peritoneal	Sweat
	Amniotic	Urine
	Cerebrospinal	Feces
	Pleural	Gastric secretions
	Synovial	
	Pericardial	

Sources: Morbidity and Mortality Weekly Report (1988;37(24):377–388), 1988, U.S. Centers for Disease Control; and Enforcement Procedures for Occupational Exposure to HBV, HIV and other Bloodborne Infectious Agents in Health Care Facilities by Occupational Safety and Health Administration, U.S. Department of Labor, 1988.

Although Universal Precautions are intended for protection against bloodborne organisms, their use would certainly protect against contact with other pathogens that might be contained in stool or in wound or skin exudates. Some hospitals have therefore eliminated the categories of Enteric Precautions, Secretion/Drainage Precautions, and the nonairborne infections in the Contact Isolation category. Other hospitals have retained all the previous categories. There is much discussion among infection control practitioners about which is the correct approach.[9]

Body Substance Isolation

A variation of Universal Precautions was developed by one group of infection control practitioners that eliminates all previous diagnosis-related categories. It, too, requires the use of barriers (i.e., gloves) for handling all body fluids, including "body substances" such as stool and wound drainage. A card at *every* patient's bed would indicate which body substances are involved. A major disadvantage is that a knowledgeable person would have to check the appropriate substances and everyone would have to read the card. The old color-coded cards helped to differentiate the type of infection without careful reading. In addition there would be some lack of confidentiality because everyone could read what was checked off. Private rooms with a sign outside would still be required for patients with airborne infections.

The variations in nomenclature for precautionary measures may seem to be confusing, and a perfect system is not possible. Each hospital must decide which system to use and what to call their isolation precautions. The author has used her personal preferences in this book, but does not wish to imply that other systems cannot be equally efficacious. Nurses must then follow the hospital's policies. To do otherwise could have serious legal implications.

Changing Concerns and Concepts in Infection Control

Infection control is a dynamic discipline. As research in the field progresses, modifications in precautionary measures will continue to be made. A case in point is the elimination of Reverse or Protective Isolation in hospitals that do not have the facility to provide "whole life islands" or laminar-flow air. Simple Protective Isolation has not produced a statistically significant reduction in infectious morbidity or mortality and is, therefore, neither cost effective nor worth the sense of true isolation experienced by patients in this category.[10] Patient care measures for reducing exogenously introduced infections for immunocompromised patients are available in the literature.[11]

Another example of change is the discontinuation of unnecessary double-bagging of soiled linen from patients on precautions or isolation. Studies have demonstrated that the number of organisms in the laundry of infected patients is no higher than in noninfected patients and the colony counts on the outside of laundry bags are similar in both types of patients.[12] Soiled linen should not be sorted prior to laundering, and gloves should be worn by those laundry workers who handle the dirty laundry. Nurses must cooperate in protecting laundry workers by not overfilling laundry hampers so that the bags can be securely closed prior to transport to the laundry.

Occasionally a particular type of precautionary measure creates a difficult problem. The tendency of the staff may then be to simply ignore the requirements. This can be a very risky decision and should not be made arbitrarily. The unit's nursing staff and the infection control practitioner should confer and possibly consult others, such as the staff of the engineering department. Compromises can usually be worked out for the safety of all concerned. One such problem occurred in a pediatric intensive care unit, where nurses would leave the door to a child's room open, even if the infection was airborne, so they could hear the child if he cried. Installation of large windows in the door and an intercom solved this particular problem.

CONCLUSIONS

Nurses as professionals are familiar with the application of theory to practice. The theoretical concepts discussed in this book should enable nurses to protect themselves from presently recognized infections and those not yet discovered or named that may be confronted in the future. Anyone who can answer the questions "how is this organism transmitted from its source," "which portals of entry does it require to infect a new host," and "how can such transmission and entry be avoided," will be able to avoid acquiring or spreading all but the most unusual infections.

REFERENCES

1. Cook E. Life of Florence Nightingale. London: Macmillan, 1913.

2. Childress JF. Hospital acquired infections: Some ethical issues. In Wenzel RP (ed). Prevention and Control of Nosocomial Infections. Baltimore: Williams & Wilkins, 1987.

3. Nottebart HC. Current legal issues. In Wenzel RP (ed). Prevention and Control of Nosocomial Infections. Baltimore: Williams & Wilkins, 1987.

4. Centers for Disease Control. Isolation Techniques for Use in Hospitals. Dixon RE, Brachman PS, Bennett JV (eds). Department of Health, Education and Welfare publication No. (CDC) 78-8314, 1975.

5. Garner JS, Simmons BP. Guidelines for Isolation Precautions in hospitals. Infection Control 1983;4(S):245–325.

6. Centers for Disease Control. Recommendations for prevention of HIV transmission in health care settings. MMWR 1987;36(2S):3S–18S.

7. Centers for Disease Control. Update: Universal Precautions for prevention of transmission of HIV, HBV and other bloodborne pathogens in health care settings. MMWR 1988;37(24):377–388.

8. Occupational Safety and Health Administration. Enforcement Procedures for Occupational Exposure to HBV, HIV and Other Bloodborne Infectious Agents in Health Care Facilities. Washington, DC: U.S. Department of Labor, 1988.

9. Lynch P, Jackson MM, Cummings MJ, Stamm WE. Rethinking the role of isolation practices in the prevention of nosocomial infections. Ann Intern Med 1987;107:243–246.

10. Nauseef WM, Maki DG. A study of the value of simple protective isolation in patients with granulocytopenia. N Engl J Med 1981;304:448–453.

11. Gurevich I, Tafuro P. The compromised host: Deficit-specific infection and the spectrum of prevention. Cancer Nursing 1986;9(5):263–275.

12. Maki DG, Alvarado C, Hassemaier L. Double-bagging of items from isolation rooms is unnecessary as an infection control measure. Infect Control 1986;7:535–537.

CHAPTER REVIEW QUESTIONS

1. What important aspect is missing from the listed "requirements for transmission of infection"? Write down the missing link.
   Reservoir of infection
   Portal of exit
   Mode of transmission
   Susceptible host

   _____

2. Transmission of infection by air can be direct (within 3 feet) and indirect. Which organisms are *not* transmitted by the indirect route?
   a. *Mycobacterium tuberculosis* and varicella virus
   b. Meningococcus and the human immunodeficiency virus
   c. Influenza virus and *Staphylococcus*
   d. b and c

3. One of the responsibilities of infection control practitioners and critical care nurses is to prevent infections in
   a. Patients
   b. Staff
   c. a and b

4. Precautionary measures (isolation and precautions) are based on the
   a. Mode(s) of transmission of the pathogen
   b. Virulence of the pathogen involved

5. Universal Precautions as mandated by the Occupational Safety and Health Administration apply to infections that are
   a. Airborne
   b. Bloodborne
   c. a and b

Answers are provided in Appendix B.

Centers for Disease Control Precautions against Blood-Borne Infections

RECOMMENDATIONS FOR PREVENTION OF HIV TRANSMISSION IN HEALTH CARE SETTINGS*

Introduction

Human immunodeficiency virus (HIV), the virus that causes acquired immunodeficiency syndrome (AIDS), is transmitted through sexual contact and exposure to infected blood components and perinatally from mother to neonate. HIV has been isolated from blood, semen, vaginal secretions, saliva, tears, breast milk, cerebrospinal fluid, amniotic fluid, and urine and is likely to be isolated from other body fluids, secretions, and excretions. However, epidemiologic evidence has implicated only blood, semen, vaginal secretions, and possibly breast milk in transmission.

The increasing prevalence of HIV increases the risk that health care workers will be exposed to blood from patients infected with HIV, especially when blood and body fluid precautions are not followed for all patients. Thus, this document emphasizes the need for health care workers to consider *all* patients as potentially infected with HIV and/or other bloodborne pathogens and to adhere rigorously to infection control precautions for minimizing the risk of exposure to blood and body fluids of all patients.

The recommendations contained in this document consolidate and update CDC recommendations published earlier for preventing HIV transmission in health care settings: precautions for clinical and laboratory staffs[1] and precautions for health care workers and allied professionals;[2] recommendations for preventing HIV transmission in the workplace[3] and during invasive procedures;[4] recom-

---

*This portion of Appendix A is reprinted from *Morbidity and Mortality Weekly Report* (1987;36(2S)), August 1987, U.S. Centers for Disease Control.

mendations for preventing possible transmission of HIV from tears;[5] and recommendations for providing dialysis treatment for HIV-infected patients.[6] These recommendations also update portions of the "Guideline for Isolation Precautions in Hospitals"[7] and reemphasize some of the recommendations contained in "Recommended Infection Control Practices for Dentistry."[8] The recommendations contained in this document have been developed for use in health care settings and emphasize the need to treat blood and other body fluids from *all* patients as potentially infective. These same prudent precautions also should be taken in other settings in which persons may be exposed to blood or other body fluids.

Definition of Health Care Workers

Health care workers are defined as persons, including students and trainees, whose activities involve contact with patients or with blood or other body fluids from patients in a health care setting.

Health Care Workers with AIDS

As of July 10, 1987, a total of 1,875 (5.8%) of 32,395 adults with AIDS, who have been reported to the CDC national surveillance system and for whom occupational information was available, reported being employed in a health care or clinical laboratory setting. In comparison, 6.8 million persons—representing 5.6% of the U.S. labor force—were employed in health services. Of the health care workers with AIDS, 95% have been reported to exhibit high-risk behavior; for the remaining 5%, the means of HIV acquisition was undetermined. Health care workers with AIDS were significantly more likely than other workers to have an undetermined risk (5% versus 3%, respectively). For both health care workers and non-health care workers with AIDS, the proportion with an undetermined risk has not increased since 1982.

AIDS patients initially reported as not belonging to recognized risk groups are investigated by state and local health departments to determine whether possible risk factors exist. Of all health care workers with AIDS reported to CDC who were initially characterized as not having an identified risk and for whom follow-up information was available, 66% have been reclassified because risk factors were identified or because the patient was found not to meet the surveillance case definition for AIDS. Of the 87 health care workers currently categorized as having no identifiable risk, information is incomplete on 16 (18%) because of death or refusal to be interviewed; 38 (44%) are still being investigated. The remaining 33 (38%) health care workers were interviewed or had other follow-up information available. The occupations of these 33 were as follows: five physicians (15%), three of whom were surgeons; one dentist (3%); three nurses (9%); nine nursing assistants (27%); seven housekeeping or maintenance workers (21%); three clinical laboratory technicians (9%); one therapist (3%); and four others who did not have contact with patients (12%). Although 15 of these 33 health care workers reported parenteral and/or other non-needle-stick exposure to blood or body fluids from patients in the 10 years preceding their diagnosis of AIDS, none of these exposures involved a patient with AIDS or known HIV infection.

Risk to Health Care Workers of Acquiring HIV in Health Care Settings

Health care workers with documented percutaneous or mucous-membrane exposures to blood or body fluids of HIV-infected patients have been prospectively evaluated to determine the risk of infection after such exposures. As of June 30, 1987, 883 health care workers have been tested for antibody to HIV in an ongoing surveillance project conducted by CDC.[9] Of these, 708 (80%) had percutaneous exposures to blood and 175 (20%) had a mucous membrane or an open wound contaminated by blood or body fluid. Of 396 health care workers, each of whom had only a convalescent-phase serum sample obtained and tested ≥90 days postexposure, one—for whom heterosexual transmission could not be ruled out—was seropositive for HIV antibody. For 425 additional health care workers, both acute- and convalescent-phase serum samples were obtained and tested; none of 74 health care workers with nonpercutaneous exposures seroconverted, and three (0.9%) of 351 with percutaneous exposures seroconverted. None of these three health care workers had other documented risk factors for infection.

Two other prospective studies to assess the risk of nosocomial acquisition of HIV infection for health care workers are ongoing in the United States. As of April 30, 1987, 332 health care workers with a total of 453 needlestick or mucous membrane exposures to the blood or other body fluids of HIV-infected patients were tested for HIV antibody at the National Institutes of Health.[10] These exposed workers included 103 with needlestick injuries and 229 with mucous-membrane exposures; none had seroconverted. A similar study at the University of California of 129 health care workers with documented needlestick injuries or mucous membrane exposures to blood or other body fluids from patients with HIV infection has not identified any seroconversions.[11] Results of a prospective study in the United Kingdom identified no evidence of transmission among 150 health care workers with parenteral or mucous membrane exposures to blood or other body fluids, secretions, or excretions from patients with HIV infection.[12]

In addition to health care workers enrolled in prospective studies, eight persons who provided care to infected patients and denied other risk factors have been reported to have acquired HIV infection. Three of these health care workers had needlestick exposures to blood from infected patients.[13–15] Two were persons who provided nursing care to infected persons; although neither sustained a needlestick, both had extensive contact with blood or other body fluids, and neither observed recommended barrier precautions.[16,17] The other three were health care workers with non-needlestick exposures to blood from infected patients.[18] Although the exact route of transmission for these last three infections is not known, all three persons had direct contact of their skin with blood from infected patients, all had skin lesions that may have been contaminated by blood, and one also had a mucous-membrane exposure.

A total of 1,231 dentists and hygienists, many of whom practiced in areas with many AIDS cases, participated in a study to determine the prevalence of antibody to HIV; one dentist (0.1%) had HIV antibody. Although no exposure to a known HIV-infected person could be documented, epidemiologic investigation did not identify any other risk factor for infection. The infected dentist, who also had a history of sustaining needlestick injuries and trauma to his hands, did not routinely wear gloves when providing dental care.[19]

Precautions To Prevent Transmission of HIV

Universal Precautions

Since medical history and examination cannot reliably identify all patients infected with HIV or other bloodborne pathogens, blood and body fluid precautions should be consistently used for *all* patients. This approach, previously recommended by CDC,[3,4] and referred to as "universal blood and body fluid precautions" or "universal precautions," should be used in the care of *all* patients, especially including those in emergency care settings in which the risk of blood exposure is increased and the infection status of the patient is usually unknown.[20]

1. All health care workers should routinely use appropriate barrier precautions to prevent skin and mucous membrane exposure when contact with blood or other body fluids of any patient is anticipated. Gloves should be worn for touching blood and body fluids, mucous membranes, or non-intact skin of all patients, for handling items or surfaces soiled with blood or body fluids, and for performing venipuncture and other vascular access procedures. Gloves should be changed after contact with each patient. Masks and protective eyewear or face shields should be worn during procedures that are likely to generate droplets of blood or other body fluids to prevent

exposure of mucous membranes of the mouth, nose, and eyes. Gowns or aprons should be worn during procedures that are likely to generate splashes of blood or other body fluids.

2. Hands and other skin surfaces should be washed immediately and thoroughly if contaminated with blood or other body fluids. Hands should be washed immediately after gloves are removed.

3. All health care workers should take precautions to prevent injuries caused by needles, scalpels, and other sharp instruments or devices during procedures; when cleaning used instruments; during disposal of used needles; and when handling sharp instruments after procedures. To prevent needlestick injuries, needles should not be recapped, purposely bent or broken by hand, removed from disposable syringes, or otherwise manipulated by hand. After they are used, disposable syringes and needles, scalpel blades, and other sharp items should be placed in puncture-resistant containers for disposal; the puncture-resistant containers should be located as close as practical to the use area. Large-bore reusable needles should be placed in a puncture-resistant container for transport to the reprocessing area.

4. Although saliva has not been implicated in HIV transmission, to minimize the need for emergency mouth-to-mouth resuscitation, mouthpieces, resuscitation bags, or other ventilation devices should be available for use in areas in which the need for resuscitation is predictable.

5. Health care workers who have exudative lesions or weeping dermatitis should refrain from all direct patient care and from handling patient care equipment until the condition resolves.

6. Pregnant health care workers are not known to be at greater risk of contracting HIV infection than health care workers who are not pregnant; however, if a health care worker develops HIV infection during pregnancy, the infant is at risk of infection resulting from perinatal transmission. Because of this risk, pregnant health care workers should be especially familiar with and strictly adhere to precautions to minimize the risk of HIV transmission.

Implementation of universal blood and body fluid precautions for *all* patients eliminates the need for use of the isolation category of ''Blood and Body Fluid Precautions'' previously recommended by CDC[7] for patients known or suspected to be infected with bloodborne pathogens. Isolation precautions (e.g., enteric ''AFB''[7]) should be used as necessary if associated conditions, such as infectious diarrhea or tuberculosis, are diagnosed or suspected.

Precautions for Invasive Procedures

In this document, an invasive procedure is defined as surgical entry into tissues, cavities, or organs or repair of major traumatic injuries (1) in an operating or delivery room, emergency department, or outpatient setting, including both physicians' and dentists' offices; (2) cardiac catheterization and angiographic procedures; (3) a vaginal or cesarean delivery or other invasive obstetric procedure during which bleeding may occur; or (4) the manipulation, cutting, or removal of any oral or perioral tissues, including tooth structure, during which bleeding occurs or the potential for bleeding exists. The universal blood and body fluid precautions listed above, combined with the precautions listed below, should be the minimum precautions for *all* such invasive procedures.

1. All health care workers who participate in invasive procedures must routinely use appropriate barrier precautions to prevent skin and mucous membrane contact with blood and other body fluids of all patients. Gloves and surgical masks must be worn for all invasive procedures. Protective eyewear or face shields should be worn for procedures that commonly result in the generation of droplets, splashing of blood or other body fluids, or the generation of bone chips. Gowns or aprons made of materials that provide an effective barrier should be worn during invasive procedures that are likely to result in the splashing of blood or other body fluids. All health care workers who perform or assist in vaginal or cesarean deliveries should wear gloves and gowns when handling the placenta or the infant until blood and amniotic fluid have been removed from the infant's skin and should wear gloves during postdelivery care of the umbilical cord.
2. If a glove is torn or a needlestick or other injury occurs, the glove should be removed and a new glove used as promptly as patient safety permits; the needle or instrument involved in the incident should also be removed from the sterile field.

*Precautions for Dentistry**

Blood, saliva, and gingival fluid from *all* dental patients should be considered infective. Special emphasis should be placed on the following precautions for preventing transmission of bloodborne pathogens in dental practice in both institutional and non-institutional settings.

1. In addition to wearing gloves for contact with oral mucous membranes of all patients, all dental workers should wear surgical masks and protective eyewear or chin-length plastic face shields during dental procedures in which splashing or spattering of blood, saliva, or gingival fluids is likely. Rubber dams, high-speed evacuation, and proper patient positioning, when

---

*General infection-control precautions are more specifically addressed in previous recommendations for infection-control practices for dentistry.[8]

appropriate, should be utilized to minimize generation of droplets and spatter.

2. Handpieces should be sterilized after use with each patient, since blood, saliva, or gingival fluid of patients may be aspirated into the handpiece or waterline. Handpieces that cannot be sterilized should at least be flushed, the outside surface cleaned and wiped with a suitable chemical germicide, and then rinsed. Handpieces should be flushed at the beginning of the day and after use with each patient. Manufacturers' recommendations should be followed for use and maintenance of waterlines and check valves and for flushing of handpieces. The same precautions should be used for ultrasonic scalers and air/water syringes.

3. Blood and saliva should be thoroughly and carefully cleaned from material that has been used in the mouth (e.g., impression materials, bite registration), especially before polishing and grinding intra-oral devices. Contaminated materials, impressions, and intra-oral devices should also be cleaned and disinfected before being handled in the dental laboratory and before they are placed in the patient's mouth. Because of the increasing variety of dental materials used intra-orally, dental workers should consult with manufacturers as to the stability of specific materials when using disinfection procedures.

4. Dental equipment and surfaces that are difficult to disinfect (e.g., light handles or x-ray-unit heads) and that may become contaminated should be wrapped with impervious-backed paper, aluminum foil, or clear plastic wrap. The coverings should be removed and discarded, and clean coverings should be put in place after use with each patient.

Precautions for Autopsies or Morticians' Services

In addition to the universal blood and body fluid precautions listed above, the following precautions should be used by persons performing postmortem procedures:

1. All persons performing or assisting in postmortem procedures should wear gloves, masks, protective eyewear, gowns, and waterproof aprons.
2. Instruments and surfaces contaminated during postmortem procedures should be decontaminated with an appropriate chemical germicide.

Precautions for Dialysis

Patients with end-stage renal disease who are undergoing maintenance dialysis and who have HIV infection can be dialyzed in hospital-based or free-standing dialysis units using conventional infection-control precautions.[21] Universal blood and body fluid precautions should be used when dialyzing *all* patients.

Strategies for disinfecting the dialysis fluid pathways of the hemodialysis machine are targeted to control bacterial contamination and generally consist of using 500–750 parts per million (ppm) of sodium hypochlorite (household bleach) for 30–40 minutes or 1.5%–2.0% formaldehyde overnight. In addition, several chemical germicides formulated to disinfect dialysis machines are commercially available. None of these protocols or procedures need to be changed for dialyzing patients infected with HIV.

Patients infected with HIV can be dialyzed by either hemodialysis or peritoneal dialysis and do not need to be isolated from other patients. The type of dialysis treatment (i.e., hemodialysis or peritoneal dialysis) should be based on the needs of the patient. The dialyzer may be discarded after each use. Alternatively, centers that reuse dialyzers—i.e., a specific single-use dialyzer is issued to a specific patient, removed, cleaned, disinfected, and reused several times on the same patient only—may include HIV-infected patients in the dialyzer-reuse program. An individual dialyzer must never be used on more than one patient.

Precautions for Laboratories†

Blood and other body fluids from *all* patients should be considered infective. To supplement the universal blood and body fluid precautions listed above, the following precautions are recommended for health care workers in clinical laboratories.

1. All specimens of blood and body fluids should be put in a well-constructed container with a secure lid to prevent leaking during transport. Care should be taken when collecting each specimen to avoid contaminating the outside of the container and of the laboratory form accompanying the specimen.
2. All persons processing blood and body fluid specimens (e.g., removing tops from vacuum tubes) should wear gloves. Masks and protective eyewear should be worn if mucous-membrane contact with blood or body fluids is anticipated. Gloves should be changed and hands washed after completion of specimen processing.
3. For routine procedures, such as histologic and pathologic studies or microbiologic culturing, a biological safety cabinet is not necessary. However, biological safety cabinets (Class I or II) should be used whenever procedures are conducted that have a high potential for generating droplets. These include activities such as blending, sonicating, and vigorous mixing.
4. Mechanical pipetting devices should be used for manipulating all liquids in the laboratory. Mouth pipetting must not be done.

---

†Additional precautions for research and industrial laboratories are addressed elsewhere.[22,23]

5. Use of needles and syringes should be limited to situations in which there is no alternative, and the recommendations for preventing injuries with needles outlined under universal precautions should be followed.
6. Laboratory work surfaces should be decontaminated with an appropriate chemical germicide after a spill of blood or other body fluids and when work activities are completed.
7. Contaminated materials used in laboratory tests should be decontaminated before reprocessing or be placed in bags and disposed of in accordance with institutional policies for disposal of infective waste.[24]
8. Scientific equipment that has been contaminated with blood or other body fluids should be decontaminated and cleaned before being repaired in the laboratory or transported to the manufacturer.
9. All persons should wash their hands after completing laboratory activities and should remove protective clothing before leaving the laboratory.

Implementation of universal blood and body fluid precautions for *all* patients eliminates the need for warning labels on specimens since blood and other body fluids from all patients should be considered infective.

Environmental Considerations for HIV Transmission

No environmentally mediated mode of HIV transmission has been documented. Nevertheless, the precautions described below should be taken routinely in the care of *all* patients.

Sterilization and Disinfection

Standard sterilization and disinfection procedures for patient-care equipment currently recommended for use[25,26] in a variety of health care settings—including hospitals, medical and dental clinics and offices, hemodialysis centers, emergency care facilities, and long-term nursing care facilities—are adequate to sterilize or disinfect instruments, devices, or other items contaminated with blood or other body fluids from persons infected with bloodborne pathogens including HIV.[21,23]

Instruments or devices that enter sterile tissue or the vascular system of any patient or through which blood flows should be sterilized before reuse. Devices or items that contact intact mucous membranes should be sterilized or receive high-level disinfection, a procedure that kills vegetative organisms and viruses but not necessarily large numbers of bacterial spores. Chemical germicides that are registered with the U.S. Environmental Protection Agency (EPA) as "sterilants" may be used either for sterilization or for high-level disinfection depending on contact time.

Contact lenses used in trial fittings should be disinfected after each fitting by using a hydrogen peroxide contact lens disinfecting system or, if compatible, with heat (78°C–80°C [172.4°F–176.0°F]) for 10 minutes.

Medical devices or instruments that require sterilization or disinfection should be thoroughly cleaned before being exposed to the germicide, and the manufacturer's instructions for the use of the germicide should be followed. Further, it is important that the manufacturer's specifications for compatibility of the medical device with chemical germicides be closely followed. Information on specific label claims of commercial germicides can be obtained by writing to the Disinfectants Branch, Office of Pesticides, Environmental Protection Agency, 401 M Street, SW, Washington, D.C. 20460.

Studies have shown that HIV is inactivated rapidly after being exposed to commonly used chemical germicides at concentrations that are much lower than used in practice.[27–30] Embalming fluids are similar to the types of chemical germicides that have been tested and found to completely inactivate HIV. In addition to commercially available chemical germicides, a solution of sodium hypochlorite (household bleach) prepared daily is an inexpensive and effective germicide. Concentrations ranging from approximately 500 ppm (1:100 dilution of household bleach) sodium hypochlorite to 5,000 ppm (1:10 dilution of household bleach) are effective depending on the amount of organic material (e.g., blood, mucus) present on the surface to be cleaned and disinfected. Commercially available chemical germicides may be more compatible with certain medical devices that might be corroded by repeated exposure to sodium hypochlorite, especially to the 1:10 dilution.

Survival of HIV in the Environment

The most extensive study on the survival of HIV after drying involved greatly concentrated HIV samples, i.e., 10 million tissue culture infectious doses per milliliter.[31] This concentration is at least 100,000 times greater than that typically found in the blood or serum of patients with HIV infection. HIV was detectable by tissue-culture techniques 1–3 days after drying, but the rate of inactivation was rapid. Studies performed at CDC have also shown that drying HIV causes a rapid (within several hours) 1–2 log (90%–99%) reduction in HIV concentration. In tissue culture fluid, cell-free HIV could be detected up to 15 days at room temperature, up to 11 days at 37°C (98.6°F), and up to 1 day if the HIV was cell-associated.

When considered in the context of environmental conditions in health care facilities, these results do not require any changes in currently recommended sterilization, disinfection, or housekeeping strategies. When medical devices are contaminated with blood or other body fluids, existing recommendations include the cleaning of these instruments, followed by disinfection or sterilization, depending on the type of medical device. These protocols assume "worst-case" conditions of extreme virologic and microbiologic contamination, and whether viruses have been inactivated after drying plays no role in formulating these strategies. Consequently, no changes in published procedures for cleaning, disinfecting, or sterilizing need to be made.

Housekeeping

Environmental surfaces such as walls, floors, and other surfaces are not associated with transmission of infections to patients or health care workers. Therefore, extraordinary attempts to disinfect or sterilize these environmental surfaces are not necessary. However, cleaning and removal of soil should be done routinely.

Cleaning schedules and methods vary according to the area of the hospital or institution, type of surface to be cleaned, and the amount and type of soil present. Horizontal surfaces (e.g., bedside tables and hard-surfaced flooring) in patient care areas are usually cleaned on a regular basis, when soiling or spills occur, and when a patient is discharged. Cleaning of walls, blinds, and curtains is recommended only if they are visibly soiled. Disinfectant fogging is an unsatisfactory method of decontaminating air and surfaces and is not recommended.

Disinfectant-detergent formulations registered by EPA can be used for cleaning environmental surfaces, but the actual physical removal of microorganisms by scrubbing is probably at least as important as any antimicrobial effect of the cleaning agent used. Therefore, cost, safety, and acceptability by housekeepers can be the main criteria for selecting any such registered agent. The manufacturers' instructions for appropriate use should be followed.

Cleaning and Decontaminating Spills of Blood or Other Body Fluids

Chemical germicides that are approved for use as "hospital disinfectants" and are tuberculocidal when used at recommended dilutions can be used to decontaminate spills of blood and other body fluids. Strategies for decontaminating spills of blood and other body fluids in a patient care setting are different than for spills of cultures or other materials in clinical, public health, or research laboratories. In patient care areas, visible material should first be removed and then the area should be decontaminated. With large spills of cultured or concentrated infectious agents in the laboratory, the contaminated area should be flooded with a liquid germicide before cleaning, then decontaminated with fresh germicidal chemical. In both settings, gloves should be worn during the cleaning and decontaminating procedures.

Laundry

Although soiled linen has been identified as a source of large numbers of certain pathogenic microorganisms, the risk of actual disease transmission is negligible. Rather than rigid procedures and specifications, hygienic and common-sense storage and processing of clean and soiled linen are recommended.[26] Soiled linen should be handled as little as possible and with minimum agitation to prevent gross microbial contamination of the air and of persons handling the linen. All soiled linen should be bagged at the location where it was used; it should not be sorted or rinsed in patient care areas. Linen soiled with blood or body fluids should be placed and transported in bags that prevent leakage. If hot water is used, linen should be washed with detergent in water at least 71°C (160°F) for 25 minutes. If low-temperature ($\leq$ 70°C [158°F]) laundry cycles are used, chemicals suitable for low-temperature washing at proper use concentration should be used.

Infective Waste

There is no epidemiologic evidence to suggest that most hospital waste is any more infective than residential waste. Moreover, there is no epidemiologic evidence that hospital waste has caused disease in the community as a result of improper disposal. Therefore, identifying wastes for which special precautions are indicated is largely a matter of judgment about the relative risk of disease transmission. The most practical approach to the management of infective waste is to identify those wastes with the potential for causing infection during handling and disposal and for which some special precautions appear prudent. Hospital wastes for which special precautions appear prudent include microbiology laboratory waste, pathology waste, and blood specimens or blood products. While any item that has had contact with blood exudates or secretions may be potentially infective, it is not usually considered practical or necessary to treat all such waste as infective.[23,26] Infective waste, in general, should either be incinerated or should be autoclaved before disposal in a sanitary landfill. Bulk blood, suctioned fluids, excretions, and secretions may be carefully poured down a drain connected to a sanitary sewer. Sanitary sewers may also be used to dispose of other infectious wastes capable of being ground and flushed into the sewer.

Implementation of Recommended Precautions

Employers of health care workers should ensure that policies exist for

1. Initial orientation and continuing education and training of all health care workers—including students and trainees—on the epidemiology, modes of transmission, and prevention of HIV and other bloodborne infections and the need for routine use of universal blood and body fluid precautions for all patients.

2. Provision of equipment and supplies necessary to minimize the risk of infection with HIV and other bloodborne pathogens.
3. Monitoring adherence to recommended protective measures. When monitoring reveals a failure to follow recommended precautions, counseling, education, and/or re-training should be provided, and, if necessary, appropriate disciplinary action should be considered.

Professional associations and labor organizations, through continuing education efforts, should emphasize the need for health care workers to follow recommended precautions.

Serologic Testing for HIV Infection

Background

A person is identified as infected with HIV when a sequence of tests, starting with repeated enzyme immunoassays (EIA) and including a Western blot or similar, more specific assay, are repeatedly reactive. Persons infected with HIV usually develop antibody against the virus within 6–12 weeks after infection.

The sensitivity of the currently licensed EIA tests is at least 99% when they are performed under optimal laboratory conditions on serum specimens from persons infected for ≥12 weeks. Optimal laboratory conditions include the use of reliable reagents, provision of continuing education of personnel, quality control of procedures, and participation in performance-evaluation programs. Given this performance, the probability of a false-negative test is remote except during the first several weeks after infection, before detectable antibody is present. The proportion of infected persons with a false-negative test attributed to absence of antibody in the early stages of infection is dependent on both incidence and prevalence of HIV infection in a population (Table A-1).

The specificity of the currently licensed EIA tests is approximately 99% when repeatedly reactive tests are considered. Repeat testing of initially reactive specimens by EIA is required to reduce the likelihood of laboratory error. To increase further the specificity of serologic tests, laboratories must use a supplemental test, most often the Western blot, to validate repeatedly reactive EIA results. Under optimal laboratory conditions, the sensitivity of the Western blot test is comparable to or greater than that of a repeatedly reactive EIA, and the Western blot is highly specific when strict criteria are used to interpret the test results. The testing sequence of a repeatedly reactive EIA and a positive Western blot test is highly predictive of HIV infection, even in a population with a low prevalence of infection (Table A-2). If the Western blot test result is indeterminant, the testing sequence is considered equivocal for HIV infection. When this occurs, the Western blot test should be repeated on the same serum sample,

Table A-1 Estimated Annual Number of Patients Infected with HIV Not Detected by HIV-Antibody Testing in a Hypothetical Hospital with 10,000 Admissions/Year*

Beginning Prevalence of HIV Infection	Annual Incidence of HIV Infection	Approximate Number of HIV-Infected Patients	Approximate Number of HIV-Infected Patients Not Detected
5.0%	1.0%	550	17–18
5.0%	0.5%	525	11–12
1.0%	0.2%	110	3–4
1.0%	0.1%	105	2–3
0.1%	0.02%	11	0–1
0.1%	0.01%	11	0–1

*The estimates are based on the following assumptions: (1) the sensitivity of the screening test is 99% (i.e., 99% of HIV-infected persons with antibody will be detected); (2) persons infected with HIV will not develop detectable antibody (seroconvert) until 6 weeks (1.5 months) after infection; (3) new infections occur at an equal rate throughout the year; (4) calculations of the number of HIV-infected persons in the patient population are based on the mid-year prevalence, which is the beginning prevalence plus half the annual incidence of infections.

and, if still indeterminant, the testing sequence should be repeated on a sample collected 3–6 months later. Use of other supplemental tests may aid in interpreting the results on samples that are persistently indeterminant by Western blot.

Testing of Patients

Previous CDC recommendations have emphasized the value of HIV serologic testing of patients for (1) management of parenteral or mucous membrane ex-

Table A-2 Predictive Value of Positive HIV-Antibody Tests in Hypothetical Populations with Different Prevalences of Infection

Test	Prevalence of Infection	Predictive Value of Positive Test*
Repeatedly reactive enzyme immunoassay (EIA)†	0.2%	28.41%
	2.0%	80.16%
	20.0%	98.02%
Repeatedly reactive EIA followed by positive Western blot (WB)‡	0.2%	99.75%
	2.0%	99.97%
	20.0%	99.99%

*Proportion of persons with positive test results who are actually infected with HIV.
†Assumes EIA sensitivity of 99.0% and specificity of 99.5%.
‡Assumes WB sensitivity of 99.0% and specificity of 99.9%.

posures of health care workers, (2) patient diagnosis and management, and (3) counseling and serologic testing to prevent and control HIV transmission in the community. In addition, more recent recommendations have stated that hospitals, in conjunction with state and local health departments, should periodically determine the prevalence of HIV infection among patients from age groups at highest risk of infection.[32]

Adherence to universal blood and body fluid precautions recommended for the care of all patients will minimize the risk of transmission of HIV and other bloodborne pathogens from patients to health care workers. The utility of routine HIV serologic testing of patients as an adjunct to universal precautions is unknown. Results of such testing may not be available in emergency or outpatient settings. In addition, some recently infected patients will not have detectable antibody to HIV (see Table A-1).

Personnel in some hospitals have advocated serologic testing of patients in settings in which exposure of health care workers to large amounts of patients' blood may be anticipated. Specific patients for whom serologic testing has been advocated include those undergoing major operative procedures and those undergoing treatment in critical care units, especially if they have conditions involving uncontrolled bleeding. Decisions regarding the need to establish testing programs for patients should be made by physicians or individual institutions. In addition, when deemed appropriate, testing of individual patients may be performed on agreement between the patient and the physician providing care.

In addition to the universal precautions recommended for all patients, certain additional precautions for the care of HIV-infected patients undergoing major surgical operations have been proposed by personnel in some hospitals. For example, surgical procedures on an HIV-infected patient might be altered so that hand-to-hand passing of sharp instruments would be eliminated; stapling instruments rather than hand-suturing equipment might be used to perform tissue approximation; electrocautery devices rather than scalpels might be used as cutting instruments; and, even though uncomfortable, gowns that totally prevent seepage of blood onto the skin of members of the operative team might be worn. While such modifications might further minimize the risk of HIV infection for members of the operative team, some of these techniques could result in prolongation of operative time and could potentially have an adverse effect on the patient.

Testing programs, if developed, should include the following principles:

- Obtaining consent for testing
- Informing patients of test results, and providing counseling for seropositive patients by properly trained persons
- Assuring that confidentiality safeguards are in place to limit knowledge of test results to those directly involved in the care of infected patients or as required by law

- Assuring that identification of infected patients will not result in denial of needed care or provision of suboptimal care
- Evaluating prospectively (1) the efficacy of the program in reducing the incidence of parenteral, mucous membrane, or significant cutaneous exposures of health care workers to the blood or other body fluids of HIV-infected patients and (2) the effect of modified procedures on patients

Testing of Health Care Workers

Although transmission of HIV from infected health care workers to patients has not been reported, transmission during invasive procedures remains a possibility. Transmission of hepatitis B virus (HBV)—a bloodborne agent with a considerably greater potential for nosocomial spread—from health care workers to patients has been documented. Such transmission has occurred in situations (e.g., oral and gynecologic surgery) in which health care workers, when tested, had very high concentrations of HBV in their blood (at least 100 million infectious virus particles per milliliter, a concentration much higher than occurs with HIV infection), and the health care workers sustained a puncture wound while performing invasive procedures or had exudative or weeping lesions or microlacerations that allowed virus to contaminate instruments or open wounds of patients.[33,34]

The hepatitis B experience indicates that only those health care workers who perform certain types of invasive procedures have transmitted HBV to patients. Adherence to recommendations in this document will minimize the risk of transmission of HIV and other bloodborne pathogens from health care workers to patients during invasive procedures. Since transmission of HIV from infected health care workers performing invasive procedures to their patients has not been reported and would be expected to occur only very rarely, if at all, the utility of routine testing of such health care workers to prevent transmission of HIV cannot be assessed. If consideration is given to developing a serologic testing program for health care workers who perform invasive procedures, the frequency of testing, as well as the issues of consent, confidentiality, and consequences of test results—as previously outlined for testing programs for patients—must be addressed.

Management of Infected Health Care Workers

Health care workers with impaired immune systems resulting from HIV infection or other causes are at increased risk of acquiring or experiencing serious complications of infectious disease. Of particular concern is the risk of severe infection following exposure to patients with infectious diseases that are easily transmitted if appropriate precautions are not taken (e.g., measles, varicella).

Any health care worker with an impaired immune system should be counseled about the potential risk associated with taking care of patients with any transmissible infection and should continue to follow existing recommendations for infection control to minimize risk of exposure to other infectious agents.[7,35] Recommendations of the Immunization Practices Advisory Committee (ACIP) and institutional policies concerning requirements for vaccinating health care workers with live-virus vaccines (e.g., measles, rubella) should also be considered.

The question of whether workers infected with HIV—especially those who perform invasive procedures—can adequately and safely be allowed to perform patient care duties or whether their work assignments should be changed must be determined on an individual basis. These decisions should be made by the health care worker's personal physician(s) in conjunction with the medical directors and personnel health service staff of the employing institution or hospital.

Management of Exposures

If a health care worker has a parenteral (e.g., needlestick or cut) or mucous membrane (e.g., splash to the eye or mouth) exposure to blood or other body fluids or has a cutaneous exposure involving large amounts of blood or prolonged contact with blood—especially when the exposed skin is chapped, abraded, or afflicted with dermatitis—the source patient should be informed of the incident and tested for serologic evidence of HIV infection after consent is obtained. Policies should be developed for testing source patients in situations in which consent cannot be obtained (e.g., an unconscious patient).

If the source patient has AIDS, is positive for HIV antibody, or refuses the test, the health care worker should be counseled regarding the risk of infection and evaluated clinically and serologically for evidence of HIV infection as soon as possible after the exposure. The health care worker should be advised to report and seek medical evaluation for any acute febrile illness that occurs within 12 weeks after the exposure. Such an illness—particularly one characterized by fever, rash, or lymphadenopathy—may be indicative of recent HIV infection. Seronegative health care workers should be retested 6 weeks postexposure and on a periodic basis thereafter (e.g., 12 weeks and 6 months after exposure) to determine whether transmission has occurred. During this follow-up period—especially the first 6–12 weeks after exposure, when most infected persons are expected to seroconvert—exposed health care workers should follow U.S. Public Health Service (PHS) recommendations for preventing transmission of HIV.[36,37]

No further follow-up of a health care worker exposed to infection as described above is necessary if the source patient is seronegative unless the source patient is at high risk of HIV infection. In the latter case, a subsequent specimen (e.g., 12 weeks following exposure) may be obtained from the health care worker for antibody testing. If the source patient cannot be identified, decisions regarding appropriate follow-up should be individualized. Serologic testing should be available to all health care workers who are concerned that they may have been infected with HIV.

If a patient has a parenteral or mucous membrane exposure to blood or other body fluid of a health care worker, the patient should be informed of the incident and the same procedure outlined above for management of exposures should be followed for both the source health care worker and the exposed patient.

REFERENCES

1. CDC. Acquired immunodeficiency syndrome (AIDS): Precautions for clinical and laboratory staffs. MMWR 1982;31:577–580.

2. CDC. Acquired immunodeficiency syndrome (AIDS): Precautions for health-care workers and allied professionals. MMWR 1983;32:450–451.

3. CDC. Recommendations for preventing transmission of infection with human T-lymphotropic virus type III/lymphadenopathy-associated virus in the workplace. MMWR 1985;34:681–686, 691–695.

4. CDC. Recommendations for preventing transmission of infection with human T-lymphotropic virus type III/lymphadenopathy-associated virus during invasive procedures. MMWR 1986;35:221–223.

5. CDC. Recommendations for preventing possible transmission of human T-lymphotropic virus type III/lymphadenopathy-associated virus from tears. MMWR 1985;34:533–534.

6. CDC. Recommendations for providing dialysis treatment to patients infected with human T-lymphotropic virus type III/lymphadenopathy-associated virus infection. MMWR 1986;35:376–378, 383.

7. Garner JS, Simmons BP. Guideline for isolation precautions in hospitals. Infect Control 1983;4(suppl):245–325.

8. CDC. Recommended infection control practices for dentistry. MMWR 1986;35:237–242.

9. McCray E. The Cooperative Needlestick Surveillance Group. Occupational risk of the acquired immunodeficiency syndrome among health care workers. N Engl J Med 1986;314:1127–1132.

10. Henderson DK, Saah AJ, Zak BJ, et al. Risk of nosocomial infection with human T-cell lymphotropic virus type III/lymphadenopathy-associated virus in a large cohort of intensively exposed health care workers. Ann Intern Med 1986;104:644–647.

11. Gerberding JL, Bryant-LeBlanc CE, Nelson K, et al. Risk of transmitting the human immunodeficiency virus, cytomegalovirus, and hepatitis B virus to health care workers exposed to patients with AIDS and AIDS-related conditions. J Infect Dis 1987;156:1–8.

12. McEvoy M, Porter K, Mortimer P, Simmons N, Shanson D. Prospective study of clinical, laboratory, and ancillary staff with accidental exposures to blood or other body fluids from patients infected with HIV. Br Med J 1987;294:1595–1597.

13. Anonymous. Needlestick transmission of HTLV-III from a patient infected in Africa. Lancet 1984;2:1376–1377.

14. Oksenhendler E, Harzic M, Le Roux JM, Rabian C, Clauvel JP. HIV infection with seroconversion after a superficial needlestick injury to the finger. N Engl J Med 1986;315:582.

15. Neisson-Vernant C, Arfi S, Mathez D, Leibowitch J, Monplaisir N. Needlestick HIV sero-conversion in a nurse. Lancet 1986;2:814.

16. Grint P, McEvoy M. Two associated cases of the acquired immune deficiency syndrome (AIDS). PHLS Commun Dis Rep 1985;42:4.

17. CDC. Apparent transmission of human T-lymphotropic virus type III/lymphadenopathy-associated virus from a child to a mother providing health care. MMWR 1986;35:76–79.

18. CDC. Update: Human immunodeficiency virus infections in health-care workers exposed to blood of infected patients. MMWR 1987;36:285–289.

19. Kline RS, Phelan J, Friedland GH, et al. Low occupational risk for HIV infection for dental professionals (Abstract). In: Abstracts from the III International Conference on AIDS, 1–5 June 1985, Washington, DC: 155.

20. Baker JL, Kelen GD, Sivertson KT, Quinn TC. Unsuspected human immunodeficiency virus in critically ill emergency patients. JAMA 1987;257:2609–2611.

21. Favero MS. Dialysis-associated diseases and their control. In Bennett JV, Brachman PS (eds). Hospital Infections. Boston: Little, Brown and Company, 1985:267–284.

22. Richardson JH, Barkley WE (eds). Biosafety in microbiological and biomedical laboratories. 1984. Washington, DC: U.S. Department of Health and Human Services, Public Health Service HHS publication no. (CDC) 84-8395.

23. CDC. Human T-lymphotropic virus type III/lymphadenopathy-associated virus: Agent summary statement. MMWR 1986;35:540–542, 547–549.

24. Environmental Protection Agency. EPA guide to infectious waste management. Washington, DC: U.S. Environmental Protection Agency. May 1986 (Publication no. EPA/530-SW-86-014).

25. Favero MS. Sterilization, disinfection, and antisepsis in the hospital. In: Manual of Clinical Microbiology, 4th ed. Washington, DC: American Society for Microbiology, 1985:129–137.

26. Garner JS, Favero MS. Guideline for handwashing and hospital environmental control, 1985. Atlanta: Public Health Service, Centers for Disease Control, 1985. HHS publication no. 99-1117.

27. Spire B, Montagnier L, Barré-Sinoussi F, Chermann JC. Inactivation of lymphadenopathy-associated virus by chemical disinfectants. Lancet 1984;2:899–901.

28. Martin LS, McDougal JS, Loskoski SL. Disinfection and inactivation of the human lymphotropic virus type III/lymphadenopathy-associated virus. J Infect Dis 1985;152:400.

29. McDougal JS, Martin LS, Cort SP, et al. Thermal inactivation of the acquired immunodeficiency syndrome virus-III/lymphadenopathy-associated virus, with special reference to antihemophilic factor. J Clin Invest 1985;76:875–877.

30. Spire B, Barré-Sinoussi F, Dormont D, Montagnier L, Chermann JC. Inactivation of lymphadenopathy-associated virus by heat, gamma rays, and ultraviolet light. Lancet 1985;1:188–189.

31. Resnik L, Veren K, Salahuddin SZ, Tondreau S, Markham RD. Stability and inactivation of HTLV-III/LAV under clinical and laboratory environments. JAMA 1986;255:1887–1891.

32. CDC. Public Health Service (PHS) guidelines for counseling and antibody testing to prevent HIV infection and AIDS. MMWR 1987;3:509–515.

33. Kane MA, Lettau LA. Transmission of HBV from dental personnel to patients. J Am Dent Assoc 1985;110:634–636.

34. Lettau LA, Smith JD, Williams D, et al. Transmission of hepatitis B with resultant restriction of surgical practice. JAMA 1986;255:934–937.

35. Williams WW. Guideline for infection control in hospital personnel. Infect Control 1983;4(suppl):326–349.

36. CDC. Prevention of acquired immune deficiency syndrome (AIDS): Report of inter-agency recommendations. MMWR 1983;32:101–103.

37. CDC. Provisional Public Health Service inter-agency recommendations for screening donated blood and plasma for antibody to the virus causing acquired immunodeficiency syndrome. MMWR 1985;34:1–5.

UPDATE: UNIVERSAL PRECAUTIONS FOR PREVENTION OF TRANSMISSION OF HUMAN IMMUNODEFICIENCY VIRUS, HEPATITIS B VIRUS, AND OTHER BLOODBORNE PATHOGENS IN HEALTH CARE SETTINGS*

Introduction

The purpose of this report is to clarify and supplement the CDC publication entitled "Recommendations for Prevention of HIV Transmission in Health Care Settings."[1]†

In 1983, CDC published a document entitled "Guideline for Isolation Precautions in Hospitals"[2] that contained a section entitled "Blood and Body Fluid Precautions." The recommendations in this section called for blood and body fluid precautions when a patient was known or suspected to be infected with bloodborne pathogens. In August 1987, CDC published a document entitled "Recommendations for Prevention of HIV Transmission in Health Care Settings."[1] In contrast to the 1983 document, the 1987 document recommended that blood and body fluid precautions be consistently used for all patients regardless of their bloodborne infection status. This extension of blood and body fluid precautions to *all* patients is referred to as "Universal Blood and Body Fluid Precautions" or "Universal Precautions." Under universal precautions, blood and certain body fluids of all patients are considered potentially infectious for human immunodeficiency virus (HIV), hepatitis B virus (HBV), and other bloodborne pathogens.

Universal precautions are intended to prevent parenteral, mucous membrane, and nonintact skin exposures of health care workers to bloodborne pathogens. In addition, immunization with HBV vaccine is recommended as an important adjunct to universal precautions for health care workers who have exposures to blood.[3,4]

Since the recommendations for universal precautions were published in August 1987, CDC and the Food and Drug Administration (FDA) have received requests for clarification of the following issues: (1) body fluids to which universal precautions apply, (2) use of protective barriers, (3) use of gloves for phlebotomy, (4) selection of gloves for use while observing universal precautions, and (5) need for making changes in waste management programs as a result of adopting universal precautions.

---

*This portion of Appendix A is reprinted from *Morbidity and Mortality Weekly Report* (1988;37(24):377–378), June 1988, U.S. Centers for Disease Control.

†The August 1987 publication should be consulted for general information and specific recommendations not addressed in this update.

Body Fluids to Which Universal Precautions Apply

Universal precautions apply to blood and to other body fluids containing visible blood. Occupational transmission of HIV and HBV to health care workers by blood is documented.[4,5] Blood is the single most important source of HIV, HBV, and other bloodborne pathogens in the occupational setting. Infection control efforts for HIV, HBV, and other bloodborne pathogens must focus on preventing exposures to blood as well as on delivery of HBV immunization.

Universal precautions also apply to semen and vaginal secretions. Although both of these fluids have been implicated in the sexual transmission of HIV and HBV, they have not been implicated in occupational transmission from patient to health care worker. This observation is not unexpected, since exposure to semen in the usual health care setting is limited, and the routine practice of wearing gloves for performing vaginal examinations protects health care workers from exposure to potentially infectious vaginal secretions.

Universal precautions also apply to tissues and to the following fluids: cerebrospinal fluid (CSF), synovial fluid, pleural fluid, peritoneal fluid, pericardial fluid, and amniotic fluid. The risk of transmission of HIV and HBV from these fluids is unknown; epidemiologic studies in the health care and community setting are currently inadequate to assess the potential risk to health care workers from occupational exposures to them. However, HIV has been isolated from CSF, synovial, and amniotic fluid,[6-8] and HBsAg has been detected in synovial fluid, amniotic fluid, and peritoneal fluid.[9-11] One case of HIV transmission was reported after a percutaneous exposure to bloody pleural fluid obtained by needle aspiration.[12] Whereas aseptic procedures used to obtain these fluids for diagnostic or therapeutic purposes protect health care workers from skin exposures, they cannot prevent penetrating injuries due to contaminated needles or other sharp instruments.

Body Fluids to Which Universal Precautions Do Not Apply

Universal precautions do not apply to feces, nasal secretions, sputum, sweat, tears, urine, and vomitus unless they contain visible blood. The risk of transmission of HIV and HBV from these fluids and materials is extremely low or nonexistent. HIV has been isolated and HBsAg has been demonstrated in some of these fluids; however, epidemiologic studies in the health care and community setting have not implicated these fluids or materials in the transmission of HIV and HBV infections.[13,14] Some of the above fluids and excretions represent a potential source for nosocomial and community-acquired infections with other pathogens, and recommendations for preventing the transmission of nonbloodborne pathogens have been published.[2]

Precautions for Other Body Fluids in Special Settings

Human breast milk has been implicated in perinatal transmission of HIV, and HBsAg has been found in the milk of mothers infected with HBV.[10,13] However, occupational exposure to human breast milk has not been implicated in the transmission of HIV nor HBV infection to health care workers. Moreover, the health care worker will not have the same type of intensive exposure to breast milk as the nursing neonate. Whereas universal precautions do not apply to human breast milk, gloves may be worn by health care workers in situations where exposures to breast milk might be frequent, for example, in breast milk banking.

Saliva of some persons infected with HBV has been shown to contain HBV-DNA at concentrations 1/1,000 to 1/10,000 of that found in the infected person's serum.[15] HBsAg-positive saliva has been shown to be infectious when injected into experimental animals and in human bite exposures.[16–18] However, HBsAg-positive saliva has not been shown to be infectious when applied to oral mucous membranes in experimental primate studies[18] or through contamination of musical instruments or cardiopulmonary resuscitation dummies used by HBV carriers.[19,20] Epidemiologic studies of nonsexual household contacts of HIV-infected patients, including several small series in which HIV transmission failed to occur after bites or after percutaneous inoculation or contamination of cuts and open wounds with saliva from HIV-infected patients, suggest that the potential for salivary transmission of HIV is remote.[5,13,14,21,22] One case report from Germany has suggested the possibility of transmission of HIV in a household setting from an infected child to a sibling through a human bite.[23] The bite did not break the skin or result in bleeding. Since the date of seroconversion to HIV was not known for either child in this case, evidence for the role of saliva in the transmission of virus is unclear.[23] Another case report suggested the possibility of transmission of HIV from husband to wife by contact with saliva during kissing.[24] However, follow-up studies did not confirm HIV infection in the wife.[21]

Universal precautions do not apply to saliva. General infection control practices already in existence—including the use of gloves for digital examination of mucous membranes and endotracheal suctioning, and handwashing after exposure to saliva—should further minimize the minute risk, if any, for salivary transmission of HIV and HBV.[1,25] Gloves need not be worn when feeding patients and when wiping saliva from skin.

Special precautions, however, are recommended for dentistry.[1] Occupationally acquired infection with HBV in dental workers has been documented,[4] and two possible cases of occupationally acquired HIV infection involving dentists have been reported.[5,26] During dental procedures, contamination of saliva with blood is predictable, trauma to health care workers' hands is common, and blood spattering may occur. Infection control precautions for dentistry minimize the potential for nonintact skin and mucous membrane contact of dental health care workers to blood-contaminated saliva of patients. In addition, the use of gloves for oral examinations and treatment in the dental setting may also protect the patient's oral mucous membranes from exposures to blood, which may occur from breaks in the skin of dental workers' hands.

Use of Protective Barriers

Protective barriers reduce the risk of exposure of the health care worker's skin or mucous membranes to potentially infective materials. For universal precautions, protective barriers reduce the risk of exposure to blood, body fluids containing visible blood, and other fluids to which universal precautions apply. Examples of protective barriers include gloves, gowns, masks, and protective eyewear. Gloves should reduce the incidence of contamination of hands, but they cannot prevent penetrating injuries due to needles or other sharp instruments. Masks and protective eyewear or face shields should reduce the incidence of contamination of mucous membranes of the mouth, nose, and eyes.

Universal precautions are intended to supplement rather than replace recommendations for routine infection control, such as handwashing and using gloves to prevent gross microbial contamination of hands.[27] Because specifying the types of barriers needed for every possible clinical situation is impractical, some judgment must be exercised.

The risk of nosocomial transmission of HIV, HBV, and other bloodborne pathogens can be minimized if health care workers use the following general guidelines:‡

1. Take care to prevent injuries when using needles, scalpels, and other sharp instruments or devices; when handling sharp instruments after procedures; when cleaning used instruments; and when disposing of used needles. Do not recap used needles by hand; do not remove used needles from disposable syringes by hand; and do not bend, break, or otherwise manipulate used needles by hand. Place used disposable syringes and needles, scalpel blades, and other sharp items in puncture-resistant containers for disposal. Locate the puncture-resistant containers as close to the use area as is practical.

2. Use protective barriers to prevent exposure to blood, body fluids containing visible blood, and other fluids to which universal precautions apply. The type of protective barrier(s) should be appropriate for the procedure being performed and the type of exposure anticipated.

---

‡The August 1987 publication should be consulted for general information and specific recommendations not addressed in this update.

3. Immediately and thoroughly wash hands and other skin surfaces that are contaminated with blood, body fluids containing visible blood, or other body fluids to which universal precautions apply.

Glove Use for Phlebotomy

Gloves should reduce the incidence of blood contamination of hands during phlebotomy (drawing blood samples), but they cannot prevent penetrating injuries caused by needles or other sharp instruments. The likelihood of hand contamination with blood containing HIV, HBV, or other bloodborne pathogens during phlebotomy depends on several factors: 1) the skill and technique of the health care worker, 2) the frequency with which the health care worker performs the procedure (other factors being equal, the cumulative risk of blood exposure is higher for a health care worker who performs more procedures), 3) whether the procedure occurs in a routine or emergency situation (where blood contact may be more likely), and 4) the prevalence of infection with bloodborne pathogens in the patient population. The likelihood of infection after skin exposure to blood containing HIV or HBV will depend on the concentration of virus (viral concentration is much higher for hepatitis B than for HIV), the duration of contact, the presence of skin lesions on the hands of the health care worker, and—for HBV—the immune status of the health care worker. Although not accurately quantified, the risk of HIV infection following intact skin contact with infective blood is certainly much less than the 0.5% risk following percutaneous needle-stick exposures.[5] In universal precautions, *all* blood is assumed to be potentially infective for bloodborne pathogens, but in certain settings (e.g., volunteer blood-donation centers) the prevalence of infection with some bloodborne pathogens (e.g., HIV, HBV) is known to be very low. Some institutions have relaxed recommendations for using gloves for phlebotomy procedures by skilled phlebotomists in settings where the prevalence of bloodborne pathogens is known to be very low.

Institutions that judge that routine gloving for *all* phlebotomies is not necessary should periodically reevaluate their policy. Gloves should always be available to health care workers who wish to use them for phlebotomy. In addition, the following general guidelines apply:

1. Use gloves for performing phlebotomy when the health care worker has cuts, scratches, or other breaks in his/her skin.
2. Use gloves in situations where the health care worker judges that hand contamination with blood may occur, for example, when performing phlebotomy on an uncooperative patient.
3. Use gloves for performing finger and/or heel sticks on infants and children.
4. Use gloves when persons are receiving training in phlebotomy.

Table A-3 Summary—Cases of Specified Notifiable Diseases, United States

Disease	24th Week Ending			Cumulative, 24th Week Ending		
	Jun. 18, 1988	Jun. 20, 1987	Median 1983–1987	Jun. 18, 1988	Jun. 20, 1987	Median 1983–1987
Acquired Immunodeficiency Syndrome (AIDS)	198	U*	187	13,918	8,486	3,267
Aseptic meningitis	98	164	123	1,855	2,374	2,102
Encephalitis:						
Primary (arthropod-borne & unspec)	10	18	17	300	405	405
Post-infectious	1	4	3	44	54	54
Gonorrhea: Civilian	11,071	14,550	17,073	303,455	363,500	383,650
Military	189	282	407	5,531	7,687	9,454
Hepatitis: Type A	419	481	439	10,868	11,471	10,071
Type B	351	479	532	9,614	11,666	11,451
Non A, Non B	51	60	74	1,137	1,461	1,623
Unspecified	23	75	102	930	1,477	2,212
Legionellosis	16	16	16	376	399	314
Leprosy	6	1	3	80	93	121

Malaria	13	17	20	304	341	349
Measles: Total†	21	92	92	1,406	2,379	1,620
Indigenous	12	73	73	1,263	2,089	1,436
Imported	9	19	10	143	290	195
Meningococcal infections	44	55	55	1,592	1,648	1,575
Mumps	84	255	93	2,749	9,053	2,000
Pertussis	43	42	58	984	800	865
Rubella (German measles)	15	15	28	115	196	302
Syphilis (Primary & Secondary): Civilian	728	719	566	17,246	15,492	12,764
Military	1	2	2	84	80	93
Toxic Shock syndrome	6	5	5	131	145	178
Tuberculosis	435	442	475	8,999	9,396	9,397
Tularemia	7	9	8	68	64	68
Typhoid Fever	6	6	5	159	136	136
Typhus fever, tick-borne (RMSF)	27	35	35	130	154	177
Rabies, animal	78	85	111	1,874	2,368	2,368

*Because AIDS cases are not received weekly from all reporting areas, comparison of weekly figures may be misleading.

†Nine of the 21 reported cases for this week were imported from a foreign country or can be directly traceable to a known internationally imported case within two generations.

Selection of Gloves

The Center for Devices and Radiological Health, FDA, has responsibility for regulating the medical glove industry. Medical gloves include those marketed as sterile surgical or nonsterile examination gloves made of vinyl or latex. General purpose utility ("rubber") gloves are also used in the health care setting, but they are not regulated by FDA since they are not promoted for medical use. There are no reported differences in barrier effectiveness between intact latex and intact vinyl used to manufacture gloves. Thus, the type of gloves selected should be appropriate for the task being performed.

The following general guidelines are recommended:

1. Use sterile gloves for procedures involving contact with normally sterile areas of the body.
2. Use examination gloves for procedures involving contact with mucous membranes, unless otherwise indicated, and for other patient care or diagnostic procedures that do not require the use of sterile gloves.
3. Change gloves between patient contacts.
4. Do not wash or disinfect surgical or examination gloves for reuse. Washing with surfactants may cause "wicking," i.e., the enhanced penetration of liquids through undetected holes in the glove. Disinfecting agents may cause deterioration.
5. Use general-purpose utility gloves (e.g., rubber household gloves) for housekeeping chores involving potential blood contact and for instrument cleaning and decontamination procedures. Utility gloves may be decontaminated and reused but should be discarded if they are peeling, cracked, or discolored, or if they have punctures, tears, or other evidence of deterioration.

Waste Management

Universal precautions are not intended to change waste management programs previously recommended by CDC for health care settings.[1] Policies for defining, collecting, storing, decontaminating, and disposing of infective waste are generally determined by institutions in accordance with state and local regulations. Information regarding waste management regulations in health care settings may be obtained from state or local health departments or agencies responsible for waste management.

Editorial Note. Implementation of universal precautions does not eliminate the need for other category- or disease-specific isolation precautions, such as

Table A-4 Notifiable Diseases of Low Frequency, United States

	Cum. 1988		Cum. 1988
Anthrax	—	Diphtheria	—
Botulism:		Leptospirosis	13
Foodborne (Md. 1)	10	Plague	2
Infant	16	Poliomyelitis, Paralytic	—
Other	2	Psittacosis	
Brucellosis (Minn. 1)	26	(Upstate N.Y. 1)	36
Cholera	—	Rabies, human	—
Congenital rubella		Tetanus	20
syndrome	3	Trichinosis (Alaska 28)	37
Congenital syphilis,			
ages <1 year	—		

enteric precautions for infectious diarrhea or isolation for pulmonary tuberculosis.[1,2] In addition to universal precautions, detailed precautions have been developed for the following procedures and/or settings in which prolonged or intensive exposures to blood occur: invasive procedures, dentistry, autopsies or morticians' services, dialysis, and the clinical laboratory. These detailed precautions are found in the August 21, 1987, "Recommendations for Prevention of HIV Transmission in Health Care Settings."[1] In addition, specific precautions have been developed for research laboratories.[28]

REFERENCES

1. Centers for Disease Control. Recommendations for prevention of HIV transmission in health care settings. MMWR 1987;36(suppl no. 2S).

2. Garner JS, Simmons BP. Guideline for isolation precautions in hospitals. Infect Control 1983;4:245–325.

3. Immunization Practices Advisory Committee. Recommendations for protection against viral hepatitis. MMWR 1985;34:313–24, 329–335.

4. Department of Labor, Department of Health and Human Services. Joint advisory notice: protection against occupational exposure to hepatitis B virus (HBV) and human immunodeficiency virus (HIV). Washington, DC: U.S. Department of Labor, U.S. Department of Health and Human Services, 1987.

5. Centers for Disease Control. Update: Acquired immunodeficiency syndrome and human immunodeficiency virus infection among health-care workers. MMWR 1988;37:229–234, 239.

6. Hollander H, Levy JA. Neurologic abnormalities and recovery of human immunodeficiency virus from cerebrospinal fluid. Ann Intern Med 1987;106:692–695.

7. Wirthrington RH, Cornes P, Harris JRW, et al. Isolation of human immunodeficiency virus from synovial fluid of a patient with reactive arthritis. Br Med J 1987;294:484.

8. Mundy DC, Schinazi RF, Gerber AR, Nahmias AJ, Randall HW. Human immunodeficiency virus isolated from amniotic fluid. Lancet 1987;2:459–460.

9. Onion DK, Crumpacker CS, Gilliland BC. Arthritis of hepatitis associated with Australia antigen. Ann Intern Med 1971;75:29–33.

10. Lee AKY, Ip HMH, Wong VCW. Mechanisms of maternal-fetal transmission of hepatitis B virus. J Infect Dis 1978;138:668–671.

11. Bond WW, Petersen NJ, Gravelle CR, Favero MS. Hepatitis B virus in peritoneal dialysis fluid: A potential hazard. Dialysis and Transplantation 1982;11:592–600.

12. Oskenhendler E, Harzic M, Le Roux J-M, Rabian C, Clauvel JP. HIV infection with sero-conversion after a superficial needlestick injury to the finger [Letter]. N Engl J Med 1986;315:582.

13. Lifson AR. Do alternate modes for transmission of human immunodeficiency virus exist? A review. JAMA 1988;259:1353–1356.

14. Friedland GH, Saltzman BR, Rogers MF, et al. Lack of transmission of HTLV-III/LAV infection to household contacts of patients with AIDS or AIDS-related complex with oral candidiasis. N Engl J Med 1986;314:344–349.

15. Jenison SA, Lemon SM, Baker LN, Newbold JE. Quantitative analysis of hepatitis B virus DNA in saliva and semen of chronically infected homosexual men. J Infect Dis 1987;156:299–306.

16. Cancio-Bello TP, de Medina M, Shorey J, Valledor MD, Schiff ER. An institutional outbreak of hepatitis B related to a human biting carrier. J Infect Dis 1982;146:652–656.

17. MacQuarrie MB, Forghani B, Wolochow DA. Hepatitis B transmitted by a human bite. JAMA 1974;230:723–724.

18. Scott RM, Snitbhan R, Bancroft WH, Alter HJ, Tingpalapong M. Experimental transmission of hepatitis B virus by semen and saliva. J Infect Dis 1980;142:67–71.

19. Glaser JB, Nadler JP. Hepatitis B virus in a cardiopulmonary resuscitation training course: Risk of transmission from a surface antigen-positive participant. Arch Intern Med 1985;145:1653–1655.

20. Osterholm MT, Bravo ER, Crosson JT, et al. Lack of transmission of viral hepatitis type B after oral exposure to HBsAg-positive saliva. Br Med J 1979;2:1263–1264.

21. Curran JW, Jaffe HW, Hardy AM, et al. Epidemiology of HIV infection and AIDS in the United States. Science 1988;239:610–616.

22. Jason JM, McDougal JS, Dixon G, et al. HTLV-III/LAV antibody and immune status of household contacts and sexual partners of persons with hemophilia. JAMA 1986;255:212–215.

23. Wahn V, Kramer HH, Voit T, Brüster HT, Scrampical B, Scheid A. Horizontal transmission of HIV infection between two siblings [Letter]. Lancet 1986;2:694.

24. Salahuddin SZ, Groopman JE, Markham PD, et al. HTLV-III in symptom-free seronegative persons. Lancet 1984;2:1418–1420.

25. Simmons BP, Wong ES. Guideline for prevention of nosocomial pneumonia. Atlanta: U.S. Department of Health and Human Services, Public Health Service, Centers for Disease Control, 1982.

26. Klein RS, Phelan JA, Freeman K, et al. Low occupational risk of human immunodeficiency virus infection among dental professionals. N Engl J Med 1988;318:86–90.

27. Garner JS, Favero MS. Guideline for handwashing and hospital environmental control, 1985. Atlanta: U.S. Department of Health and Human Services, Public Health Service, Centers for Disease Control, 1985; HHS publication no. 99-1117.

28. Centers for Disease Control. 1988 Agent summary statement for human immunodeficiency virus and report on laboratory-acquired infection with human immunodeficiency virus. MMWR 1988;37(suppl no. S4:1S–22S).

Answers to the Chapter Review Questions

Chapter	Answers
1. The Infectious Patient	1b, 2d, 3d, 4b, 5c
2. The Immune System	1b, 2a, 3b, 4d, 5c
3. Collection of Specimens	1b, 2d, 3d, 4c, 5c
4. AIDS	1a, 2a, 3b, 4d, 5d, 6b, 7c, 8b
5. Hepatitis B and Delta Hepatitis	1c, 2b, 3d, 4b, 5a
6. Hepatitis A and Hepatitis Non-A, Non-B	1b, 2a, 3d, 4b, 5c, 6b, 7a, 8c, 9a, 10b
7. Pulmonary Tuberculosis	1e, 2d, 3b, 4b, 5c
8. Epstein-Barr Virus and Cytomegalovirus	1e, 2a, 3b, 4b, 5a
9. Herpes Simplex and Varicella-Zoster	1b, 2a, 3e, 4a, 5c
10. Meningitis	1b, 2a, 3c, 4b, 5c
11. Pregnancy and the Risk of Infection	1b, 2a, 3d, 4b, 5c
12. The Infection Control Practitioner and the Critical Care Nurse	1 portal of entry, 2d, 3c, 4a, 5b

Index

253

Humoral immunodeficiency, age,
32–33
Hyperbilirubinemia, 92

I

IgA, functions, 27
IgD, functions, 27
IgE, functions, 27
IgG
  age, 31
  functions, 27
IgM, functions, 27
IgM titer, 29
Immune response, 26–27,
28
Immune system, 15–33
  components, 15–33
  pregnancy, 182–183
Immunodeficiency virus, 60–61
Immunoglobulin, 26–30
  diagnosis, 28–30
  functions, 27
Immunosuppressive drug, 25
Index of suspicion, 11
Infected wound, 37
Infection
  covert, 3
  overt, 3
Infection control
  critical care, 208–211
  prevention, 10–12
Infection control practitioner,
  6, 7, 11
  consultation, 11
Infectious disease
  entry portal, 204, 205
  exit portal, 204, 205
  immunoglobulin diagnosis,
    28–30
  infection reservoir, 204
  pregnancy as risk factor, 180–182
  subtle manifestations, 11
  susceptible host, 204, 207
  symptoms, 11
  transmission, 204, 205–207
    barriers, 208

Infectious mononucleosis, 137
Interferon, 21
Interleukin, 22
Intracellular pathogen, 16, 24
Intravascular line, blood culture, 42–43
Intravenous catheter, blood culture,
  42–43
Invasive candidiasis, 53
Invasive procedure, precautions,
  225–226
Isolation, 211–217
  category-specific precautions,
    212–214
  decision, 39
  disease-specific precautions, 214, 215
  historical aspects, 211
  tuberculosis, 129–130
    discontinuation, 130
Isoniazid, tuberculosis, 131–132
  contraindications, 132
Isopora belli, 52

J

Jaundice, 85

K

Kaposi's sarcoma, 64
Kernig's sign, 167

L

Laboratory
  infection control department,
    cooperative relationship, 9
  precautions, 228–229
Lactic acid, bacterial meningitis,
  169–170
Legal issues, 209–211
Leukemia, 25
  chronic lymphocytic, 32–33
Leukocyte, count in infectious processes,
  17
Leukocytosis, 16
Leukopenia, 18–20
  causes, 19